Advance Praise for *Zionist Diplomacy*

"No one gets (and shapes) Israel's global stance like Ron Prosor—seasoned diplomat, UN ambassador, and a multi decade insider to Israel's leadership. In this urgent, eye-opening book, he unpacks Zionist diplomacy from its early wins to today's battles for legitimacy and a sustainable future. Sharp, timely, essential."

—**Ambassador Dennis Ross,** Former U.S. Envoy to the Middle East

"Ambassador Ron Prosor has delivered a bold, timely, and essential book. *Zionist Diplomacy* captures the high-stakes reality of Israel's diplomatic frontlines like no one else can."

—**Ronald S. Lauder,** President, World Jewish Congress

"Ron Prosor is one of the absolute gems of Israeli diplomacy. In this important book he brings a lifetime's experience to bear in a book which is thoughtful, insightful, and wise. With any luck it'll help bring us more Ron Prosors. Israel—and the world—needs them."

—**Douglas Murray,** Bestselling Author of On Democracies and Death Cults

"Ambassador Prosor is one of the most important figures in the history of Israeli foreign affairs. *Zionist Diplomacy* is his witty, incisive, forceful, and proud account of how men and women in the Zionist movement and then in the State of Israel have advanced the national cause of the Jewish People in the arena of world politics. It is a history and memoir that entertains and illuminates."

—**Douglas J. Feith,** Under Secretary of Defense for Policy in the George W. Bush administration

ZIONIST DIPLOMACY

ZIONIST DIPLOMACY

HOW ISRAEL FOUND ITS PLACE AMONG THE NATIONS

AMBASSADOR RON PROSOR

WS
WICKED SON

A WICKED SON BOOK
An Imprint of Post Hill Press
ISBN: 978-1-63758-449-1
ISBN (eBook): 978-1-63758-450-7

Zionist Diplomacy:
How Israel Found Its Place Among the Nations

Cover Design by Jim Villaflores

This is a work of nonfiction. All people, locations, events, and situations are portrayed to the best of the author's memory.

Post Hill Press
New York • Nashville
wickedsonbooks.com
posthillpress.com

Published in the United States of America
1 2 3 4 5 6 7 8 9 10

TABLE OF CONTENTS

PROLOGUE

THE DAY THE MASKS CAME OFF

After more than forty years of public service, I am no longer required to put on a uniform, grab a rifle, and report for duty with the Israel Defense Forces (IDF) when war breaks out. But the eruption of October 7, 2023, was a call to arms louder than anything I have ever experienced.

Like hundreds of thousands of other Israelis, from reservists and ambulance volunteers to countless others who would give their time, money, and energies to support the families of hostages, the devastated business, and the evacuees—I, too, woke up that Saturday morning, on the Jewish festival of Simchat Torah, to find my life overturned. Not just by the unfathomable brutality of Hamas's invasion of Israel's southern communities. But also by the instantaneous, collective mobilization of Israelis, as well as Jews and other allies around the world, all of whom were driven by a sense of immediate and almost infinite responsibility for the fate of our nation.

I am an Israeli diplomat. Over the past four decades, I have filled some of my country's most important diplomatic and foreign-policy roles, including as ambassador to the United Kingdom, director-general of the Foreign Ministry, and ambassador to the United Nations. October 7 found me in Berlin in my latest role, as ambassador to Israel's most important ally in Europe, the Federal Republic of Germany.

In some respects, what happened on October 7, and the intense efforts that many hundreds of Israeli diplomats like me have undertaken every day since, have been unprecedented in my career. In others, however, they have relied heavily on decades of experience fighting for Israel's good name and its national interests abroad. This experience has, in turn, been deeply informed by a unique diplomatic tradition more than a century in the making, beginning with the origins of the Zionist movement in the 1890s and carrying through to the founding of Israel in 1948 and until our day.

This fascinating tradition of *Zionist diplomacy* is the subject of this book.

It is, of necessity, also a book about the Jews—and the tireless efforts, spanning a century and a half, of an ancient people trying to find a place among the nations as a sovereign state after thousands of years of exile. Zionist diplomacy is, if nothing else, a major front in the legitimate and just struggle of the Jewish people to live a sovereign life in the face of what appears to be an infinite wellspring of hatred, violence, mendacity, and depravity aimed at preventing such a sovereign life from existing in our world.

The new period in our history, which began on October 7 and continues today, is therefore but another, especially brutal, chapter in a long story that will only come to an end when our enemies have gone silent, and our people may live alongside others in the peace, prosperity, and richness of life that every Jew is both entitled to and has held up as a central communal aspiration since time immemorial.

***

Hamas's assault began at 5:29 a.m. Berlin time, and within hours, the entire embassy staff was working. Our information was incomplete—it would take days before the magnitude of the assault was understood—but nonetheless we began an intense diplomatic operation, one that was repeated in Israel's embassies and consulates across Europe and around the world.

We did not wait for detailed instructions from Jerusalem. We knew that the first interpretive lens to reach the public is often the one that sticks, and that we therefore had to get out there immediately with the obvious truths: Israel had been the victim of an unprecedented genocidal assault by a known terror organization, aimed primarily at civilians, in violation of every accepted norm of conflict. The coming Israeli response, consequently, would be both inevitable and entirely justified—as just as any war that had ever been waged.

Our first order of business was to map out an immediate diplomatic initiative across Germany's sixteen states as well as its federal government. We began by building a list of people who could be relied on for help—sympathetic politicians, journalists and commentators, pro-Israel Christians, the German-Israeli Friendship League, and more. Each would need to be approached by the right contact, with clear messaging and a clear request for specific assistance.

Second, we crafted a strategy for what is known as public diplomacy—turning directly to broader audiences. But which ones? In addition to sending our messages to the general public through traditional and social media, we set specific audience goals for our messaging, including journalists both international and domestic, influencers, decision-makers and politicians at both the state and federal level, and Jewish communities in Germany and abroad. Here, too, audiences were assigned to different members of our staff depending on their contacts and expertise.

Finally, what exactly were the messages we needed to get out? Again, there was no time to wait for specific guidance—though there would be intensive coordination with Jerusalem as the days and weeks went by. (Indeed, I would end up making no fewer than twelve trips home for consultations in the ensuing three months.) We needed to be exceptionally clear about what had happened, who was to blame, and why we had every right to defend ourselves militarily.

Beyond this, however, there were deeper messages that had to get out. We needed people to understand not just what happened on October 7, but what had been happening for years and decades that led up to it, both in Gaza and around the world.

No less important, we had to channel all of this into messaging that would hold not just for the first week or two, when the atrocities were fresh in everyone's minds and dominated the headlines, but also in the weeks and months to follow, when Israel would mount a long, grueling effort to eradicate the military and political presence of Hamas in Gaza and to secure the release of Israeli hostages.

***

Our biggest challenge would concern what Israeli policymakers and diplomats refer to as the "hourglass."

For decades, Israel's wars and major military operations were always undertaken with an acute awareness of limited time: Regardless of the justice or necessity of the battle, regardless of our operational needs to achieve legitimate goals, international powers and especially the United States would, eventually, insist that we stop—and would even threaten sanctions, whether through the United Nations Security Council, the withholding of arms shipments, or the International Criminal Court (ICC), if we did not. Whenever Israel fights to defend itself, its most powerful allies in the world stand with an hourglass of unclear size, and the sand keeps pouring.

This creates immense pressure on Israel to get as much done on the battlefield as quickly as possible. Yet at the same time, there is counter-pressure that pushes the other way. Not just because war is complicated, and achieving objectives takes time; but also because Israel is held, by these same international actors, to an unbearable, unique standard when it comes to the conduct of war. The extreme efforts to avoid civilian casualties require that Israel operate slowly, carefully, with a constant eye towards potential legal and public-opinion exposure, in every battlefield. Over time, its freedom to maneuver effectively becomes increasingly constrained—as seen since the October 7 war began, in which every major operation or shipment of advanced weaponry becomes a matter of international concern.

As diplomats, one of our main objectives during every military conflict is to put more sand into that hourglass, so that our nation's forces can have the time they need to create effective deterrence and prevent or delay future rounds of conflict. And so, one of my central messages, which I passed to our team that morning, was to remind our German interlocutors that their sympathy and support were absolutely needed, not just now, but also in the coming weeks and months. "You stand by us today," I told German political leaders. "But as images of destruction in Gaza begin to be appear on television, will you still be there for us?"

Another crucial message concerned the background that had led to this moment. In 2005, I was director-general of Israel's foreign ministry when our government, under the leadership of Ariel Sharon, decided to withdraw all military bases and civilian towns from the Gaza Strip in a policy known as Disengagement. For generations, we had been told that settlements were the principal obstacle to peace. I, too, was among those who had believed that by ending our occupation of the Gaza Strip, we could build our international legitimacy and possibly set the stage for a new order in the Strip. If we gave residents of Gaza full control over their destiny, we believed, they could create a prosperous and peaceable alternative to the complex reality they faced in the West Bank. We were strong, we believed, and that strength gave us the flexibility to take risks.

We were indeed strong—but also wrong.

Hamas, it turned out, viewed Disengagement through an entirely different lens. The Zionists, they said, had tucked tail and run, and now was the time to go on the offensive. Less than a year after the last Israeli citizen was removed and the last IDF base dismantled, Hamas violently overthrew the Palestinian Authority's government in Gaza. For the next seventeen years, this internationally recognized terror organization ruled with an iron fist, controlling everything that happened in the Strip. It commandeered all the agencies of government, including health and education—through the aegis of the United Nations Relief and Works Agency (UNRWA)—and created a vast system of underground tunnels that extended both into Israel, for conducting assaults, and also into Egypt, from which it smuggled arms and cash. Hamas confiscated all humanitarian aid, whether it was in the form of money or healthcare supplies, food or building materials. No less important: As has been well documented, all reporting by journalists took place, as in North Korea or the Soviet Union in its day, under strict censorship of Hamas authorities.[1]

Worst of all, Hamas built a vast arsenal including tens of thousands of rockets, many of which were homemade, which its members periodically launched at Israeli civilian centers, or allowed other terror organizations, such as the Palestinian Islamic Jihad (PIJ), another Iran-backed group in Gaza, to do so.

After several rounds of limited war between Israel and Hamas—in 2009, 2012, 2014, 2018, and 2021—a new narrative began to take hold: Hamas, we told ourselves, had no interest in direct conflict. It much preferred to invest its resources in eliminating internal opponents and cementing its rule over the Gaza Strip. The last round of fighting, in 2021, was almost entirely conducted between the IDF and the PIJ. Hamas sat on the sidelines for this one, and Israelis saw it as proof that deterrence was working. Many Israelis convinced themselves that despite Hamas's founding as an Islamist organization with the aim of wiping out Israel and spreading Islamic rule far beyond, its true goals could be influenced through a series of carrots and sticks—and that we had successfully limited not only its capabilities but also its intentions.

I, too, was among the believers.

So were the Germans—a fact of which I reminded them at this crucial moment. "We are all responsible," I told them, "for trivializing Hamas's intentions and their absolutist ideology. We all believed Hamas had been 'contained,' and that their stated belief in global conquest was irrelevant in light of their weakness. Today, however, we must all understand: If we do not stand up to them now, this war will not end at Israel's borders. It will expand into Europe as well."

History, and specifically the history of Germany in World War II, teaches that radical ideology can never be altered. It can only be destroyed,

---

[1] See, for example, Matti Friedman, "An Insider's Guide to the Most Important Story on Earth," *Tablet*, August 26, 2014, https://www.tabletmag.com/sections/israel-middle-east/articles/israel-insider-guide (accessed October 8, 2024); and Mark Lavie, "Why Everything Reported from Gaza Is Crazy Twisted," *The Tower*, No. 17 (August 2014), https://www.thetower.org/article/why-everything-reported-from-gaza-is-crazy-twisted/ (accessed October 8, 2024).

as the Nazi regime was. Only a thorough a process akin to German denazification can one hope to bring fundamental change and, ultimately, peace.

***

It was also important for the world to understand what exactly had made it possible for Jews and Israelis to be dehumanized, even demonized, to the point at which there could actually be a public debate about whether rape, kidnapping, and murder of civilians was somehow a legitimate form of "resistance." This was not just the rhetoric of Hamas or other terror organizations. It was reflected in spontaneous demonstrations around the world beginning that same day—a protest movement that has only gotten stronger as Israel has effectively defeated Hamas on the battlefield. This movement is based on a widespread ideology, generations in the making, according to which Israel's very existence, and the very lives of every Israeli, were illegitimate. This expressed itself, in the months that followed, in activist organizations across the West which called for "globalizing the intifada"; in scholars and books that had captured the imagination of young students in elite institutions; in university administrators who considered Jews to be part of the "oppressor" class and therefore not entitled to protections against violence, hatred, or exclusion; in structures at the UN that had been created for the purpose of turning Israel into a pariah; in NGOs that viewed any act of Israeli self-defense as a form of "apartheid"; and on and on.

Jews are familiar with being dehumanized. It was a frequent part of life in the pre-Israel era. Not just in Russia, Nazi Germany, and the Arab world, where institutionalized discrimination made it impossible for us to live as equals even when we were not being actively persecuted; but even in France in the late nineteenth century and the United States in the pre-civil rights era. Our past experience has hardened us—but also sensitized us, so that there could be no doubt in our own minds about what we were facing. As diplomats, our obligation was to share that experience and sensitivity with the world. We understood that while Israel's armed forces and intelligence services could fight against enemies like Iran, Hamas, and

Hezbollah, the burden of fighting this international battle of ideas would fall mainly on the shoulders of Israeli diplomats, as well as the broader community of pro-Israel advocates and Jewish communal leaders around the world.

Another messaging line involved changing the way people talked about the broader conflict, and its potential resolution, in the wake of October 7. The mantra of the "two-state solution," which continues to be the central paradigm held by many foreign ministries for eventually resolving the conflict, would not help them now. While we Israelis had for decades been pushing for two states for two peoples, nobody in Israel was interested right then in hearing about a Palestinian state—and, given the overwhelming support among Palestinians for the Hamas assaults of October 7, neither, did it seem, was anyone on the other side. I made it clear that addressing a brutal invasion of our country with parroted calls for giving the aggressors a sovereign nation-state would be utterly unhelpful. Now was not the time for anything other than unequivocal condemnation of Hamas and unequivocal support for Israel to respond in full.

What we witnessed in the coming days and weeks was a strange combination of unprecedented international affronts and equally unprecedented diplomatic successes.

In some quarters—specifically officials of UN agencies like UNICEF, UN Women, and the UN Human Rights Council, as well as human rights NGOs like Amnesty International and Human Rights Watch—Hamas's actions were deemed understandable, even justifiable, *even after the scope and barbarity of the atrocities became evident*. Hamas members had filmed themselves butchering civilians, kidnapping, raping, and violating every law of war ever imagined. They even used the victims' cell phones to post the videos of their atrocities on the victims' own social media accounts. Yet none other than the secretary-general of the UN, António Guterres, had the gall to say, just days later, that the assault "did not happen in a vacuum." Volker Türk, UN High Commissioner for human rights, declared that while Hamas had committed war crimes, so had Israel—concluding that "the solution to this situation is the end of the occupation, and full respect for the right to self-determination for Palestinians." The NGOs meant to advocate for human rights were far swifter in justifying Hamas. Amnesty's press release on October 7 claimed that "the root causes of these repeated cycles of violence must be addressed"—the root causes, of course, being Israel's alleged "occupation" of Gaza.

At this point in my career, very little genuinely surprises me. What shocked me now, however, was not the words themselves so much as the timing. These so-called leaders, these institutions created to represent the hope of humanity, did not wait weeks or months to justify the unjustifiable crimes of Hamas. They did not spend the requisite few weeks condemning the horrors that looked far too much like the actions of Nazis and other genocidal actors in history. Instead, the apologetics began almost immediately. It was almost instinctive.

The masks had come off. The moral bankruptcy of entire swaths of the "international community" was revealed for all to see.

As an Israeli official, it became clear to me that October 7 was a turning point not just in Israeli history, but specifically in the history of Zionist diplomacy. From that moment on, I would draw a clear line between us and them, between those leaders, dignitaries, organizations, and others who accepted our existence and recognized the evil of our enemies—with whom I would warmly continue to work—and those who, through word or deed, sought to normalize the terror, those who rationalized or contextualized their brutality. With the latter, I felt a red line had been crossed, and I wanted nothing to do with them.

So revelatory a moment in history, in which the two sides—that of peace and that of endless, fruitless conflict—reveal themselves so starkly, is an unusual thing. The willingness to support, condone, and enable the most heinous crimes was not only a shock, but also a clarifying moment: Nations and other global powers were choosing sides, and the public was watching it all in real time. This, for me, became a litmus test of whether we could have a common future together. The die had been cast.

And yet, ultimately it was not Guterres or Türk or the NGOs whose opinions mattered most to the fate of Israel. The people who really count are the political leaders of countries. They are the ones who control budgets, militaries, and votes in the UN Security Council, which far more directly affect the fate of our people. When a nation's top leaders clear their schedules, get on a plane, and come to Israel in the middle of a crisis to show support, it means something much more powerful. US President Joe Biden, whose immediate reaction was to dispatch a carrier group to the eastern Mediterranean to deter Hezbollah from opening a second front of the war, came to Tel Aviv on October 17, as did the secretaries of state and defense as well as the national security advisor. So, too, did the leaders of the United Kingdom, France, Italy, and many other countries—all of whom expressed profound sympathy and support for Israel.

But of all the nations that sent top-level delegations, none perhaps was as robust, repeated, and supportive as Germany. This was, to a large extent, the fruit of our immediate and intensive diplomatic campaign. Within weeks of the attacks, Israeli received visits from Chancellor Olaf Scholz, Defense Minister Boris Pistorius, and Foreign Minister Annalena Baerbock. The German parliament passed a rare unanimous resolution condemning Hamas and supporting Israel's right to defend itself. In early November, Interior Minister Nancy Faeser banned all activity of Hamas, as well as the international pro-Palestinian NGO Samidoun. Germany even went so far as to demand of all new immigrants, as a condition for their naturalization, that they recognize Israel's right to exist.

Nowhere was Germany's support more evident than in its handling of the hundreds of Israeli hostages taken by Hamas on October 7. Germany took a leading role in applying international pressure to secure their release and in offering support for families of the hostages, using diplomatic, financial, and other leverage far beyond what any other European country did.

For the most powerful nation in Europe, support for Israel at this moment was a matter of *Staatsräson*, the fundamental national interest often referred to also as *raison d'état*—a term I directed our diplomats to use regularly, reminding Germans of the core moral norms on which their nation was founded after World War II.

Because of its foundation on the ashes of the Holocaust, Germany has always seen the protection of the Jewish people as a central element of its *Staatsräson*—whereas the *raison d'être*, the very reason for existing, of

Hamas is, explicitly, the destruction of the Jews. Germany is founded on rejection of Nazism, and Hamas is the closest thing to Nazism. This was a message every German official needed to hear.

***

I tell this story because it is, in effect, symbolic of not only my entire career, but also of more than 130 years of Zionist diplomacy. It has been a long tale of constant motion, of vigilance and resilience, and of patient behind-the-scenes investment and maneuvering, leading up, at the most decisive moments, to aggressive, creative, collective action on a global scale.

As of this writing, more than a year has gone by since that horrible day. And while the memories remain raw and the trauma stifling—perhaps they will always be—we can now take stock of the central role that diplomacy has played, and continues to play, in Israel's survival and success in the world.

Despite everything that Israelis have experienced over the past year, despite the hit we took and all the trauma and feelings of helplessness that accompanied it, a few important facts must be recalled.

Israel is a much stronger nation today than it was the last time it was the victim of a major surprise attack, fifty years ago with the 1973 Yom Kippur War.

When the combined forces of Egypt and Syria launched a surprise attack on the holiest day in the Jewish calendar on October 6, 1973, Israel was not only much weaker militarily and economically, but also far more isolated diplomatically than it is today, lacking even minimal recognition not only from the entire Arab world but also from the entire Soviet bloc of nations. Nor was Europe anywhere near as supportive as it is today: In 1973, Israel had so little leverage there that, at the crucial moment in which our nation's fate hung in the balance, European states refused to allow American planes to refuel on their way to delivering existentially crucial military resupplies for Israel—a story discussed later in depth.

The difference between then and now could not be greater. Over the past half century, Israel built productive and at times even flourishing relations with Russia and the rest of the former Soviet states, as well as the broader Soviet bloc. It made peace with the two Arab nations sharing its longest borders, Egypt and Jordan, and more recently with two key Gulf states, the United Arab Emirates (UAE) and Bahrain, through the Abraham Accords which offered a far warmer, people-to-people kind of peace. Decisively, Israel reached agreement with the most powerful nation on Earth to ensure that it always enjoyed a qualitative military edge (QME) over its adversaries.

Even after a year of war, after the accusations of "war crimes" and "genocide" echoed throughout the halls of elite institutions from human rights NGOs to elite American campuses to the World Court to mass demonstrations across Europe with hundreds of thousands of protestors—after all of it, Israel continues to enjoy major political support from Germany, France, and the United Kingdom, while the United States continues to offer powerful military support as well as financial and diplomatic cover, reflecting the overwhelming popular support our country still enjoys. Nor has Israel suffered significant sanctions, or the severing of diplomatic relations with any country other than South Africa, Bolivia, and Colombia. Even the UAE, Bahrain, Egypt, and Jordan have maintained relations; even Russia, which supports Iran and is furious at Israel's support of Ukraine, has not broken off ties.

To top it off—and this is almost impossible to have imagined only recently—even Saudi Arabia, which has a keen interest in normalizing ties with Israel, joined an informal military coalition along with the U.S., the United Kingdom, and Jordan to *defend* Israel against the hundreds of Iranian missiles and drones that were launched at our country in the early morning hours of April 14, 2024.

And so, while many Israelis may believe we are once again "surrounded by enemies" as we once were, an objective take yields a different picture: It seems that Israel will continue, despite all the harsh reactions to the Gaza war, to enjoy fruitful relations—not just diplomatic, but also economic, cultural, tourism, and more—with nearly the entire globe. It is far from perfect, but when compared with the state of affairs of decades past, we may observe that Israel has, in fact, become an integral member of the family of nations.

How did this happen? Certainly there are many contributing factors. Israel's economy opened up beginning in the 1980s, unleashing its entrepreneurial and technological abilities, and expanding its economic power immeasurably, making it worthwhile for other countries to deepen their ties with Israel. More wealth also meant more military power, and Israel grew stronger, while its enemies either made their peace with it or, as in the case of Syria, Iraq, Yemen, and Lebanon, more or less collapsed.

There is another component. Israel's success can also be traced, in large part, to some impressive acts of diplomacy—without which the Jewish state would likely have never reached the global position it has today.

***

It is widely believed, particularly among the country's supporters around the world, that the State of Israel has generally been either unwittingly incompetent or willfully negligent in the art of diplomacy. This is most often expressed in the context of public diplomacy. As Yaakov Katz, former editor-in-chief of *The Jerusalem Post*, recently put it: "Israel is failing miserably in its public diplomacy, we're just really bad at it.... There's no discipline and there's no unified message."[2] We hear constantly from critics and friends alike, about "Israel's PR problem," a commonplace phrase appearing in op-eds and blog posts almost daily. It assumes that the success or failure of a country depends on its ability to market itself as a kind of product.

Part of this presumptive criticism stems from a carefully crafted image projected by many of its leaders over generations. Gruff, socialism-inspired prime ministers like David Ben-Gurion, Golda Meir, and Yitzhak Rabin

---

[2] Quoted in Ruth Marks Eglash, "Israel losing the hasbara battle because of a broken public relations playbook, experts say," *Jewish Insider,* March 21, 2024, https://jewishinsider.com/2024/03/israel-hasbara-public-diplomacy-war-gaza-hamas/ (accessed October 8, 2024).

often behaved as if they had no interest in diplomacy's bourgeois affects, its cocktail parties and the compulsive equivocation of diplomats.

Another part of this belief flows from what looks, at first glance, like the repeated failure of Israel on the diplomatic playing field over a period of decades. After all, it is only Israel that is routinely singled out for censure by UN bodies that choose to ignore the evils of the world's worst regimes. Only Israel has global conferences hosted about it whose central aim is to delegitimize the country and plot its destruction. That Israel came into being and has survived for more than seven decades at all seems to be despite, not because of, its diplomacy.

In recent years, Israel has further added to this anti-diplomatic image through the systemic downgrading—reflected first of all in its budgetary allocations—of old-fashioned diplomacy. Its foreign ministry, its embassies, its training programs have all suffered from regular cutbacks, as modern technology has enabled political leaders to run global messaging campaigns and communicate with foreign leaders without the input of Israeli diplomats.

And then, of course, there is the simple fact that Israelis like to criticize their government's performance even when it is successful, and they do so not only in Hebrew, but in every language at their disposal.

Yet despite all this, much of this image is false. The belief that Israel is either endemically inept or constitutionally ill-disposed to diplomacy, including public diplomacy, is simply wrong. And the refutation of this belief constitutes the central aim of this book.

***

Beyond the vindication of more than a century of Zionist diplomacy, however, there are a few crucial stories that will be told along the way. These stories tell a great deal about the aims and methods of Zionist diplomacy from its earliest days until our own time, as well as the successes and failures of Israeli diplomacy surrounding the major wars and conflicts of its history. I also delve deeply into the major arenas in which diplomacy has its most decisive impact on Israeli security and prosperity today: the United Nations, Europe, and the Arab states.

But the most important story, perhaps, concerns the single most determinative relationship Israel has with any other country—namely, the United States of America.

Indeed, my aim is to make the case that a great many of the beliefs voiced by commentators, politicians, and policymakers in both Israel and the United States are grounded in fundamental misconceptions about why, exactly, that relationship exists and has taken the form that it does: as a strong, multilayered, bedrock alliance that includes a veto in the UN Security Council against harmful resolutions against the Jewish state, as well as the allocation of more foreign aid to Israel than to any other country. The misconceptions result in wildly incorrect assessments about what threatens that relationship and which benefits the two sides derive from it, and also in countless policies, statements, and actions that are at best a waste of breath, and at times do more harm than good.

To be clear: America has supported Israel over the past five decades, whether under Democratic or Republican administrations, chiefly as a matter of its own national security interests, and only secondarily as a matter of principle, politics, or public sentiment.

Throughout this book, I contend that this remains the case today—and that there is absolutely nothing wrong with it. Why is this important? Because a great deal of confusion has arisen from the contrary belief, according to which America supports Israel mainly because of Jewish or Evangelical support, and is therefore extremely vulnerable to the fluctuations of support that may arise at moments of disagreement. Today, at a time when the United States constantly advances its strategic interests through innumerable channels in its relationship with Israel, including through its financial support, the belief that this engagement is mainly due to sentiment has distorted the conversation of both the pro-Israel and anti-Israel camps.

This does not mean that public support for Israel is unimportant or that the growth of opposition to Israel among younger Americans is not a cause for concern. It is not impossible that the day will come when

American public support for Israel wanes to a point where the United States will find reason to become far less friendly to the Jewish state. But to tell the difference between real and perceived threats, and between real and perceived achievements in this long battle, one must first understand what truly undergirds the kinds of support that are of greatest importance to the future of Israel. And that begins with understanding how it began—a story that this book tells in detail.

***

I write this book not as a professional historian, but as a practitioner. Over the past three decades, I have participated directly in every major arena of Israeli diplomacy: first, as first secretary in Israel's embassy in Bonn as the Cold War came to an end; then as spokesperson for Israel's embassy in London in the mid-1990s, just after the Oslo Accords; then, from 1998 to 2002, as political counsel in our embassy to the United States in Washington, D.C., during the 1998 Wye River talks, the 2000 Camp David talks, the transition from the Clinton to Bush administrations in 2001, and the horrific terror attacks of 9/11; then, in the mid-2000s, as director-general of Israel's Foreign Ministry in Jerusalem; later on as Israel's ambassador to the United Kingdom from 2007 to 2011; and then as ambassador to the United Nations during the tumultuous period of 2011 to 2015. In 2022, as the first draft of this book was being completed, I took up my most recent posting, as Israel's ambassador to Germany.

Along the way, I have had occasion to study, to draw inspiration from, and in some cases even to work directly with, the greatest diplomats and foreign ministers in Israel's history.

To be clear, I will not argue that Zionist diplomacy has been an unmitigated success on every front. No country with a shred of honesty can make such a claim—certainly not one as embattled as Israel. Rather, my main claim is twofold. First, once the central aims of Israel's diplomacy are fully understood, it will emerge that the Israelis have developed a style that is uniquely suited for the interests and *raison d'état* of the Jewish state.

And second, that this style has served Israel exceptionally well in its most critical moments in history—especially in the wake of October 7.

Just like Israel's military and economic enterprises, Israeli diplomacy has a method of its own, and a surprisingly impressive record of success. If the political and economic walls around Israel have been coming down, it is due in no small part to its diplomatic efforts.

In what follows, I retell the story of Zionist diplomacy as I have understood and experienced it. It requires both a retrospective view—not a full-blown history, but more of a focus on key moments and figures since the dawn of the Zionist revolution—as well as my own personal account of the past three decades of Israel's history. From a literary perspective, it therefore requires telling two distinct stories: first, that of Zionist and Israeli diplomacy dating back to Theodor Herzl and up to the 1990s; and second, the story that I have witnessed personally as one of Israel's most senior diplomats. Such a hybrid approach—part history, part memoir—provides the necessary perspective to discover that Zionist diplomacy has not simply been adequate to the task of creating and building a thriving Jewish state. It has, in fact, been one of Zionism's most important achievements.

Along the way, we will encounter many of the central luminaries and key historical events of our history: from Theodor Herzl, who not only wrote several of the founding texts of the Zionist movement but also laid the institutional and diplomatic foundation on which the entire enterprise would be ultimately built; to Chaim Weizmann, who successfully negotiated the Balfour declaration in 1917 and contributed decisively to the passage of the UN Partition plan three decades later; to Abba Eban, the greatest of Israel's diplomats in the country's first decades of statehood; to Menachem Begin, who led Israel in its first-ever peace treaty with the Arab world; to the many leaders that I've had the profound honor to work with directly—including Shimon Peres, Ariel Sharon, and Benjamin Netanyahu. As a whole, these historical giants were a resourceful, determined, articulate, and exceptionally creative group, and each of these individuals, at his own special moment in time, played an irreplaceable role that helped lead to the establishment and success of the Jewish state.

As a first step, then, I trace the threads that connect them all, the unique approaches to diplomacy that have served the Jewish homeland so well in the nearly century and a half since the Zionist movement launched.

PART I

THE LEGACY

CHAPTER 1

HERZL, WEIZMANN, AND THE FOUNDING OF ZIONIST DIPLOMACY

Dreams mean little without actions that convert them into reality. For decades and centuries before the late 1800s, Jews dreamed of a return to the biblical land of their forefathers, and even made repeated small-scale attempts to realize that dream.[3]

The story of modern Zionism begins, of course, with the feverish, creative work of its founding visionary Theodor Herzl, the black-bearded Viennese journalist and playwright who somehow, in the span of just one epoch-changing decade, from his first epiphany in the wake of the Dreyfus Affair in 1894 until his sudden death at age forty-two in 1904, managed to give birth to the movement that realized the dream.

In those few years, Herzl laid the groundwork for what eventually became the State of Israel. He did this both in the realm of ideas, through writings both futuristic and programmatic; and also through the creation of key institutions, including the Zionist Congresses as well as the Zionist Organization which contained almost all of the movement's practical organs in embryonic form—parliamentary governance, land acquisition, banking, immigrant absorption, and more.

---

[3] See Arie Morgenstern, "Dispersion and the Longing for Zion, 1240–1840," *Azure*, No. 12 (Winter 2002), pp. 71–132.

But Herzl's most intensive energies were reserved for diplomacy. He managed to meet personally with leaders around the world, from Kaiser Wilhelm II of Germany to the Russian interior minister to the king of Italy and the Pope. To each he described his outlandish-sounding dream of bringing the Jews back to the Promised Land. To each, he coupled that dream with proposals that attempted to win over both the hearts and the calculating minds of his interlocutors. In 1901, for example, he offered the Ottoman Sultan Abdulrahim II the proposition that the Jews would consolidate the empire's unbearable international debt in exchange for permission to create a national homeland in Palestine. As in almost every other case, he came away more or less empty-handed.

Herzl was not the first to dream or agitate for a modern-day Return to Zion. Across the nineteenth century, books were written—such as Moses Hess's *Rome and Jerusalem*—and movements were started, like Hibbat Zion, to prepare the Jews for the physical labor and self-defense that a Jewish homeland would require. Herzl, however, understood a few things that they did not about the nature of geopolitics in the age of emerging nation-states and competing colonial empires. As a journalist, he understood that without the official, public support of world powers, the Jews would have little hope of ever coming home.

When Herzl published his 1896 manifesto *The Jewish State*, it sent shock waves across the Jewish world. Here are the words of Chaim Weizmann, who would later lead the Zionist movement and eventually become Israel's first president. Weizmann had come from the *shtetl*, spoke Yiddish and Russian, had come to Germany to study chemistry, and by the time Herzl appeared on the scene, had been involved in Zionist activism for many years:

> I was in my second year in Berlin when, in 1896, Theodor Herzl published his tract, now a classic of Zionism, *Der Judenstaat—The Jewish State*. It was an utterance which came like a bolt from the blue.... Not the ideas, but the personality which stood behind them appealed to us. Here was daring, clarity, and energy. The very fact that

> this Westerner came to us unencumbered by our own preconceptions...what had emerged from the *Judenstaat* was less a concept than a historic personality.[4]

Herzl's principal operational goal as a statesman was to convince the world powers to grant the Jews a "charter" to create such a homeland—and to organize the Jewish people in such a way that those powers would take the idea seriously.

To achieve this goal, Herzl used diplomacy as perhaps no Jew since King Solomon had done. He effectively created something out of nothing. Riding the wave of his manifesto's success, in 1897 he organized the first Zionist Congress in Basel, Switzerland, pulling together leaders from around the Jewish world and establishing bodies that would become the core organs of the movement. Herzl was a master of theater, converting a casino into an august assembly hall, designing a flag for the Jewish nation, and making everyone dress up as if for royalty.

The success of the Congress, in turn, opened doors for Herzl to meet with global leaders, thus creating a virtuous circle that allowed the movement to take off: World leaders took him seriously because the Jews took him seriously, and vice versa. Zionist Congresses would be held almost every year after that, and the word "Zionism" became known around the world, not just among Jews but also in the loftiest halls of statecraft. Herzl's boundless energy, his ability to dream and articulate, his pragmatic side, all of it together constituted one of the most remarkable feats of bootstrapping that the political world has ever seen, anywhere on Earth.

But despite all these efforts, Herzl did not actually get very far with his diplomacy. It is no coincidence that, having failed to win over the world powers to the idea of Zionism, the movement he launched stalled out and very nearly expired when he himself suddenly passed away in 1904.

Part of his failure was due to his own limitations. As an assimilated Western European Jew, he spoke little Yiddish and had a hard time resonating with the larger masses of Eastern European *Ostjuden*, who saw

---

4 Chaim Weizmann, *Trial and Error: The Autobiography of Chaim Weizmann* (New York: Harper Brothers, 1949), p. 43.

the return of the Jews to the Promised Land in ancient, often religious categories. Even the more secular Jews in the East were suspicious of his top-down solution of a charter granted by the great powers as a result of diplomatic efforts. Many of them had long believed that the first steps needed to be practical—large numbers of Jews needed to learn Hebrew, to learn agriculture, to move there, to build a new civilization. Even as they attended the Congresses and called themselves Zionists, many saw Herzl as alien to the spirit that animated much of Jewish life, and did not hesitate to say so. These divisions were not lost on the world leaders he met with, undermining his credibility.

Herzl, however, was nothing if not the embodiment of Zionist urgency. And from the Jews' perspective, the urgency was entirely warranted. Cruel winds were swirling across Europe that were seen by many as small horrors that could lead to far bigger ones. Beginning with the Russian pogroms of 1881 and the rise of antisemitic political parties in Central Europe, culminating during Herzl's life with the Kishinev pogrom in 1903, in which dozens of Jews were murdered, hundreds of Jewish homes and shops destroyed, and a wave of shock rippled across the global Jewish community, it was becoming increasingly clear that Jews needed a way out. Zionism under Herzl offered immense hope. A messianic figure had appeared, and he had a plan.

But Herzl's biggest blunder flowed from the impatience that such urgency engendered. At the Sixth Zionist Congress in 1903, just months after Kishinev, he delivered what he believed to be wonderful news: the "Uganda plan." Miraculously, it seemed, Great Britain had offered him thirteen thousand square kilometers of mostly undeveloped land, about the size of Connecticut, east of Nairobi in modern-day Kenya. This could serve as temporary refuge for the Jews, as they awaited the possibility of finding their permanent home in Palestine. In the wake of Kishinev, and given the prevailing sense that antisemitism had been rising all over Europe for two decades, the prospect of an immediate refuge seemed too good to pass up.

Herzl's formidable powers of persuasion convinced a majority of the participants in the Congress to support this proposal, as bizarre as it may seem today. But for many others, the Uganda plan was nothing less than blasphemy. Men like the Ahad Ha'am (a pen name for the author Asher Ginsberg) and Chaim Weizmann, who had spent their lives, well before Herzl appeared on the scene, organizing and agitating for a return of the Jewish people to Zion, suddenly found Zion betrayed by a Congress that called itself Zionist.

The Uganda plan was, it turned out, a disastrous move for a political movement that had up to that point been fueled by a supreme clarity of purpose. The idea of Palestine as both a refuge and the subject of ancient longing, as a permanent home—that was Herzl's original dream on which the whole movement had been based, and for most Jews it was far more enticing than relocating to eastern Africa. The magic of Zionism had been fueled principally by Herzl's unique ability to take the ancient longing and make it seem plausible in the modern world. Uganda offered a shelter, not a home. For a large minority it was a non-starter. (Another part of the movement, led by the British-Jewish leader Israel Zangwill, was so enamored with the idea of a temporary refuge that, for years after Herzl's death, it continued to scour the Earth for suitable territory that frankly only a tiny number of Jews would have ever agreed to relocate to.)

The 1903 Congress ultimately voted in favor of the Uganda plan—but nearly half the delegates either voted against it or abstained. Herzl himself understood the danger that such a plan had of dividing, even destroying, the movement. The opposition was so harsh, and the minority against it so important to the movement's future, that Herzl withdrew his support for the plan. The Seventh Zionist Congress, held in 1905, put the issue to bed once and for all.

But as bad a political move as Uganda may have been, there's one thing that should be pointed out to Herzl's credit. Amid all his failures gallivanting about the courts of the world, Herzl successfully cultivated the one potential great power ally that would prove to be all the Zionists really needed—indeed, the only political force that could, one day in the future, realistically have both the desire and the power to facilitate the creation of a Jewish national home in Palestine.

He inspired an important group of men within the United Kingdom's political leadership of both the Liberal and Conservative parties.

Men like Arthur Balfour, who was prime minister when the Uganda offer was made to Herzl, and who would ultimately issue the famous Balfour Declaration as foreign secretary in 1917; David Lloyd George, who would become prime minister during World War I and shepherd the Balfour Declaration; and Joseph Chamberlain, the colonial secretary who personally made the African offer to Herzl. (Chamberlain's son Neville would, as prime minister in the late 1930s, prove far less helpful to the Zionist cause and to the Allied efforts against Nazism more broadly.)

These were pragmatic men with a soft spot for biblical romanticism and a grand vision of British expansion. They understood, through their own Protestant lens, the historical meaning of potentially being the ones who had saved the Jews and brought them, like the Persian King Cyrus in the sixth century BCE, back to the Promised Land.

Herzl understood, as early as 1898, the central role that Britain would one day play in the future of world affairs and, by extension, in fulfilling the Zionist dream. "From the first moment I entered the movement," he wrote, "my eyes were directed towards England because I saw that it was the Archimedean point where the lever could be applied."[5]

The trouble was, of course, that for all the vast land holdings of the British empire, stretching across Africa, India, and Southeast Asia, Great Britain did not actually control the Land of Israel. Palestine was still under the rule of the slowly decaying Ottoman Empire.

If politics is the art of the possible, as Bismarck said, then a Jewish homeland in Palestine was simply not possible in Herzl's time. Indeed, the biggest reason why Herzl didn't get what he wanted from the world leaders he met with was that the world, seen as a geostrategic map of great power calculations, was not ready for a Jewish national home in Palestine. And for all his prophetic consumption towards this one goal, Herzl seemed to understand this was the case, as well.

---

[5] Cited in Conor Cruise O'Brien, *The Siege: The Saga of Israel and Zionism* (New York: Touchstone, 1987), p. 122.

For their part, the Ottomans, who controlled Palestine, had no intention of fanning the flames of Arab nationalism by giving the Zionists the rights to immigration and land ownership that they desired. Their allies the Germans had no desire to upset the Ottomans, who were seeing their own empire gradually slipping away. The Western powers—Great Britain, France, and the United States—were perhaps more sympathetic in principle but powerless to deliver. And Czarist Russia had too many revolutionary movements threatening its regime to encourage any of them, including Zionism.

Herzl had managed, through remarkable self-propelled diplomatic legerdemain, to get in the door. He built connections, he cajoled and begged, he got the meetings with the most important men on Earth. He was infectiously impassioned and capable of getting down to business. These successes, such as they were, went a long way to convincing Jewish communities across Europe and beyond that something was changing, that the hope of salvation for millions of dispersed Jews was not a vain one, a hope that lingered even after the devastating news of his death.

Herzl's diplomacy lit a torch that would be carried by generations of Zionist diplomats. He taught the Jews that not only could they be full-fledged players in the geopolitical Great Game, but that they could do so on behalf of the Jewish people. He may not have delivered, but he made the fantastical seem suddenly plausible. Deliverance would come later.

From the perspective of world leaders, as well, there can be no doubt that Herzl left a powerful impression everywhere he went. But his direct influence on their policy was minimal. His dream of a charter for the Jews in Palestine was, for the time being, left flapping in the wind. He may have laid the foundation, conceiving the baby as it were. But the baby was quite nearly stillborn.

It is only in retrospect that we see how the institutions Herzl established, like the Zionist Congresses, the Zionist Organization, the Jewish Colonial Trust, and the tens of thousands of Jews who founded farms and defensive militia, kibbutzim, towns, and even small cities in Palestine in the first decade of the twentieth century—how all of these became the beginning of something much larger, and eventually the modern State of Israel.

***

Another decade would pass after Herzl's death before the global restructuring that accompanied World War I would lend his dream any semblance of real-world plausibility in the eyes of the great powers. And in fact, by the time the Allies were dissecting the remains of the Ottoman Empire, the establishment of a Jewish national home in the Land of Israel had somehow, almost miraculously, become a central feature of discussions among the victors at the highest levels. How did this happen?

The best-known moment in this part of the story is, of course, the Balfour Declaration, issued on November 2, 1917. In it, Lord Arthur Balfour, now foreign secretary, declared that "Her majesty's government view with favor the establishment in Palestine of a Jewish national home, and will use their best endeavors to facilitate the achievement of this object...." For the first time, a major world power had declared its official support for a Jewish homeland in Palestine.

Nor were the British acting alone. The United States, France, and other Allies had all expressed their support behind closed doors prior to the British declaration. Even Germany, the principal enemy of the Allied forces, was suddenly forced to take Zionism seriously, not least because of the country's large Jewish population and organized Zionist movement. As Weizmann writes:

> Perhaps the most interesting evidence of the seriousness with which the Zionist movement was being taken was the effort of imperial Germany to make use of it for her own ends. The German Zionist leaders were approached with the request to offer their services as intermediaries for peace negotiations.[6]

These talks didn't lead anywhere, and within just a few months, British troops would sweep through the Holy Land, the Great War would be over, and the commitments of the Balfour Declaration would become enshrined

6 Weizmann, *Trial and Error*, p. 185.

in the establishment of the British Mandate across the southern half of the Middle East. The San Remo conference of 1920, which formally carved up the conquered lands among the Allies, explicitly confirmed that the goal of the British administration in Palestine would be no less than the "establishment in Palestine of a national home for the Jewish people."

The Balfour Declaration and the San Remo conference were the first great diplomatic achievements of Zionism. But Herzl had been dead for thirteen years by the time Balfour signed his letter, and this miraculous moment in Jewish history did not happen on its own. The Balfour Declaration was, in fact, the product of an intensive diplomatic effort undertaken by Herzl's heirs.

And the chief diplomat of them all, the man who became Zionism's greatest guiding light of that period, was Chaim Weizmann, the founding father of Zionist diplomacy.

***

If Herzl's background made him an unlikely candidate to lead a long-exiled nation to freedom, Chaim Weizmann was, on paper at least, a preposterous choice as his successor. Skinny, bald, with a goatee and a heavy Eastern European accent, more comfortable in a chemist's laboratory than at a diplomatic dinner, it was much easier imagining him in a lab coat shouting "Eureka!" than as the leader of the movement to bring the Israelites out of two thousand years of bondage. He was in many ways the opposite of Herzl, who had traipsed around with his top hat and colossal beard. By contrast, the only time in his life that Weizmann ever wore a top hat was for his sole audience with the king of England.

But what made Weizmann even more unlikely is that until Herzl's death, he had staunchly opposed Herzl's focus on diplomacy. He had been one of the more vocal adherents to the camp of "practical" Zionism, led by Herzl's nemesis Ahad Ha'am. As opposed to Herzl's "political" Zionism, Weizmann and Ahad Ha'am believed that Herzl was wasting his time running around to world capitals peddling a vision of a Jewish state and seeking some kind of "charter" before any significant Jewish population had moved to Palestine and built the homeland's infrastructure. They viewed Jewish settlement, rather than a Jewish charter, as the necessary precursor to everything else, a proof of concept without which any charter or other international declaration would scarcely be worth the paper it was written on.

Weizmann came to England in 1904, the same year Herzl died, and took up a research position in chemistry at Manchester University. He spoke barely any English, and was in no position to justify his later achievements.

Weizmann found himself quite alone in England at first. While he could take counsel with Ahad Ha'am whenever he went to London, the great majority of the leadership of British Jewry were either anti-Zionist or followed Zangwill's increasingly tenuous version of the political approach. Despondent yet willing to bide his time, he spent most of his time in Manchester focused on his chemistry, while building his contacts and influence among Zionist sympathizers across the country.

With Herzl's sudden death in 1904, the Zionist organization found itself rudderless. Even the horrors of Kishinev were not enough to open the gates to Ottoman-ruled Palestine, and while a few tens of thousands of Jews were able to arrive and found new communities in what was known as the Second Aliyah, their ability to purchase land or immigrate freely was extremely limited.

Without Herzl around to offer a compelling case for diplomatic activity, Weizmann began to feel less of a need to focus solely on practical Zionism and started thinking about an approach that combined the practical with the political.

It is easy in hindsight to take for granted what the early Zionists had to learn for themselves: that without more than half a million Jews in Palestine, without the functioning cities and school systems and universities and the military force and economy they had built, there would never have been a UN Partition vote in 1947; and even if there were, there would not have been any chance of victory in the War of Independence. In this sense, the practical Zionists were right. But at the same time, without the diplomatic achievements of the Balfour Declaration and San Remo

Conference, and then later the Partition vote in the UN, the Jewish state would have remained an empty dream.

Weizmann understood this, and without Herzl leading the charge among the leaders of nations, he slowly fit himself into the role. He sold this amalgam to the movement as "synthetic Zionism," a synthesis of the practical and the political. But within a few years, he proved himself to be a master diplomat, a worthy successor to Herzl.

There is nothing like a world war to bring a man's hidden abilities to light.

For the world, too, was changing, in ways that required hard choices for the Zionist movement. To survive, Zionism had to include the major Jewish communities across Europe comprising the bulk of global Jewry. From England and France to Czarist Russia and the United States, Jews organized Zionist groups that all were part of the movement Herzl built and took part in the Zionist Congresses.

But Europe was lurching towards war, and the question of loyalty would become a portentous one. As the alliances became clearer, with the British, French, and Russians on one side, and the Germans, Austro-Hungarians, and Ottomans on the other, the Zionists relocated their headquarters to Copenhagen in neutral Denmark. Zionist groups existed on both sides, and the movement, they believed, had to stay neutral.

Weizmann disagreed. He was convinced that not only would war soon engulf the nations and change the composition of the world—which was widely understood—but that it would end with an Allied victory, which not many people believed at the time. And the greatest of the Allies, Great Britain, would soon have immense influence over the vast territories that made up the Ottoman Empire, including the Land of Israel. If the Zionists wanted the nations to take the Jews into account when dividing up the Middle East, they would have to bet on the right horse as early as possible.

Weizmann had gotten to know England during his years shuttling between Manchester and London. He knew that unlike the Catholic French, the British were Protestants with an innate sense of nostalgia for ancient Israel who could be inspired by the story of the return of Jews to their homeland. They also had a far greater strategic interest in Palestine than the French did: Having a highly developed Jewish protectorate there would provide a crucial buffer to their interests in Egypt, especially the Suez Canal. Wooing the British would also be helpful in bringing aboard the United States, which had the largest and most influential Jewish community in the world outside Europe.

So determined was Weizmann to sell the idea of a Jewish national home to the British that he quietly cut his ties with the Zionist headquarters in Copenhagen, telling them not to send him any more correspondence. He understood that only by going all in for Britain would he gain the trust of its political leaders. He thereby laid the groundwork for a century of Zionist and Israeli diplomacy.

***

One of the most important insights I have gained in my career as a diplomat is that there is a world of difference between *access* and *influence*. Many people have, for various reasons, the ability to gain the attention of those who wield power. But it is one thing to get in the door, and entirely another to change people's minds once inside the room.

Weizmann had this ability—and in this, he succeeded precisely where Herzl did not. One may imagine that whenever Herzl left the room, there was a stunned silence followed by furtive glances and perhaps even some nervous laughter. Herzl was a biblical prophet, a glorious kingly type who had, through force of his own fiery will, crafted a dream and rallied representatives of Jewish communities around the world behind it. He was a charismatic wonder who beamed into the room from another planet and, having departed, left the impression of a hurricane that had passed through, leaving people scrambling for a return to normalcy. The impression was immense—but not always effective.

Weizmann, on the other hand, brought with him a sense of clarity, integrity, and gravity. As a scientist, he believed deeply not just in the rigorous logic that undergirds reality, but also in the necessity for practical confirmations of theoretical imaginings. He was thus able to convey not just the plausibility, but the *inevitability*, of Zionist success in a way that moved people to change their minds and to keep their word. One simply did not want to fail Weizmann's implicit test of character. Nobody wanted to be on the wrong side of history, or to disappoint this noble force. Weizmann, Abba Eban wrote in his autobiography, "had a special capacity to believe and to convince others that the needs of Jewish history must ultimately prevail against all obstacles of rationality."[7]

How did he do this? Part of it was theater. Like Herzl, he presented himself as nothing less than the embodiment of thousands of years of history dating back to the time of the Bible. Like Herzl, Weizmann attended to the details, acting as though he were already a head of state of an important nation. As Eban recalls:

> One of his devices for promoting a Jewish state was to behave as though it already existed. His appearance—tall, and with a goatee and a prodigious bald pate—like a well-nourished Lenin, all his mannerisms, his air of tranquil superiority and of social ease, as well as his material habits such as riding around London in a chauffeured Rolls-Royce, were those of a chief of state engaged in a permanent summit conference. He addressed foreign statesmen as though his status were already equal to their own. They and he knew that it was not strictly true, but something in his bearing and in their own historic imagination forbade them to break the spell.[8]

Herzl rarely received this kind of praise, much as he might have wished for it. "His manner," the historian Howard M. Sachar put it, "transcended the regal and approached the dictatorial."[9] As a scientist of the first order, by contrast, Weizmann naturally occupied a more respected place in the

7 Abba Eban, *Abba Eban: An Autobiography* (New York: Random House, 1977), p. 8

8 Eban, *Autobiography*, p. 12.

9 Howard M. Sachar, *A History of Israel: From the Rise of Zionism to Our Time* (New York: Alfred A. Knopf, 1985), p. 64.

cultural hierarchy of any Western country than did Herzl the journalist, and acted as though he had far less to prove.

In some respects, he really did have less to prove. Unlike Herzl, Weizmann had the credentials of being a true *Ostjud*, an Eastern European Jew raised on the rafts of Ukrainian rivers, who could, precisely because of his foreignness, more plausibly play the role of "King of the Jews" than Herzl ever could. When Weizmann told you, in his Russian-Yiddish accent, that in spite of all the obstacles, masses of Jews would come to Palestine and build a beautiful, powerful civilization there, you believed him in a way you didn't necessarily believe Herzl, because you believed that Weizmann knew the hearts of the Jewish masses and the real-world challenges that such a vision entailed.

Weizmann also proved to be a consummate networker. Through his chemical research, he got to know the Jewish industrialist Charles Dreyfus, who was so moved by Weizmann's Zionism that he introduced him to then-former Prime Minister Arthur Balfour. (A key lesson I have learned as a diplomat is the value of cultivating relationships not just with those in power, but also with those among the opposition. They generally have more time on their hands, and eventually they return to power, at which point the investment pays off handsomely. I would apply this lesson to great effect in Washington in the late 1990s, as we shall see.)

Weizmann also struck up a friendship with C.P. Scott, editor of the Manchester *Guardian*, a major conservative paper. Scott found Weizmann's case for Zionism highly compelling and introduced him to other leading figures of the British establishment, including the Conservative Party politician Sir Mark Sykes, the Jewish rising star of the Liberal Party Herbert Samuel, and David Lloyd George.

No less important were the steps that Weizmann took to prove his value to the British as a chemist. By the time he was actively pitching them for a Jewish national home during World War I, many in the government already felt a debt to him for his crucial contribution to the war effort.

Lloyd George was minister of munitions and then minister of war before he became prime minister in December 1916, and it was Weizmann the chemist who, at his encouragement, had resolved one of most vexing problems of the war. The production of cordite, the smokeless gunpowder used by the Allied forces, required large amounts of acetone, which was difficult to come by. Weizmann discovered a process through which acetone could be extracted from corn and mass-produced—which Winston Churchill would refer to as the "Weizmann process."

In his memoir, Lloyd George describes the fateful exchange that set into motion a process that would result, the following year, in the Balfour Declaration:

> I said to him: "You have rendered great service to the State, and I should like to ask the Prime Minister to recommend you to His Majesty for some honour."
>
> He said: "There is nothing I want for myself."
>
> "But is there nothing we can do as a recognition of your valuable assistance to the country?" I asked.
>
> He replied: "Yes, I would like you to do something for my people." He then explained his aspirations as to the repatriation of the Jews to the sacred land they had made famous. That was the fount and origin of the famous declaration about the National Home for Jews in Palestine.[10]

In this, too, Weizmann was a superior diplomat to Herzl. For Herzl, every meeting was a cold call. At best, he was a bedazzling stranger offering his interlocutor a possible win-win by artificially inflating the global power of the Jews and his own role among them, leaving behind lingering doubts about whether he could actually deliver. At worst, he was being entertained only as a favor to someone else and was quickly sent packing, along with his top hat and his preposterous dreams.

---

[10] David Lloyd George, *War Memoirs*, Vol. I (London: Odhams Press Limited, 1936), p. 349.

Weizmann, by contrast, entered meetings with British officials carrying an unspoken assumption that it was they who owed *him* their attention, not the other way around.

The most important development from the perspective of the Zionists of that time was the resignation of Prime Minister H.H. Asquith and the rise of Lloyd George to replace him in December 1916. Now it could be said that a genuine Zionist ally—who had personally represented Herzl in talks about the Uganda plan—had moved into Number 10 Downing Street, just as the Allies were about to gain the upper hand in the war and conquer Palestine. Shortly after he took office, Weizmann, along with allies like Herbert Samuel, began actively lobbying the government on behalf of the Zionist dream.

***

The task, however, was far from simple, in part because the British had no interest in imposing the establishment of a Jewish homeland on their allies. The Balfour Declaration, issued on November 2, 1917, stands out as the first time a major power publicly announced support for a Jewish national home. But it came only in the wake of significant diplomatic efforts by the Zionists around the world. The preceding April, the government of France sent what became known as the Cambon Letter to Nahum Sokolow, one of the Zionist leaders, declaring that "it would be a deed of justice and of reparation to assist, by the protection of the Allied Powers, in the renaissance of the Jewish nationality in that Land from which the people of Israel were exiled so many centuries ago."

The French commitment, which was not publicized, was crucial for several reasons. First, because unbeknownst to the Zionist leadership, France and Britain had reached a secret agreement, known as the Sykes-Picot agreement, to rule jointly over Palestine once it was conquered from the Ottomans. (Later, once the British marched through, that agreement was quietly dropped.) Thus the French endorsement of the Jewish national home potentially would be no less important than that of Britain.

The following month, in May 1917, Sokolow traveled to France and Italy together with Mark Sykes and secured the blessing of Pope Benedict XV, who described the return of the Jews to Palestine as "providential." Meanwhile, Sokolow and Weizmann benefited from the support of the American Zionist Louis Brandeis, who the previous year had become the first Jew on the United States Supreme Court, to bring President Woodrow Wilson around to supporting the idea as well.

Indeed, it would turn out that by the time the fall of 1917 came about, the principle of creating a Jewish national home in the historic Land of Israel had been largely accepted by the Allied Powers. (Only Russia, overcome by two revolutions that year, had little to contribute.)

Meanwhile, a rumor had spread—which proved unfounded and, for all one knows, may have been the result of disinformation—that the Germans were considering a declaration of their own in support of the Jewish national home, beating Britain to the punch, in order to win over the support of global Jewry for the cause of the Central Powers. Balfour would use this rumor, along with the professed support from France and the United States, in his arguments before the British War Cabinet favoring the declaration.

One can tease out from all these efforts the outlines of a robust diplomatic strategy—one that would repeat itself in later years. Herzl had demonstrated the possibilities inherent in international diplomacy, and the advantage that having a broad network of well-connected Jews in different countries could give the Zionist movement. His success as a diplomat may have been limited, but Weizmann, Sokolow, and others understood the potential inherent in his diplomacy, and pressed it to much greater success.

They did so, first of all, by understanding the limitations of what they had already achieved: Even having the prime minister and foreign secretary of the United Kingdom on their side was no guarantee that a plan so bold and controversial as the establishment of a Jewish homeland would actually be implemented. They never knew where opposition could come from, especially in time of war, to disrupt their efforts. They pressed every lever they had in every country that could be seen as helpful. Whether an emerging great power like the United States, a centuries-long competitor like France, or an enemy in war like Germany—each would bring a different kind of pressure in the minds of different members of the British government.

And indeed, the biggest obstacle, it would quickly turn out, would be within the War Cabinet itself, embodied in the person of a Jew by the name of Edwin Montagu, who joined the government as secretary of state for India in August 1917. Like many prominent British and American Jews of the time, Montagu opposed Zionism, seeing it as fanning the flames of suspicion of disloyalty, even violence, against Jews around the world. Around the time of his appointment, he issued a memo arguing that the idea of endorsing a Jewish national home would be "anti-Semitic in result [and] will prove a rallying ground for anti-Semites in every country in the world."

The virulent opposition of a Jewish member of cabinet, however, did not prevent the Balfour Declaration from being issued. In part, this owed to the fact that in addition to the Protestant sympathizers like Lloyd George and Balfour, the idea was also supported by Montagu's cousin Herbert Samuel, who until recently had served as home secretary and was close to Lloyd George.

But such was Montagu's impassioned opposition, combined with Lloyd George's desire to avoid dividing the government and to provide a unified statement from the cabinet, that the resulting declaration was significantly watered down. Whereas the well-known, final version of the Balfour Declaration announces that the government "view with favor the establishment in Palestine of a national home for the Jewish people," the earlier version was far more full-throated, calling for nothing less than the "reconstitution of Palestine as the National Home of the Jewish People."

Weizmann was furious at the last-minute changes. "There cannot be the slightest doubt," he later wrote, "that without outside interference—*entirely from Jews!*—the draft would have been accepted early in August, substantially as we submitted it."[11]

Yet at this juncture, the Zionists made the crucial decision to accept the final text—a tactic that the Zionists would exercise again and again,

[11] Weizmann, *Trial and Error*, p. 204.

and which would Arab leaders would repeatedly fail to embrace: *When the negotiation has reached its end, take what you can get*. Half of something is better than nothing. Weizmann understood that a weaker first-ever world power declaration favoring the Jewish national home was still a thousand times better than none at all. The Zionists accepted it and declared victory.

Three decades later, a similar question would arise, in 1947, when the United Nations voted on Resolution 181 to divide the land west of the Jordan River between Jewish and Arab states. David Ben-Gurion and other Zionist leaders balked at a UN Partition plan that divided the proposed Jewish state into three barely connected regions and excluded Jerusalem. Despite this, Ben-Gurion decided—at the elderly Weizmann's urging—to accept the plan and to declare independence on May 14, 1948, understanding that war would anyway redraw the lines, and the flat-out rejection of the plan by the Arab countries would effectively render them irrelevant. Because an internationally recognized Jewish state in any part of the land, no matter how small, was infinitely better than none at all.

***

Weizmann's achievements came from a wide range of innate diplomatic skills he cultivated over many years. It wasn't just his networking or the sense of debt he created by the development of industrial acetone. A crucial part of his success was his uncanny ability to cast the Zionist cause differently for every interlocutor, without betraying the core of his truth. To find the terms that would speak to each person's sense of both personal and ideological interest.

All political actors live in a permanent state of weighing and re-weighing consequences. To change their decisions, one must not just inspire them, but also alter their calculus. The costs of actively helping the Zionists needed to be seen as less than the benefits. And while those costs were often clear—the need to override the wishes of one's own diplomats, to avoid upsetting allies, to trigger a harsh response from the Arab world, and so on—the benefits were not so easily measurable. An appeal to potential public support of the cause did not come with sophisticated modern polling. An appeal to the biblical resonance of Zionism required tapping into the listener's hidden sentiments and childhood religious yearnings.

Indeed, Weizmann had a remarkable ability to tailor his arguments to the specific interests of the person he spoke with. Here is Sir Charles Webster, who met Weizmann in 1917:

> With unerring skill, he adapted his arguments to the special circumstances of each statesman. To the British and Americans he could use biblical language and awake a deep emotional undertone; to other nationalities he more often talked in terms of interest. Mr. Lloyd George was told that Palestine was a little mountainous country not unlike Wales; with Lord Balfour the philosophical background of Zionism could be surveyed; for Lord Cecil the problem was placed in the setting of a new world organization; while to Lord Milner the extension of imperial power could be vividly portrayed.[12]

In 1918, as British forces advanced, Weizmann traveled into modern-day Jordan north of Aqaba to meet with Emir Faisal, the Hashemite leader of the British-backed Arab revolt and future king of Iraq. Weizmann convinced Faisal that there was nothing to fear from Jewish settlement in Palestine, that indeed it would be crucial for the development of a successful independent Arab kingdom. Faisal even lent his support to the Balfour Declaration in an agreement he and Weizmann reached, though that support was short-lived, as the Arabs came to utterly reject any kind of Jewish national home in Palestine.

Similarly, when trying to win the cooperation of the Soviet Union, Weizmann knew how to pivot straight into the rhetoric of Soviet Communism. In a letter he sent to Ivan Mikhailovich Maisky, Stalin's ambassador to Great Britain, in 1943, Weizmann wrote:

---

[12] Cited in Sacher, *A History of Israel*, p. 98.

> Three of the most fundamental aspects of Soviet social philosophy are embodied in the national system being built in Palestine by the Zionist movement: collective welfare and not individual gain is the guiding principle and goal of the economic structure; equality of standing is established in the community between manual and intellectual workers; and consequently the fullest scope is provided for intellectual life and the development of labor. There are no fundamental psychological barriers to mutual understanding, and the Zionist movement has never felt antagonistic to Soviet social philosophy.[13]

But despite Weizmann's chameleon-like ability to modify the language of his arguments, he never budged from their essence. Indeed, perhaps Weizmann's most important diplomatic skill was not his flexibility and adaptability, so much as his ability to combine these with a tendency to be, for lack of a better word, "undiplomatic."

Intuitively, Weizmann understood that a diplomat's greatest asset is not his personal likeability or the changing light he casts his arguments in, but rather the respect he earns in the eyes of others. And that respect comes less from how friendly or accommodating he is than from his absolute dedication to the principles and interests of the people he represents.

There is no question that Weizmann had a certain powerful magic about him—more subtle than Herzl's yet more serious because of it—when he met with people privately. In his first meeting with Balfour, in 1906, he presented himself not as some activist from a tiny, dispersed, and beleaguered people seeking acts of charity, but as the leader of an ancient, proud nation that had come to reclaim its role in history.

For his part, Balfour had been surprised at the opposition Weizmann and others had shown to the Uganda plan, which Balfour had proudly offered Herzl, and the former prime minister was hoping to convince

---

[13] Martin Kramer, "Who Saved Israel in 1947?" *Mosaic*, November 6, 2017, https://mosaicmagazine.com/essay/2017/11/who-saved-israel-in-1947/ (accessed October 11, 2024).

Weizmann of its benefits. The conversation, however, ended up going the other way, with Weizmann convincing Balfour of the centrality of the Land of Israel to any Jewish national home. Here is part of Weizmann's account of the meeting:

> Then suddenly I said: "Mr. Balfour, supposing I were to offer you Paris instead of London, would you take it?"
>
> He sat up, looked at me, and answered: "But, Dr. Weizmann, we have London."
>
> "That is true," I said. "But we had Jerusalem when London was a marsh."
>
> He leaned back, continued to stare at me, and said two things which I remember vividly. The first was: "Are there many Jews who think like you?"
>
> I answered: "I believe I speak the mind of millions of Jews whom you will never see and who cannot speak for themselves, but with whom I could pave the streets of the country I come from."
>
> To this he said: "If that is so, you will one day be a force."
>
> Shortly before I withdrew, Balfour said: "It is curious. The Jews I meet are quite different."
>
> I answered: "Mr. Balfour, you meet the wrong kind of Jews."[14]

It was through the strength of his personality, his articulate and impassioned commitment to his people, his bearing as a leader of equal stature

[14] Weizmann, *Trial and Error*, pp. 110–111.

to his interlocutors, and his ability to make the argument from a place of absolute certainty—that he found the path from access to influence.

A diplomat who is unwilling to say "no" will have difficulty getting others to say "yes."

It is such a lovely word, "no." In any struggle of wills, any act of sales, any attempt at persuasion—"no" suggests that the speaker is a person of strength, clarity, and command. We are oddly attracted to those who say "no" in ways that people who only say "yes" never seem to understand. For of what value is "yes" when it comes from someone who never says "no"?

This is not often understood in the diplomatic world. Indeed, even veteran diplomats often become so smitten with the ease and extravagance, the red carpets and accolades, the hotels and first-class travel—that they become lulled into neglecting to serve fully the interests and policies of their own governments. And the more they do so, the more they are feted and recognized by the "international community," the more it becomes difficult for the home government to correct their course.

Indeed, one might go so far to say that much of all that pampering of diplomats is aimed at precisely that goal—to help them to forget why they are really there. Many of the world's diplomats, I have come almost to believe, live in and ultimately serve a different country entirely, one I call "Diplomacy-land." With capitals in New York, Brussels, Geneva, and Davos, it almost acts as a separate sovereign entity, staking a powerful claim to every diplomat's true loyalty. It is by advancing this non-existent country's interests, no less than those of the home country, that reward, praise, and career advancement often become possible. And the material life of an ambassador and his family is often far more enticing than that of anyone back home at the Foreign Ministry (including, as I learned, even that of the director general).

Israeli diplomats are no less susceptible to this temptation than anyone else. This is surprising, given that most of them have personally experienced the horrific consequences of failed diplomacy, whether through the suicidal terror campaign of the Second Intifada or the missile attacks of the Second Lebanon War. Yet the temptation is inherent in the life of the diplomat. And it can be expressed in something as innocuous as putting less than your best efforts into defending controversial policies with which you may not fully agree.

This may sound self-evident, yet you would be surprised how often in my diplomatic career I found myself nearly alone, even among my fellow Israeli diplomats, in vigorously defending the policies of our nation.

There is, however, a second path to success in diplomacy—the path that follows Weizmann's example. And for the Zionists then and now, it has been in my mind the only one available to us: to remain true to principle and to one's national interests, no matter the short-term cost.

Or, to put it another way: Something about Weizmann's commitment to principle, his unflinching and consistent defense of the honor of his people, made other leaders trust him—even demanded a degree of personal loyalty to him. Decades later, in March 1948, U.S. President Harry S. Truman faced immense pressure to go back on his word to Weizmann and thwart the establishment of a Jewish state. And yet, he ultimately did not. As Truman confided to his friend Judge Samuel Rosenman, as he wrestled with the question of whether to recognize the Jewish state that was to be declared two months later: "I have Dr. Weizmann on my conscience."

***

Indeed, it is not unreasonable to suggest that many of Israel's greatest failures in foreign policy and diplomacy over the years have arisen in moments when they chose the path of conciliation and submission to pressure rather than adherence to principle and national honor.

On clear-cut matters of defense security, this principle has usually been fairly obvious to most Israeli decision-makers, who have been willing to endure intense international pressure, including threats of all-out war, in order to defend the key security interests of the country, from borders to preventing the sale of sophisticated weapons to our enemies, to bombing nuclear facilities in Iraq and Syria, to launching a major military retaliation in Gaza in the wake of October 7.

But in foreign relations and diplomacy, Israeli leaders have too often underplayed their own hands, gaining short-term agreeability at the expense of long-term national respect.

A few examples will make the point clear. By 1979, Egypt had lost every war it had fought with Israel and was ready for peace. A new era dawned, Egyptian President Anwar Sadat spoke in Jerusalem, U.S. President Jimmy Carter brought leaders together at Camp David, and then a treaty was signed on the White House lawn. It was wonderful. And from a security perspective, there was indeed peace. Armies stood down, Israel could demobilize its southern border, and the threat of war receded, more or less permanently.

And then—what? Beyond the military peace, there has been precious little in terms of economics and business, cultural exchanges, people-to-people relations, or major tourism. I exaggerate only slightly, but it's been made all too clear that Egypt, a nation of more than 100 million souls, is in no rush to enjoy the fruits of peace with Israel. And it's reflected in the nature of our diplomatic posture there: The entire relationship between our governments is run, from our end, out of the Defense Ministry. Again—this itself is no small achievement. When Hosni Mubarak's regime was overthrown in 2012 by Mohamed Morsi and the Muslim Brotherhood, a significant diplomatic effort was required to get Morsi to stop hinting at ending the state of peace between the countries. Morsi did not last long, and was replaced by a far more sympathetic figure, from Israel's perspective, in Abdel Fattah a-Sisi. But it's all relative, and the relationship remains today primarily one of warmer or colder defense relations—and not much beyond that. A similar relationship exists with Jordan, which made peace with Israel in 1994.

Why do we tolerate this? Why do we endlessly congratulate ourselves for achieving "peace" with two neighboring nations who continue to attack us virulently in international forums, who blame us for the violence that continues—even though it was their own countries that had started it all by going to war against us from day one? I do not wish to gainsay the strategic importance of the end of Israel's wars with Egypt and Jordan. Israel has benefited tremendously and in countless ways from it. But still, it is a cold peace, indeed, and Israel has not done much to change that, despite its being in a stronger position than ever to do so.

Other examples come to mind. In 2010, the government of Turkey actively encouraged a flotilla of ships—civilian vessels whose members were armed with axes and clubs—to break a naval blockade that Israel had imposed on the Hamas-controlled Gaza Strip. The organizing group, a Turkish NGO named IHH—which calls itself Humanitarian Relief Foundation in English—is a known material supporter of Hamas and has been designated by Israel as a terror organization. When Israeli naval commandos attempted to board the ship *Mavi Marmara*, as is their right under international law, they were attacked by these "nonprofit" activists, resulting in violent clashes and ten deaths.

Israel had every right, both in law and policy, to both create and enforce the blockade. Hamas, a globally recognized terrorist group, was importing missiles and other military equipment by sea to use against Israeli civilians. Boarding the vessel was Israel's basic obligation, and violent resistance should reasonably have been expected from commandoes defending themselves. Yet Turkey threw a fit, threatening Israel militarily and calling for UN inquiries. Under intense American pressure, Israel eventually issued an apology in 2014.

Perhaps Israel's leaders felt that apologies are merely words, meaningless in essence, while maintaining relations with Turkey was of paramount importance. Yet relations with Turkey never really improved much after that, whereas Israel's apology became the main thing people would remember about the incident. Israel was, in the world's eyes, wrong by its own admission. But it was not. Today, in the wake of October 7, Israel's relations with Turkey are at a nadir, with trade frozen, flights between the countries cancelled, and a constant stream of belligerent barbs emanating from Ankara.

We do this too often. By now we should have learned that diplomacy, to invert Clausewitz's famous dictum, is war by other means. Apologies may sometimes be essential in one's relations with friends and loved ones, but are usually extremely counterproductive at the international level, akin to a prevailing army suddenly losing heart and retreating.

Israel's greatest diplomats, from Herzl to Weizmann to Eban, understood this even before we had a recognized sovereign state of our own. If you act with dignity, stick to principle, and act from a position of strength, you will gain the respect of nations *even if in reality you have very little power*. And the reverse is also true: If you act as though you have little and deserve less, then all your tanks and sophisticated weaponry and money will mean very little as you play the game of nations.

CHAPTER 2

THE ROAD TO PARTITION

Three decades, to the month, passed between the issuance of the 1917 Balfour Declaration and the vote of the UN General Assembly on November 29, 1947, to divide the land of the British Mandate in Palestine into a Jewish and an Arab State.

The intervening years were marked by the remarkable growth of the Zionist enterprise, with the Jewish population in the Land of Israel ballooning from a few tens of thousands to more than 600,000. But the period was also marked by deep frustration and anxiety.

Under a new government, the British authorities progressively rolled back the commitments of the Balfour Declaration and San Remo Conference. They began limiting Jewish immigration to Palestine and responded weakly as the local Arabs escalated violence by organized Arab militias and mobs against Jewish civilians. The sense of urgency and despair grew as Europe darkened and the unfathomable horrors of the Holocaust and World War II unfolded.

The 1930s were marked by a policy of appeasement by the government in London, not just towards the rise of Hitler in Germany, but also towards the forces of Arab nationalism that coalesced and, in some cases, won independence in the territories under British control. (This approach, especially towards the Arab world but also towards other nations formerly under British colonial rule, continues to leave its mark in the United

Kingdom today, as I discovered in my two stints as a diplomat in London, as we shall see.)

As the British grew increasingly resistant to Jewish immigration—even as untold numbers were trying to escape the coming horror in Europe—the Jews of Palestine responded with increasing military activity of their own, not just in defense against the Arabs, but also against the British occupation forces. The mainstream underground Haganah paramilitary group—which would become the core of the Israel Defense Forces after independence—was joined by independent militias on the Right: Irgun (led by the future Prime Minister Menachem Begin) and Lehi (whose leaders included the future Prime Minister Yitzhak Shamir).

At a certain point, the British had had enough. Neither the Arabs nor the Jews were interested in making British rule an easy undertaking, and in February 1947 the British, under the Labour leadership of Prime Minister Clement Atlee, decided to toss the entire question of the Mandate into the lap of the newly established United Nations, which would meet in April to address the issue. The hope, it seems, was that the UN would recommend the continuation of British rule and lend it renewed international backing.

But the British Empire was looking smaller and weaker around the world, not entirely unlike the Ottomans a half-century earlier, and the UN wanted to establish itself as a body of global consequence. So it set up a Special Commission on Palestine (UNSCOP) to explore the possible end of the British Mandate—either through Partition into separate Jewish and Arab states, a confederation, or some other solution.

What happened next is well known. To the surprise of the British, UNSCOP recommended not the continuation of the Mandate, but a Partition of Palestine between Jewish and Arab states. The UN Partition plan was formulated as Resolution 181 of the UN General Assembly, and a vote was set for November. We have all heard the famous recordings of the roll-call vote that took place on November 29, 1947—"Argentina, *abstain*; Australia, *yes*," and so on. Enraptured Jews listened to the vote with transistor radios all around the world.

It passed. The Jews accepted partition, while the Arabs—who had refused to cooperate with UNSCOP and denied the UN any right to address the matter—rejected it and threatened all-out war. On May 14, 1948, the British finally withdrew from Palestine, and war arrived as promised. It was ultimately decided in favor of the Zionists, who captured additional territory and secured independence for the Jewish homeland, now known as the State of Israel.

What is less often mentioned is the remarkable diplomatic blitz undertaken by the Zionist leadership, with the help of Jewish and non-Jewish allies around the globe, over the course of a full year from the spring of 1947 until May 1948. It is a spectacular tale of diplomatic achievement, one that took advantage of half a century of experience, dating back to Herzl, using whatever means they had at their disposal.

There was a trigger to this effort—a moment that surprised everyone, including the Zionist leaders who had grown largely numb to the machinations of the British government and the "international community." Contrary to all expectation, it was the Soviet Union that started a process that ended with the establishment of the Jewish State. Despite the Soviets' record of overt hostility to Zionism, seeing it as a kind of fascist, bourgeois tool for Western imperialism, suddenly their tone changed. During the UN sessions of April 1947, in which UNSCOP was established, Soviet Foreign Minister Andrei Gromyko spoke almost warmly about the possibility of creating a Jewish state in Palestine. The British Mandate, Gromyko said, was irredeemable and should be dismantled. While he did not endorse Partition per se, he did see fit to suggest that perhaps it was time to give recognition to "the aspirations of the Jews to establish their own state."

What caused the sudden shift? Nobody knows for sure, but one reasonable explanation has to do with the Soviets' desire to accelerate the decline of the British Empire. In this they were not alone. A similar feeling, example, may have lent support to France's last-minute decision to support Partition when it finally came to a vote in November. As Abba Eban recounts in this context:

> I found that Zionism had a strong public echo in France. It has always been a major French enjoyment to benefit

> from Britain's troubles, and we were providing this sensual satisfaction in full degree.[15]

Once the Soviets had signaled that the idea of Partition had a fighting chance, the Zionists got to work, sending emissaries of the Jewish Agency and other Zionist bodies around the world. This sudden, unexpected Soviet support represented the best moment of hope for a Jewish homeland since the British first marched into Jerusalem in 1918.

Here, too, three decades after the Balfour Declaration, Chaim Weizmann played a crucial diplomatic role, particularly in securing the support of President Truman, not just in advance of the vote but also in the months that followed. Of course, there were also intensive efforts of American Jews, led by Abba Hillel Silver, to apply pressure on the administration. But it seems that at the key moments, it was not the American Zionists as much as Weizmann's unique personal chemistry with Truman that made the difference, particularly in a meeting at the White House on November 19, 1947, just days before the Partition vote.

Weizmann had a relationship with Truman that was not necessarily close or intimate, but resonated deeply. Truman saw in Weizmann a man of such rare qualities, such integrity, that he did not want to disappoint him. Surely, Truman saw this as a historical opportunity, an incredible moment of millennial proportions. To get the meeting, Weizmann took advantage of the network of Jewish connections that were crucial for the Zionists not just back then but, I would argue, today as well. In particular, a former business partner of Truman's, a Jew by the name of Eddie Jacobson, was crucial to getting Weizmann a private meeting with the president on more than one occasion.

But most important, Weizmann understood the one thing that could serve as a proper counterweight to the intense pressure against Partition coming from the State Department and other government officials worried about relations with the Arab world: the American voter. Truman knew America, and it was an election year, and he understood that the Zionist story resonated deeply, not just with Jews but across the country. Like the

---

[15] Eban, *Autobiography*, p. 73.

British, Americans were mainly Protestant, and they loved their biblical tales. Americans especially also loved an underdog. Less than three years after millions of Jews had been murdered by the Nazis, this group of Jews was struggling for independence in their ancient homeland, looking for a solution to hundreds of thousands of Jewish refugees stuck in displaced person camps, and about to face the military onslaught from the entire Arab world. No Hollywood film could do this underdog tale justice. (Indeed, none ever has.)

Yet while Weizmann was busy trying to secure American support, the other Zionists were engaged in a global diplomatic operation of supreme complexity and urgency. This all-hands-on-deck campaign was directed mainly by Moshe Sharett, who the following year would become the State of Israel's first foreign minister and, later, its second prime minister after Ben-Gurion, as well as the American-Zionist leader Nachum Goldmann and others.

The vote was set for November 26 and would require a two-thirds majority. Countries that either abstained or were absent would not be counted. So changing a "no" to "abstain" was almost as important as moving states into the "yes" column.

Well into November, the math did not look good. Muslim countries held ten of the fifty-seven seats and were a powerful bloc voting solidly against. As for the countries of Western Europe and Latin America, each would decide based on its own considerations. Even with both Soviet and American votes in favor, getting to two-thirds would be exceptionally difficult.

***

One by one, the votes had to be whipped. In some cases, the Zionists took advantage of connections through Jewish communities around the world; in others, through sympathetic non-Jews who knew the right people. The United States, having decided in mid-November to vote in favor, now pressed its allies as well and was able to secure several last-minute changes of heart.

Wednesday, November 26, 1947, was the last travel day before the Thanksgiving holiday—less than ideal for urgent diplomatic activity in the United States. But this did not deter the Zionist leaders gathered at the UN's temporary headquarters in Lake Success, New York. It became clear that not enough yes votes had been lined up. The president of the General Assembly, Oswald Aranha, who was something of a Christian Zionist himself, encouraged the delegates who supported Partition to stretch out their speeches in order to force a delay in the vote. In this, he had the backing of the UN secretary general, a Norwegian by the name of Trygve Lie, who was no Zionist but favored Partition as a way of proving the importance of the United Nations itself, which was barely three years old.

The filibuster worked. The following day was a holiday, so the vote had to be pushed to Friday, November 28. But even this two-day delay was not enough to get to two-thirds, and again they needed to drag out the proceedings to have a chance to twist a few more arms. It was only on Saturday, November 29, in the late afternoon New York time, that voting finally began.

During these few days, the Zionist diplomatic operation went into high gear, with a big assist from Washington—and revealed itself to be one of the most sophisticated, well-oiled diplomatic machines ever to enter the international arena.

One by one, votes were turned. The Belgian vote was swayed by an ex-roommate of the Belgian delegate to the UN, a Jew by the name of Chaim Perelman, who had served in the Jewish underground during the Holocaust and was now recruited into the effort.

France, too, had been leaning towards abstaining, and threatened to take other Western European countries with it. Abba Eban, then a young diplomat just getting his feet wet in New York, convinced Weizmann to send a cable to Léon Blum, the Jewish former prime minister of France who wielded considerable influence in the Élysée Palace. "Does France wish to be absent," Weizmann asked Blum, "from a moment unfading in the memory of man?" The French voted in favor.

Jews and other Zionists around the world were recruited to help. This was especially important in Central America, where an American-born Jew by the name of Sam Zemurray may have played a pivotal role in turning Costa Rica, Panama, Nicaragua, and Guatemala into yes votes. Zemurray, also known as "Sam the Banana Man," was the owner of United Fruit Company, the world's leading grower of bananas. He had met Weizmann in 1922 and became enamored with the rebellious Zionist spirit. Something of a rebel himself—among his exploits, Sam had hired American mercenaries to stage a coup in Honduras in 1930 in order to ensure his competitive advantage in the growing North American banana market—Sam had arranged for ships to help Jews break the British blockade to immigrate into Palestine, and would later play an important role in supplying arms to Israel during the 1948 War of Independence. So dominant was Sam's power in the economies of these Central American "banana republics" that in advance of the UN decision on partition, he was able to work the phones and secure, it seems, at least four votes in favor.

Other votes were threatened by miscommunication. To get the Philippines on board, agents from the Haganah's London office recruited the support of an American-Jewish civil servant by the name of Julius C.C. Edelstein, who had spent time in Manila and was close with Philippine President Manuel Acuña Roxas. He had already received assurance of a favorable vote from Roxas, but as the vote drew near, it turned out that the Philippine ambassador at the UN hadn't received any instructions.

The Haganah agents tracked Edelstein down at his London hotel at 3 a.m. local time. The ringing phone woke him up. They told him to call Roxas again.

On the other end of the line, there was silence. The agents got nervous. "Mr. Edelstein? Are you still there?"

"Hang on, I'm thinking," he said. "What time is it in the Philippines?"

The call was made, the Philippine UN delegate was summarily replaced, and the vote was cast in favor.

In the case of one South American country that had promised a yes vote, the ambassador chose to hide in the men's room at the UN as the voting was about to begin. The Jewish Agency's Argentinian liaison was sent to look for him, recognized his shoes from under the walls of a bathroom stall, and dragged him back to the plenum to cast his yes vote.

Haiti had planned on voting against, but Nachum Goldmann made a last-minute call to Adolf Berle, a former assistant secretary of state under President Franklin Roosevelt. Berle then managed to convince the relevant people in Washington to extend a significant loan to the Haitian government. Haiti voted in favor.

To sway the vote of Liberia, help was enlisted from Edward Stettinius, the former secretary of state and first American ambassador to the UN. Stettinius turned to his friend Harvey Firestone, Jr., whose Firestone tire company employed more than 12,000 Liberians in its rubber-tree plantations in the African nation. Firestone then reached out to William Tubman, the Liberian president, and threatened to pull out of the country entirely. The threat was taken seriously, and another yes was tallied.

Thailand had voted against Partition in committee only a few days earlier. Weizmann cabled the White House, which exerted pressure on the Thais. Suddenly, a dispute arose surrounding the legitimacy of the delegation amid a transition of power back home. On the morning of Wednesday, November 26, General Assembly President Aranha received an oddly fortuitous call from the Thai embassy in Washington declaring the credentials of the UN delegation to be null and void. By the time the final vote was cast three days later, the Thai ambassador had, miraculously, already set sail on the *Queen Mary*. Thailand was the only country listed as "absent" in the vote on partition.

Yet perhaps the most surprising example involved China. Because of its significant Muslim population, China was inclined to vote against, and probably would have done so if not for the intervention of one Morris "Two-Gun" Cohen, a Jew from Poland who, by way of England and Canada, somehow became an aide de camp to Sun Yat-sen, then a major-general in the Chinese army prior to the Communist revolution in 1949. When he learned that China was going to vote against partition, Cohen flew to San Francisco and persuaded the Chinese delegation to abstain.

By the end of it all, the Muslim bloc was able to muster only three additional "no" votes, from India, Cuba, and Greece. Thirteen in all voted against, while thirty-three voted in favor—that is, 72 percent—along with ten abstentions and the one Thai absence. The motion just barely cleared the two-thirds threshold.

The United Kingdom, humiliated by the whole affair and unable to spin the developments into anything favorable, abstained.

Jews around the world, listening to the roll being called in a live broadcast, broke into spontaneous celebration. Unaware of the vast diplomatic operation that had brought it to pass, it was for them a miraculous event, coming just a few years after the Holocaust.

In Jerusalem, where it was well into the night, thousands of Jews filled the plaza outside the Jewish Agency building on Keren Hayesod Street and roared with song and dance.

Ben-Gurion had been taking a much-needed respite on the shores of the Dead Sea. Fearing attack from Arab marauders angered by the developments at the UN, he had rushed back to Jerusalem. Now, as the celebrations carried on outside his headquarters, he sat at his desk with his head in his hands, overwhelmed by the responsibility and the shock of the historical moment.

A similar scene took place at that exact same moment in a car heading out of the UN temporary headquarters on Long Island. Abba Eban's wife Suzy, who herself had participated as a Zionist liaison to UNSCOP and was in New York for the vote, recalled how she, Eban, and Moshe Sharett made their way back to Manhattan immediately after the vote. "We sat in the car, Sharett, my husband and myself, from Lake Success to Manhattan," she would later recount, "and nobody said a word. It was overpowering."[16]

The lessons from 1947 continue to resonate today with Israel's diplomats. First, that everything one does to build relationships of trust around the world—all the meetings, the favors, the honors—might be needed at a crucial moment in one's nation's history. There is a point to all of it, which is to build up a war chest of friends, allies, and personal trust that cannot be easily replaced with military or economic might. Even superpowers like

[16] Toldot Yisrael, "November 29, 1947: The Story of a Vote," November 23, 2010, video including interviews with participants, https://www.youtube.com/watch?v=QrIjzUK0FKg (accessed October 11, 2024).

the United States frequently discover, much to their chagrin, the limits of "hard" power in getting their way.

Second, that the Jewish state owes much of its success on the world stage—to this day, if not always in the same way—to the Jewish Diaspora. Israel was created as a state for the Jewish people, a Jewish homeland, and without the aggressive, coordinated efforts of Jews around the world, the votes could never have been turned.

It seems that many Jews, both in Israel and in the Diaspora, have in recent years enjoyed flirting with the idea that these two communities have reached a moment of severe crisis in their relations. On both sides, one often saw expressions of disgust or anger about the behavior of the other—even talk of a "divorce" between Israel and the Diaspora. But the events of October 7 and their aftermath have dramatically changed that dynamic. Today, for a great many Israelis and Diaspora Jews, it is every bit as clear as it was in November 1947 that their fates are inextricably bound. Whether that feeling continues into the future remains an open question—and it will depend, in no small part, on the lessons learned by Israeli diplomats and pro-Israel Diaspora activists.

***

Yet despite the passage of Resolution 181 in November 1947, the campaign was far from over. Almost immediately, opponents to Jewish statehood began looking for ways either to overturn Partition or at least to shrink the size of the Jewish territory to the point of its becoming utterly unviable. The British declared their intention to withdraw their troops on May 14, 1948, and in the months that passed between November and May, a number of proposals tested the commitment of those who had voted in favor, especially the United States.

During that time, President Truman had largely soured on the Zionists—mainly because of what he saw as endless harassment from the American branch of the movement, led by Abba Hillel Silver, who appeared to be backing the Republicans in the coming election. Things got sufficiently bad that Truman instructed his chief of staff not to allow any Zionists into the White House.

It was here, again, that Weizmann was called upon—despite being elderly, ailing, and nearly blind—to turn the tide. He reached out to Eddie Jacobson, his former business partner. Jacobson spoke with the president, who did everything in his power to avoid a meeting. It was only when Jacobson compared Weizmann to Truman's hero Andrew Jackson that the president finally agreed. Weizmann was instructed to come in on March 18, 1948, and to enter through the back door.

It was during that meeting that Truman reaffirmed his commitment to the Partition plan and to Jewish independence. He promised—despite intense pressure, not least from his own secretary of state—to recognize the Jewish state immediately upon its upcoming declaration.

And then, the very next day after that meeting, the American delegate to the UN Security Council proposed a special session of the General Assembly to discuss the creation of an "international trusteeship" instead of Partition. Truman could not believe his ears. But he couldn't disavow his own State Department, either, especially not in an election year. Weizmann, however, remained firm in his belief that Truman would stay true to his word.

He did. On May 14, 1948, eleven minutes after Ben-Gurion declared independence for the Jewish state and named it the "State of Israel," Truman declared American recognition of Israel, and it may not be an exaggeration to say that his action—on which the fate of my country truly hinged—came about in large part due to the specific relationship that Weizmann had cultivated with him. "The old doctor will believe me now," Truman said to an aide at that moment.

It goes without saying that over the coming three-quarters of a century, relations between Israel and the United States would ultimately emerge as the most important international relationship for Israel and as a central feature of American foreign policy in general. These relations are built, as we shall see, on a broad foundation of both interests and public sentiment, and express themselves through many layers and across cultural, business, and governmental ties—ties that, for the most part, cannot be linked directly to the historical moment of Truman's decision.

But Truman's yes vote is worth focusing on when considering the enduring lessons of Zionist diplomacy. *The old doctor will believe me now*. It is fascinating to consider how this—his need to make good on his promise to Weizmann—escaped Truman's lips at that moment. Not the historic nature of the decision, not the religious moment, certainly not placating American Zionists, nor anything else. For him, the decision ultimately wasn't about politics, or history, or religion. It wasn't about his prospects for re-election. For Truman, it was about keeping a specific promise to a specific man.

It was about trust.

***

Diplomacy is a broad label that is often wildly misunderstood. True, sometimes it is about having fancy dinners with decision-makers, or about eloquent speech-making. Sometimes it's about creating a certain impression—the theater of it all. Sometimes it's about networking, or working a room, or simply representing your country with dignity in formal settings.

But there are moments when all these investments need to be fed into something much larger and centrally directed. Something that looks almost like a military operation. It is the *machinery* of diplomacy, the ability to mount a sophisticated, coordinated campaign of well-trained, well-connected, and well-spoken individuals with the singular aim of achieving a result in the interest of your nation, that national survival can depend on.

In the diplomatic history of Israel, the effort to pass the United Nations Partition plan in 1947 stands out as the ultimate campaign, where success and failure meant the difference between the life and death of a nation. It is an example that sits in the back of every Israeli diplomat's mind and reminds us all exactly what we are capable of achieving.

It also relies on an invisible diplomatic infrastructure, on successful programs that recruit and train diplomats over many years, on budgetary battles with the Finance Ministry, and on excellent internal communication.

It relies on having people in place who can read the diplomatic map, give decisive orders, and allocate resources accordingly.

It requires learning the lessons of Herzl, Weizmann, and the great diplomatic actors of the Zionist movement—lessons that become no less important in an era in which the Jewish homeland has become a relatively powerful actor on the world stage, in which the temptation to neglect diplomacy in favor of "hard" power has never been greater. Zionist diplomats today must draw upon these historical figures' remarkable ability to deploy pre-existing informal networks, both Jewish and non-Jewish, to recognize where the nodes of power reside, to cast a broad net in terms of which nations we seek to influence, and to make our pitch within the framework of those nations' interests rather than our own. At the same time, we must insist on the dignity and honor of our nation—including the prolific deployment of the word "no"—to help to frame all conversations in a way that advances our nation's interest. We must be creative and energetic, and deploy a preemptive sense of urgency in order to be remain a step ahead.

Above all, it requires a clarity of purpose that is shared across a country's entire diplomatic corps.

The new Jewish state that emerged after the War of Independence in 1948 learned an important lesson from the three decades between Balfour and Partition, and especially from the campaign to get Resolution 181 passed. True, sovereign independence would mean enjoying the freedom to live our lives and wage our own battles. But it also meant that we could no longer rely on anyone to save us.

Indeed, the inescapable fact that glared at the Zionist leaders on the morning of November 30, 1947, was this: Every single nation that voted in favor of UN Resolution 181 the day before could easily have gone the other way. The United States had backed Israel mainly on the strength of Weizmann's unique relationship with Truman, at a time when the days of institutionalized American bipartisan support for Israel, with which we are so familiar, were still decades away. The brief window of support from the Soviet Union snapped shut the moment the Soviets understood that Israel would not become a Communist client state like East Germany.

No, the new State of Israel would have to learn to defend itself, first of all against the military might of the Arab world, mostly on its own. Perhaps there were nations on Earth that could get away with subordinating their fundamental interests to the decisions of larger powers. Israel was not one of them.

Indeed, this idea—that Israel *would defend itself, by itself*—became the central pillar of its foreign and defense doctrines for the decades to come, and no less so of its diplomatic messaging.

Across the 1950s and 1960s, one man stood out as far and away the most able of these diplomats, the one who rightfully bore the torch of Zionist diplomacy that had been lit by Herzl and carried forward by Weizmann.

That man was Abba Eban. It is to his remarkable role in the history of Zionist diplomacy that we now turn.

CHAPTER 3

DEFENDING OURSELVES, BY OURSELVES (WITH AMERICAN HELP)

At no point in his life would it have been appropriate to describe Abba Eban as "dashing." Like his predecessors, there was something unusual, even funny looking, about him. Tall and portly with thick glasses and a double chin that inflated dramatically over the years, Eban was, like Herzl and Weizmann before him, striking in appearance without being cut from any particular aesthetic cloth.

Yet his oratory skills, especially in English, were unparalleled in Israeli history, before or since. In November 1956, as Israel's UN ambassador, Eban delivered a speech at the height of the Suez Crisis that was not just broadcast around the world, but re-broadcast on radio and television for days afterwards, and then commercially released as a record sold in stores. In June 1967, as Israel's foreign minister, Eban delivered a speech at the United Nations in the middle of the Six Day War that was so powerful, and resonated so broadly among American listeners, that President Lyndon Johnson said it was "worth several divisions" in Israel's war effort. A graduate with high honors from Cambridge University, Eban was a master of the quick retort. When complimented once for his perfect "Oxford English," he immediately quipped: "Cambridge, actually. But in politics one expects to be slandered."

The classic story of Israel's first decades usually focuses on the outcomes of the various military conflicts that were forced upon the fledgling Jewish state. For reasons that baffled a great many people, not least the founding generation of Israelis, Israel became the immediate focus of the violent ire of a broad swath of humanity—across the Arab and Muslim worlds and throughout the Soviet sphere of influence. And this anger expressed itself not merely in rhetoric or protest, but in repeated attempts to destroy the nation by force of arms.

It began with our War of Independence, an effort of five Arab armies to reject Partition through military invasion. Israel won that bloody war, establishing itself by 1949 as a fully sovereign state with Jerusalem as its capital. Yet it remained in a fragile strategic state, under constant threat from the far larger Arab forces that surrounded it—which led to another war, in 1956 against Egypt, known as the Sinai Campaign. In 1967, the Six Day War erupted after Egypt cut off Israel's southern shipping routes, which resulted in a lightning victory for Israel and the capture of territory that had been controlled by Egypt, Syria, and Jordan—including the reunification of Jerusalem. In 1973, the combined forces of Egypt and Syria, again with Soviet support, launched a massive surprise invasion on Yom Kippur, Israel's holiest day—which Israel managed to rebuff only after weeks of intensive fighting and heavy losses. Even after Israel made peace with Egypt in 1977, hostilities continued from Palestine Liberation Organization (PLO) militias across Israel's northern border in Lebanon, leading to the First Lebanon War in 1982, which drove the PLO out of Lebanon. And so on.

But the classic story, built as it is on the outcomes of military battles, oversimplifies the situation to the point of distortion. From the day that David Ben-Gurion stood at the Tel Aviv Museum in May 1948 and declared the independence of the "state of the Jews, to be known as the State of Israel," the nation's prospects of success or failure, and the contours of its borders, depended on the outcome not only of wars, but also of an intense diplomatic struggle that raged in New York, Paris, Washington, London, and around the world without respite for years and decades to follow.

The Partition plan embodied in UN Resolution 181 in 1947 was accepted by the Jews of Palestine, but it was rejected, *in toto*, by the entire Arab world. It included a map that was dramatically different from the one that emerged with the end of the War of Independence in 1949. Jerusalem, according to that resolution, was not to be divided between Israel and Jordan, but rather designated as a "condominium" under international authority. Large parts of the western Galilee as well as a sizable section of the Negev and the Judaean desert, including the city of Beersheba, were meant to be outside the Jewish state's borders. In sum, the "Jewish state" according to the UN map consisted of three barely connected cantons in the eastern Galilee, the coastal plain from Tel Aviv to Haifa, and the vast emptiness of the Negev and Arava deserts south to Eilat.

These borders were, again, better than nothing. But they were not even remotely defensible against the coming onslaught of the combined armies of the Arab world. Even with the war's gains—western Jerusalem, the corridor leading to the coastal plain, and the whole Galilee were, by 1949, in Israel's hands—Israel's strategic position remained precarious, with the country's midsection still only nine miles wide from the Mediterranean coast to the hostile Jordanian border in the West Bank. Eban famously referred to these armistice lines as "Auschwitz borders."

From a diplomatic perspective, the new State of Israel was not much better off. Even if Israel enjoyed the formal recognition of both the United States and the Soviet Union, this was not enough to prevent the Arab states from acting as a solid, rejectionist voting bloc in subsequent UN resolutions; nor did it ensure that the territorial gains won in the War of Independence would enjoy global recognition. True, the great powers continued to utter statements of recognition for Israel and a rejection of the obvious aggression of the Arabs. But the logic of power—the Arabs really were Goliath to Israel's David—suggested that world support could be short-lived.

It was in the UN that many of these battles were fought, with a constant flow of new plans for the effective dismembering of the Jewish state, with walkouts by the Arabs every time the Israeli representative spoke, with questions of Israel's legitimacy constantly in the air.

Nor was territory the only matter up for constant discussion. Early in the war, the UN openly debated whether Israel even had the right to allow free immigration. Hundreds of thousands of Jewish refugees were now pouring into the country, and those who were able-bodied were immediately enlisted into the war effort. According to Shimon Peres, "We had started the war in May 1948 with fewer than thirty-five thousand troops. Before the end of the fighting in 1949, more than one hundred thousand had taken up arms for the Zionist cause."[17] Immigration, in other words, was seen a form of armament, and not just by the Arabs.

The work of fighting this diplomatic battle fell primarily on two men: Foreign Minister Moshe Sharett and, above all, the nation's first UN ambassador, Abba Eban. Eban had played a crucial supporting role to Sharett's and Weizmann's efforts in New York in 1947 and 1948. With independence, he was the obvious choice for the UN post.

On May 26, 1948—less than two weeks into Israel's independence, in the thick of the war that would either define a new nation or result in its annihilation—Eban spoke powerfully before the United Nations Security Council. The United Nations had been founded three years earlier on a core principle that rejected wars of aggression, he said. But the Arab states had launched precisely such a war, in the process attacking not only the recognized Jewish state, but also the entire dream on which the United Nations itself was founded. And now the Arabs were defying repeated UN calls for ceasefire while simultaneously pressing for resolutions that would effectively undo the Partition plan. Eban stated:

> Here is a flat and defiant rejection of the Security Council's cease-fire resolution. In its place, we have a proposal for revoking Israel's statehood and independence. The sovereignty regained by an ancient people after its long march through the dark night of exile is to be surrendered at pistol-point.

---

[17] Shimon Peres, *No Room for Small Dreams: Courage, Imagination, and the Making of Modern Israel* (New York: HarperCollins, 2017), p. 48.

> It becomes my duty to make our attitude clear. If the Arab states want peace with Israel, they can have it. If they want war, they can have that too. But, whether they want peace or war, they can have it only with a sovereign State of Israel.[18]

Over the course of the 1948–1949 war, in meetings of the General Assembly, the Security Council, and various committees taking place in New York, Paris, and Geneva, the UN continually pressed for, and sometimes passed, ceasefire resolutions based on the present state of battle. Every time, a ceasefire would mean, on the one hand, that Israel's forces could rest and replenish. But the same was, of course, true for the Arab side, which was stunned by its failures in battle and loss of territory.

Besides ceasefire efforts at the UN, there was also a constant effort to formulate an international trusteeship for the city of Jerusalem, an exercise that grew increasingly fantastical as the front lines hardened in the city, with neither Israel nor Jordan the least bit interested in relinquishing control over half of the holy city.

It was during this early phase that Israel's enemies, having failed to prevent the nation's establishment either by arms or in the halls of the United Nations, began to inject their venomous opposition to Israel's very existence into the fledgling institutions of the UN wherever they could. By December 1949, to cite one of several examples, they had lobbied for the creation of the UN Relief and Works Agency (UNRWA), which focuses on helping Palestinian refugees. This agency exists completely independently of the UN High Commission for Refugees (UNHCR), which was established by a separate resolution of the General Assembly the *same month* as UNRWA was founded, and covers refugees of wars around the world.

Even today these institutions are separate: While UNHCR invests immense efforts to help people around the world end their refugee status, UNRWA—through entirely different definitions and practices—is designed to perpetuate the problem from one generation to the next and to educate successive generations of Palestinians about the alleged injustice

[18] Eban, *Autobiography*, p. 120.

of Israel and the need to resist it. (In the Gaza Strip, the world has now learned, UNRWA went far beyond even this mandate, effectively integrating with, and providing civilian cover for, the Hamas terror apparatus that ruled the Strip.)

This difference in goals is reflected in budgets, curricula in UNRWA schools, and more. But the most obvious example is in the two different bodies' basic definition of who is considered a refugee. Because UNHCR is meant to alleviate the humanitarian crisis that individuals face from displacement, it naturally defines a refugee as someone who has been displaced and has neither returned home nor been absorbed elsewhere. The UNRWA definition of refugee, by contrast, is a hereditary status handed down from one generation to the next—the assumption being that Palestinian refugees, *and they alone*, should enjoy a permanent status that extends to infinity regardless of their actual humanitarian needs, even as subsequent generations build new lives in other countries. The result is as predictable as it is absurd: An estimated Palestinian refugee population of no more than 860,000 in the 1950s has, under UNRWA, ballooned to more than five million people around the world.

What is the purpose of UNRWA? It is, in its essence, a political tool in the struggle against Israel, not a tool for humanitarian relief.

I will return to the UN's perpetual assault on Israel in greater detail. Suffice it to say at this stage that while many UN agencies, from the very beginning, were created to promote universal ideals, human rights, and peace, not all were, and many others no longer do.

As Israel's ambassador to the United Nations, I personally saw how decades-old anti-Israel structures, introduced during the Cold War at a time when fighting Israel's very existence was a high-priority goal not only of the Arab world but of the Soviet empire as well, continue to operate to this day.

The result is that in too many cases, instead of serving as a vehicle for a better world, the UN merely replicates the bad things of the world through more polite means—or makes them worse.

***

And yet, despite the diplomatic challenge of Arab rejectionism during and after the War of Independence, Israel also gained from it. From the moment the Arab nations took an absolute stance against Jewish statehood, they put themselves at a distinct diplomatic disadvantage. Over and over, their belligerence towards Israel was demonstrably stronger than their willingness to improve their own people's lives—a fact that did not sit well with the core principles on which diplomatic structures in the postwar era were built. As Eban famously put it, "the Arabs never miss an opportunity to miss an opportunity."

They refused, for example, to participate in the 1947 UNSCOP process, which meant that they had nobody working with the commission to influence the results, whereas the Zionists did. They refused to accept the Partition plan, which in practice meant that the Jewish state was established, whereas a Palestinian Arab state was not, and still has not been. In the context of ceasefire efforts during the war, their radical rejection of the entire legitimacy of the debate, coupled with their inability to admit publicly their battlefield defeats, caused them to reject any ceasefire resolutions that did not substantially downgrade Israel's achievements or its very existence. The result of that, however, was that Israel continued to press its advantage on the ground. "Indeed," Eban writes, "our successes in the ten days after the Arab rejection of the July 1948 cease-fire were more decisive in fixing our map than our successful resistance in May before the truce."[19]

Eban and Sharett maintained the classic Zionist diplomatic posture since the days of the Balfour Declaration: working with the powers, compromising where possible, but maintaining the most unbending posture where it was not, amid a crucible of international pressure that kept pushing for Israel to give back what it had gained either diplomatically or in war. At one UN committee session, a British representative explained, in his Scottish accent, "how useless, sterile, barren and unpromising" the southern Negev was, in his efforts to conjure a deal in which the Israelis would trade it for the western Galilee. Eban took the floor to answer. "I

[19] Eban, *Autobiography*, p. 132.

have never heard of anything so undesirable," he said, "being coveted by the United Kingdom with such intensity."

It was in the first years of Israeli statehood that Eban's eloquence first came to the attention of the broader public—not just to Israelis, most of whom had never heard of him before he appeared as UN ambassador, but also to the English-speaking world. It was in the radio and television broadcasts, especially in the United States, that he developed an iconic status as a noble fighter for the underdog, for Zionism, and for downtrodden Jews everywhere. In 1950, Eban was named Israel's ambassador to the United States alongside his UN role, and would hold both positions, shuttling between New York and Washington, until 1959.

Abba Eban, it can be fairly said, understood something that the previous generations of Zionist diplomats had not: the importance of appealing, especially in an age of radio and television broadcasts, directly to the American public and the world. If Chaim Weizmann was the father of Zionist diplomacy as a whole, Abba Eban can be fairly seen as the father of the specific genre of Zionist *public* diplomacy.

He would use this form of diplomacy to great effect over a period of three decades. At a time when most Israeli leaders, with the exception of Golda Meir, spoke a broken or heavily accented English, Abba Eban demonstrated with remarkable fluency, consistency, and grandiloquence not only the Israeli predicament but also the historical magnitude of every moment and the righteousness of Israel's cause. He created a model to be emulated by generations of talented diplomats and pro-Israel activists, and set the tone and content of Israel's messaging towards the English-speaking world for half a century to come.

Today we can look back, listening to Abba Eban's recorded speeches with the static in the background, or watch the old black-and-white films, and easily forget just how innovative his methods were. Eban recognized the power of new technologies to deliver Israel's message directly to the masses—creating pressure on political actors to the Jewish state's advantage.

Indeed, Eban was probably the greatest exemplar of what I call "innovative diplomacy"—a kind of urgent, entrepreneurial approach. Israel has always been at a radical disadvantage in terms of numbers: Our country is small, our enemies and rivals numerous, and unlike them we only get a single vote at the UN. The only way we can hope to survive is through creativity, energy, and flexibility that looks for opportunity in every new situation. Our world is rapidly changing: It was only a few years ago that Facebook and Twitter were the newest levers of public influence—and then came Instagram and TikTok and YouTube and Reddit and Substack and whatever else may blossom by the time you read this. One cannot know which platforms will emerge or how long they will last—but each has its own unique way of getting messages across. Nor is it just about technology: Innovative diplomacy means using the levers of culture, business, and ties with different levels of government to build an overall effect that is beneficial to the national interest. I will return to this later.

***

Perhaps the most important aspect of Eban's early speeches, however, was his assumption—echoing his mentor Weizmann—that the Jews, despite their previous centuries-long status as a tiny and often persecuted minority, now possessed a *state*, and therefore had an absolute claim on all the sovereign dignity and rights of every recognized nation under international law—and would defend them unilaterally and by force if necessary.

Eban was a master at appealing to the principles on which the United Nations was founded—sovereign rights of states, repudiation of military aggression, and the hope for a better world—to advance Israel's cause. In a meeting of the Security Council on July 13, 1948, Eban was faced with one of the countless attempts of the time to undo the gains of Partition and independence. He dispensed with the traditional legalistic formulations familiar to the United Nations delegates, and instead ripped into his adversaries with unexpected alacrity:

> There is not a single person in this room or outside it who does not know in the depths of his heart that the

> Arab states, by resuming their attacks upon Israel, have committed an act of aggression....
>
> Israel is the product of the most sustained historic tenacity which the ages recall. The Jewish people has not striven towards this goal for twenty centuries in order that, having once achieved it, it will now surrender it in response to an illegitimate and unsuccessful aggression. Whatever else changes, this will not. The State of Israel is an immutable part of the international landscape. To plan the future without it is to build delusions on sand.

Of course, aggression against Jews was nothing new, especially in the half-century prior to independence. But now, with the emergence of the United Nations, "aggression" carried a different weight than in the past: It was now a legal term in a legal context, one that stood at the heart of what gave the UN its own legitimacy. When it came to attacking Jews, Eban was saying, the rules of the game had changed irrevocably.

Israel would insist on its rightful place in the community of nations.

Even his casual use of the word "Israel"—this was less than two months after independence and before Israel was even accepted as a voting member of the body—was controversial. The nameplate before his seat continued to read "Jewish Agency," and he had to wait until the rotating president of the Security Council became somebody favorable to get the Council to change it. Full recognition, both legally and substantively, would take time, but it began with Israeli representatives speaking, behaving, and making demands that assumed the Jewish national home had already earned its place at the table.

This was entirely new in modern history, not least to Diaspora Jews. When the Jewish Agency's office on the east side of Midtown Manhattan suddenly transformed into the Consulate General of the State of Israel, adorned with national flags and symbols, the building was flooded with Jewish visitors who just wanted to see with their own eyes the imponderable trappings of sovereignty.

But it was also the Israelis who needed to adjust. In fact, they had only now *become* "Israelis," a new word to replace the "Zionists" and "Jews" of the "Yishuv." "There was the sense of a new tomorrow," Eban wrote of his first trip back to Israel after independence in August 1948. "Israelis were frankly savoring the pride of statehood. Flags on ministerial cars were a little too large, and the proceedings in cabinet and parliament were enacted with solemn relish, as though by men and women who could hardly believe the titles by which they were called."[20]

Not everyone accepted the new reality, of course, and this was felt on the diplomatic front far more consistently over time than on the battlefield.

From a diplomatic standpoint, Israel was locked in an existential war from the day of its declared independence and for many years after, long after the guns fell silent and an armistice was reached in 1949. Though Israel declared its capital to be Jerusalem, establishing its parliament and main bodies of state in the holy city, almost no countries were willing to establish embassies there, preferring Tel Aviv—a bizarre and frankly humiliating situation that continues to prevail today, with the notable exception of the United States as of 2017, and a few others that relocated their embassies in its wake. No less humiliating was the fact that the Egyptians banned passage of Israeli cargo ships through the Suez Canal, preventing Israel, and only Israel, from participating as equals in maritime shipping, in blatant violation of international treaties. This situation would remain in place until a peace accord was reached with Egypt in 1979.

As if that were not enough, questions about Israeli withdrawal from certain parts of its already meager territory, or of relinquishing Jerusalem in favor of an international protectorate of some sort, continued to occupy the minds of great-power diplomats for the better part of the coming decade.

***

With the election of General Dwight D. Eisenhower to succeed Truman as president of the United States in 1952, and the increasing hostility of the Soviet Union towards Israel, the Jewish state no longer enjoyed the

[20] Eban, *Autobiography*, pp. 128-129.

kind of support it had in 1947. The U.S. stuck to a position of formal neutrality, looking to deepen its ties with the Arab world while banning sales of weapons to the Middle East and encouraging allies to do the same.

The Soviets, on the other hand, embraced an increasingly virulent form of antisemitic rhetoric, and as for the Middle East, they went all in with the Arabs. Israel, which had relied on Soviet-controlled Czechoslovakia as its principal supplier of weapons in 1948, no longer had a major source of arms. Meanwhile, Egypt's monarch had been overthrown by a group of officers led by Colonel Gamal Abdel Nasser, whose militancy in the name of Arab nationalism echoed across the region. Arab armies were bring upgraded with sophisticated Soviet weaponry. And across all of Israel's borders, Arab *fedayeen* militia conducted terror raids, butchering Jewish civilians in their homes and on the roads.

For Eban, shuttling between New York and Washington during that time was exceptionally difficult.

> To be Israel's ambassador in Washington and to the United Nations in those days was clearly no prescription for a relaxed life. Israel's difficulties were the only possessions that nobody was trying to take away. I made a definition of my aims: in Washington to strive for a viable, if not an affectionate relationship with the Eisenhower Administration; at the United Nations to use the international platform to give some special resonance to Israel's cause; in American Jewry to create around my embassy and myself an atmosphere of solidarity and confidence; and in the general arena of American opinion to break out of diplomatic confinement so as to become a spokesman of a cause to which most Americans might be able to respond. My vocation was to develop an American-Israeli tradition based on a public sympathy that might transcend, and sometimes correct, the direction of official policy.[21]

[21] Eban, *Autobiography*, pp. 174-175.

Indeed, it was in these years, in the 1950s, that the fundamental patterns of Israel's diplomatic relationship with the United States were forged.

***

The United States has always required special attention from Israeli diplomats—even before Jerusalem began receiving significant military and economic assistance from Washington in the 1970s. Part of this stems from America's unique role in the postwar era, as the preeminent superpower defending democracy and freedom, and which displays a broad public sympathy for the Jewish state among Jews and Christians alike.

But part of it also has to do with the unique structure of American government. In most democracies, the prime minister and cabinet rule as a direct product of the confidence of parliament. In practice, this means that the number of people who require convincing of a given set of foreign-policy decisions is, at the end of the day, rather small. The same group of people involved in allocating budgets and getting laws passed are, more or less, those who also approve the sale of weapons or votes in the UN. In the United States, by contrast, fundamental decisions are made not just by the president and his vast administration stretching from the Pentagon to the State Department to the National Security Council—but also by an entirely independent Congress, on which allocations, treaty ratifications, and everything requiring legislation depends.

This requires Israeli diplomats to apply themselves not just through direct relationships in the administration, but also with key members of Congress of both parties. In recent decades, the emergence of the American Israel Public Affairs Committee (AIPAC) and other American organizations supporting the relationship have played an important role in managing all this. But in the early years, most of it fell on Israel's diplomats, especially its ambassadors in Washington and at the UN—both of whom, in the 1950s, were Abba Eban.

America's form of governance also requires a direct appeal to the public in ways that relations with other countries often do not. While the administration is formally subordinate to the president and his electoral considerations, in Congress *every* member, especially in the House of Representatives, is in a permanent state of running for office. Successful pursuit of Israel's key interests therefore requires appealing to different sectors of the electorate—the Jewish community, religious Christians, and supporters of Israel from a wide variety of additional communities. As Eban writes:

> At any given moment there are always several major problems on which the understanding of the American government is urgently needed. In almost every case there is no substitute for that support. The pressure of Israel's demands on the Administration is so intense that there is always a danger of exhausting our welcome by pressing too many cases too often and too hard. I thought that the best guarantee of success lay in the creation of a public sympathy that would take Israel out of the diplomatic routine and elevate it to a special place in American confidence. This meant that I had simultaneously to pursue contacts in Washington and take a leading share in bringing Israel's cause to millions of Americans.

This is a pyramid of responsibilities that no man, regardless of his energies, can handle alone. In his first few years in the United States, Eban ran himself quite ragged:

> Indeed, on two occasions in 1951, once in the Security Council and once at a meeting in Tulsa, Oklahoma, I found myself delivering impassioned speeches after lack of sleep and on a completely empty stomach, with the result that my energy ebbed away and I briefly fainted. When this happened during a discussion in the Security Council about our contested irrigation rights, the alarm of my family and friends was shared by David Ben-Gurion, who was then on his first official visit to the United States.

> He sent me a message suggesting that I take it easy, since, as he said blandly, "People like you are not to be found running round the streets."[22]

The United States, of course, was not the only focus of Israeli diplomacy in its first decade. And that is a good thing, since Israel was above all desperate for arms, and the Eisenhower administration had no intention of supplying them.

In the 1950s, after the Soviets pivoted into a powerful anti-Israel posture, which meant that Israel could no longer rely on Czechoslovakia for material support, Israel developed an unusual, profound, and historically crucial relationship with France—which included the supply of advanced arms and, later, the creation of a nuclear project in the desert town of Dimona.

Israel also developed a particularly strange relationship with the United Kingdom. The British, for whom the Partition plan had signaled a defeat and loss of global status, had acted obstreperously towards Israel in the aftermath of independence, supporting Arab diplomatic initiatives to undo the effects of 1947–1949, to limit Jewish immigration, to internationalize Jerusalem, and to dismember a portion of the Jewish state's territory. But the return of Winston Churchill to Downing Street in 1951 and the emergence of the Soviets as full-throated Cold War backers of the Arab side changed the atmosphere between London and Jerusalem.

These two surprising new relationships, with France and Great Britain, came together rather inelegantly in the Suez Crisis of 1956.

***

Again, the broad notes of that crisis are well known. In July 1956, Nasser declared that Egypt was nationalizing the Suez Canal, which had been built, owned, and operated by the British and French. Egypt was also cutting off all shipping through the Straits of Tiran, a recognized international waterway that any ship had to cross to get from the Red Sea to the

22 Eban, *Autobiography*, pp. 157 and 158.

Gulf of Aqaba and, from there, to Israel's southern port of Eilat. Nasser had reached an agreement with Syria placing both countries' forces under a unified command, and had been clamoring for war. "Egypt will strive to erase the shame of the Palestine War even if Israel should fulfill all UN resolutions," a leading member of the Egyptian government said. "It will not sign a peace with her. Even if Israel should consist only of Tel Aviv, we should never put up with that."[23]

In a secret meeting of leaders in an isolated house in Sèvres, France, from October 22 to 24, 1956, a plan was hatched among the British, French, and Israelis. Israel would launch a surprise invasion of the Sinai Peninsula up to the Suez Canal, which would include the capture of the peninsula's southern point at Sharm El-Sheikh, thereby reopening the Straits of Tiran. The British and French would use that invasion as a pretext to send forces into the Canal zone, ostensibly to separate the Egyptian and Israeli armies, but in fact to retake the Suez Canal.

The United States had been left out of the decision, after having explicitly warned the parties not to take unilateral action. Again: This was the 1950s, before the U.S. and Israel became clear and deep allies.

The Israelis held up their end, conducting a lightning assault on October 29, known as the Sinai Campaign, that included the first and only airdrop of paratroopers in combat in its history. The British and French offered air cover and also began to take the Canal.

What they hadn't counted on was the degree of Soviet opposition. Moscow began massively calling up its own soldiers and threatened the use of nuclear weapons.

The partners also grossly miscalculated the American response. A week before a presidential election, combined with the potential for nuclear conflict with the Soviets—Eisenhower was beside himself with fury. He threatened to cut all support for Israel, and also threatened to withhold a very large loan from the International Monetary Fund to the United Kingdom, which it desperately needed to support its postwar economy.

23 Eban, *Autobiography*, p. 183.

The British and French agreed to withdraw their forces immediately. The Israelis were left holding the bag. The ruse became known, and thus began a process of withdrawal from Sinai that took half a year to complete.

The Suez Crisis offered the first real test of U.S.-Israel relations after Truman left office. Most American Jews were Democrats, and Truman's profound commitment to his word to Weizmann was not disconnected from his electoral considerations. But Eisenhower was a Republican. He had led the Allied forces to victory in World War II, and had been outraged by the discovery of the German death camps. He had shown a profound understanding of the plight of millions of defenseless Jews. But as for Zionism and the Jewish state, he had few sentimental attachments—and neither, he believed, did his voters.

The 1956 war, despite universal condemnation, the outrage of the superpowers, the betrayal by its allies, and the eventual retreat, nonetheless offered important lessons both for Israeli leaders and diplomats. Suddenly, Israel was not merely a beneficiary of the generosity of the United Nations, which had "allowed" it to exist in the first place. It was now seen around the world as a force of its own, one that would continue to fight for its vital interests, by force of arms if necessary. Although it withdrew from Sinai, it did not leave immediately as the British and French had. It demanded—and received—assurances that its rights would be protected, especially with regard to the Straits of Tiran.

At the end of the day, Israel had stood before the combined outrage of the Americans and the Soviets and successfully overturned Nasser's attempt to choke off its shipping to Eilat. It was prepared to defend itself, by itself. Despite much evidence at the time to the contrary, the truth is that the 1956 war improved Israel's standing, its freedom to operate, and its long-term prospects immeasurably. This new State of Israel was confident, perhaps a little crazy, and unwilling to brook challenges to its sovereign rights. Perhaps the most surprising outcome of 1956 was that from that moment on, serious international efforts to roll back the achievements of 1947–1949 suddenly vanished, never to return.

It cannot be stated often enough: One does not measure diplomatic success or failure by the objections of other governments. Condemnations and protests, no matter how loud, do not mean you are doing something wrong from the perspective of your nation's *raison d'état*. To the contrary: Very often they are evidence that you are doing something right.

The goal of diplomacy, in other words, is not for your nation to gain external public approval, nor even necessarily to prevent conflict or condemnation. *It is to secure, through diplomatic means, the vital interests of your nation.* Yes, efforts should be made to act with precision and sensitivity, taking into account the sensibilities and possible reactions of other actors. But these are not the ultimate goal, and if eventually the diplomatic actions are required that do not follow the "international book of good manners," so be it.

We see this in the impact that 1956 had on American-Israeli relations. Yes, Israel had to withdraw from Sinai in the face of explicit threats from Washington. But Washington also came face to face with the new reality of Israeli power. Eisenhower had been taken by surprise—not just by the Sinai invasion itself, but by the domestic diplomatic campaign that followed. Lyndon Johnson, the Democratic leader in Congress, had turned support for Israel into a powerful political lever. He spoke with Abba Eban every few days during the negotiations over withdrawal. "They're not going to get a goddam thing here [from Congress] until they [treat you fairly]," he told Eban.[24] On February 19, 1957, the Democratic Policy Committee voted unanimously to oppose any efforts by the White House to impose sanctions on Israel.

It was at this moment that the fruits of Abba Eban's public diplomacy efforts came to light. Suddenly, American policy on Israel was revealed to be dependent not just on the sympathies of a given president, but also on those of the American people as expressed through its representatives on Capitol Hill. Congress had not just the ability, but also the will, to stand up to the president in Israel's defense.

Eisenhower began to soften his tone, and sent Secretary of State John Foster Dulles to negotiate with Eban over Israel's withdrawal. An agreement was reached: The U.S., together with other maritime powers, would assure Israel's right of shipping through the Straits of Tiran. A United

---

[24] Sachar, *A History of Israel*, p. 509.

Nations Emergency Force (UNEF) would remain in Sharm El-Sheikh, the crucial southern point of Sinai that would ensure the safety of ships going through the straits. Israel would withdraw from the entirety of Sinai—but not without having achieved spectacular success in securing its own interests.

***

For Egypt's Nasser, 1956 was a mixed bag. On the one hand, he had successfully nationalized the Suez Canal, permanently evicting the British and French—the former being the colonial power that Egypt had overthrown, the latter an enemy to Arab nationalist aspirations in Algeria, Tunisia, and Morocco for which Nasser stood as the champion. He had brazenly defied the UN, had gained full Soviet backing, and now stood as a hero of Egypt and the legitimate icon of Arab peoples across the Middle East.

At the same time, the ease with which Israel had taken Sinai rankled him.

Nasser had miscalculated, taking back Suez but needlessly closing the Straits of Tiran, provoking Israel to conquer Sinai and thus revealing the flimsiness of his own military. Britain and France had horribly miscalculated, too, being forced to retreat quickly and to abandon their possession of the Canal—marking, according to some historians, the final blow to their status as world powers. Eisenhower miscalculated as well, as he later admitted, by failing to recognize the importance of Israel both as a long-term ally and as a focus of American public sympathy.

But Israel learned lessons, too. Israelis were elated, suddenly seeing the extent of their military power. Military planners discovered the tremendous benefits of a large-scale first strike in neutralizing Israel's inherent territorial, numerical, and material disadvantages. Israelis had made clear that they would use force, aggressively and without warning, to respond to attacks on their vital national interests.

At the same time, and despite the strategic gains it afforded the Jewish state, 1956 was not seen as an outright victory. Israelis including Ben-Gurion had, briefly, entertained the hope that they might annex the Sinai and hold on to what they had gained. This hope was shattered swiftly by the combined threat of Soviet and American intervention, however, and the implication was obvious: Despite having every right to go to war in the context of Egyptian actions, Israel did not have the diplomatic standing it needed to pocket its gains and protect its shipping on its own. On the flip side, it was the Israelis' unwillingness to capitulate rapidly as the British and French had, instead digging in their heels and negotiating from a position of strength, that resulted in a decade of free passage for ships heading to Eilat. This, in turn, allowed Israel to take advantage of the coming decade to build its economy, including the transport of Iranian oil over land from Eilat to Haifa and on to Europe, offering an alternative to the Suez Canal.

And thus, the most important revelation of 1956 was that the doctrine according to which Israel would *defend itself, by itself*, came with an asterisk: The real-world outcome of its acts of legitimate self-defense would heavily depend, whether the Israelis liked it or not, on smart diplomatic maneuvers undertaken before, during, and after any conflict.

This lesson would be applied masterfully in the next round of war, in 1967. The most stunning, glorious moment in the short history of Israel's military would also be the finest hour of its diplomacy.

***

By 1967, Abba Eban was now in his early fifties. After finishing his stint in New York and Washington in 1959, he decided to return to Israel and capitalize on his newfound popularity by trying his hand in politics. Ben-Gurion was forced to resign in 1963 due to a scandal known as the Lavon Affair.[25] After briefly serving as education minister and deputy prime

[25] Named after Defense Minister Pinhas Lavon, this scandal involved a failed 1954 false-flag operation in which Israeli agents planted bombs at civilian targets in Egypt, with the aim of blaming it on the Muslim Brotherhood. The revelation of the affair resulted in the agents' arrest in Egypt and ended Lavon's career and, with time, Ben-Gurion's dominance over the governing Mapa'i Party. On June 16, 1963, Ben-Gurion resigned, presumably with the intention of returning by popular demand—but by that point, his standing in the party had deteriorated more than he knew, and his replacement by Levi Eshkol as party leader signaled the end of his career as a significant force in Israeli politics.

minister, Eban was named foreign minister in the government of Prime Minister Levi Eshkol in 1966.

Few conflicts in history demonstrate the importance of diplomacy, and the specific success of Israeli efforts in the field, as brilliantly as did the Six Day War of June 5 to 10, 1967.

The stage was set on May 14, 1967, when—after more than a decade nursing the loss of 1956—Nasser began sending huge numbers of armored and infantry forces into the Sinai, near the Israeli border. Five days later, he ordered the UN forces that had been stationed in Sinai since 1956 to leave. On May 23, Nasser, for the second time in eleven years, declared a blockade on the Straits of Tiran, again strangling Israel's key southern shipping route. Meanwhile, Syria and Jordan built their forces up as well. On May 30, Jordan formally put its army under the command of Egypt, and then invited Iraq to deploy troops and armored units in Jordan as well. Egypt declared it was withdrawing forces from its yearslong conflict in Yemen in order to redeploy them on the Israeli front.

The Arab leaders made every sign, in word and deed, of their intention to mount a massive invasion that would, once and for all, eliminate the Jewish state. The president of Iraq, Abdul Rahman Arif, said that "the existence of Israel is an error which must be rectified." Hafez el-Assad, the Syrian defense minister who would soon become its president for a period of decades, declared that his army was ready "to explode the Zionist presence in the Arab homeland...the time has come to enter into a battle of annihilation."

Israeli military planners prepared an ambitious preemptive strike from the air, with the aim of disabling the Arab aircraft on the ground and swiftly establishing air superiority. Again, Israel had learned in 1956 the tremendous military advantages of a first strike against a powerful, well-equipped enemy.

But while the Soviets were actively encouraging war, the Western countries were dead set against it, and made clear that they would not condone an Israeli first strike. So now the question was: How could Israel win not just the war, but also the peace?

Israelis over a certain age recall May 1967 as an especially traumatic period in the nation's history. Just over two decades had passed since the Holocaust, and now another fearsome enemy was preparing to vanquish the Jews. Israeli leaders made preparations but delayed action. Trenches were dug in Tel Aviv to prepare mass graves. Ordinary life shut down as a full call-up of reserves paralyzed the economy. Unlike Ben-Gurion, Prime Minister Levi Eshkol was untested in war. The delay was perceived as indecision or even weakness. Days and weeks passed as Egypt and Syria continued to build up their forces. Eshkol delivered a stuttering radio address on May 28 that added to the sense of panic.

But in reality, the delays had a purpose.

During that time, Eban was engaged in an intense diplomatic campaign that laid the groundwork for a remarkable Israeli diplomatic victory. Western countries and the United Nations had promised Israel after 1956 that the right to pass through the Straits of Tiran would be protected, as would Israel's right to defend itself against Arab aggression. Now it was time to fulfill those promises.

And indeed, as the days and hours ticked away, as war grew more and more imminent, the world powers were revealed to be quite impotent. They didn't condemn Egypt's actions; they scarcely could call a Security Council meeting on the subject to order. The Soviets, it was clear, would veto anything reasonable from Israel's perspective; they were busy making speeches comparing Israel to the Nazis, and refused to even convene a meeting of the Four Powers (the U.S., Britain, France, and the USSR) to discuss the issue.

Behind the scenes, Israel's putative friends were imploring it not to launch a preemptive strike, but instead allow the powers to work together and defuse the situation. "*Ne faites pas la guerre*" ("Don't go to war") French President Charles de Gaulle shouted at Eban. "At any rate, don't shoot first. It would be catastrophic if Israel were to attack." In London, Prime Minister Harold Wilson was less vehement in his opposition, but made clear that the United Kingdom would let the United States take the lead.

In Washington, Eban met three times with Secretary of State Dean Rusk, to little avail. President Lyndon Johnson, who had led congressional opposition to Eisenhower's threats against Israel in 1956, nonetheless took the same position as France did in 1967. "I must emphasize the necessity for Israel not to make itself responsible for the initiation of hostilities," he wrote to Eshkol on June 3. "Israel will not be alone unless it decides to go alone. We cannot imagine that it will make this decision."[26]

The Israeli diplomatic message during the weeks before the war was straightforward: We do not want war. Israel is prepared to listen, to delay action as long as possible, to see whether the "international community" can keep the peace. But Israel knows its rights under international law and will not tolerate a blockade. Egypt, to be clear, has already begun the hostilities. "A state could be attacked by many methods apart from gunfire," Eban recalls telling De Gaulle. "Civil law recognized no distinction between assault through strangulation and assault through shooting. Nor did international law."[27]

Indeed, Israel eventually took action against the advice of every one of its allies. It did so not out of folly but out of the recognition, which was in fact the core insight of the Zionist movement from the beginning, that in this new phase of history, the Jewish state would be the sole determiner of its national interests, and that sacrificing those interests in order to be agreeable to the world risked the new nation's demise. This decision would reverberate for decades to come.

The goal of Israel's diplomatic effort now was not merely to buy time, but also to demonstrate, both to the world and to Israelis, that they were every bit as committed to the international order, to the UN, to national rights, and especially to peace, as the Western powers were. The Israelis had listened, they had sought peace, they had waited to respond as long as humanly possible. It was an immense risk, of course. But the risk of allowing the Arabs to "shoot first," as De Gaulle had demanded, was far

---

[26] US Department of State Office of the Historian, "139. Letter from President Johnson to Prime Minister Eshkol, Washington, June 3, 1967," https://history.state.gov/historicaldocuments/frus1964-68v19/d139 (accessed October 13, 2024).

[27] Eban, *Autobiography*, p. 342.

greater. At some point, a preemptive strike becomes impossible, and one never knows when that point will come.

On the morning of June 5, 1967, in defiance of the world powers, Israeli fighter jets launched a large-scale assault on the airfields of Egypt and Syria, destroying the vast majority of their Soviet-built air arsenals. The Six Day War had begun.

***

The first days of the war were a fog, and the most alarming information was coming from Arab leaders declaring tremendous advances—often, we now know, based on lies they were being told by their own generals—against the "Zionist entity." The UN Security Council convened to consider resolutions demanding a ceasefire and withdrawal of forces—but because the Arabs were unwilling to admit that they were actually losing on the battlefield, they also could not agree to a ceasefire resolution calling for the *withdrawal* of forces, for that would be tantamount to conceding that it was Israeli, rather than Arab, forces that needed to do the withdrawing.

Indeed, the Arabs' propaganda machine was so busy projecting the end of Israel that it came as an overwhelming shock when Abba Eban mounted the dais at the United Nations on June 6, the second day of the war, and announced before the assembled delegates along with millions of stunned listeners around the world:

> I have just come from Jerusalem to tell the Security Council that Israel, by its independent effort and sacrifice, has passed from serious danger to successful and glorious resistance.

Eban recounted before the transfixed audience the precarious reality that had faced Israel prior to the onset of war, and called to account those nations, especially the Soviets, that had encouraged Arab aggression. Then he ended with a call to peace directed, above all, at Nasser:

> As he looks around him at the arena of battle, at the wreckage of planes and tanks, at the collapse of intoxicated hopes, might not the Egyptian ruler ponder whether anything was achieved by that disruption? What had it brought him but strife, conflict and the stern criticism of progressive men throughout the world? Israel in recent days had proved its steadfastness and vigor. It is now willing to demonstrate its instinct for peace. Let us build a new system of relationships from the wreckage of the old. Let us discern across the darkness the vision of a better and a brighter dawn.

Much of Israel's success in the diplomacy after the Six Day War can be attributed to the positioning that was outlined in this speech. Israel presented itself as facing unimaginable odds against an implacable and enormous aggressor, the underdog dedicated to peace, which viewed war as an absolutely last resort. Territories were captured, it was implied, but could be returned in exchange for peace.

The reality, naturally, was more complicated. The territories conquered in 1967 varied greatly in the extent to which Israelis felt willing to part with them. Sinai was a vast desert that had never been part of ancient Jewish history (unless one included the forty years of Israelite wanderings)—and it should not surprise anyone that it was seen by most Israelis as a potential bargaining chip in a future peace agreement—but which, in the absence of full peace, served by its sheer enormity as an irreplaceable strategic buffer against Egyptian assault.

The Golan Heights, taken from Syria, were more complicated, being both a major strategic asset—Israel's northern communities were no longer vulnerable to Syrian assault from higher ground—and also more integral to ancient Israel. The West Bank, by contrast, was both the biblical heartland and, with its rolling highlands and proximity to the narrow waist of pre-1967 Israel's midlands, the strategic solution to the "Auschwitz borders" of 1949.

As for Jerusalem and its holy sites—well, that was the very thing that had put the "Zion" in "Zionism." Having finally, after thousands of years of longing and prayer, returned the Jews to historic Jerusalem and the Western Wall, the site of King Solomon's Temple, Israel intended to stay in its eternal capital forever.

All of the captured territories, in other words, conferred legitimate strategic benefits to Israel, making future wars less likely in the absence of permanent peace. Some of them, however, were far more than that. Indeed, while most Israelis could be convinced to exchange *some* of the conquered lands for full peace, there was an equally strong consensus that others—above all Jerusalem—could never be relinquished.

So, Israel's long-term intentions regarding the lands were a mixed bag that would depend, in part, on its own internal struggles. From a diplomatic perspective, however, Eban articulated a narrative that was tailor-made for the Western audience of the moment, which had the added benefit of being mostly true. As foreign minister, he was expressing not just messaging but policy of which he was one of the principal architects: Israel, the democratic, hopeful, modern, rights-based, peace-loving state was prepared to hold these territories, especially Sinai, for as long as it took to bring the Arabs to abandon war and make peace with Israel.

Indeed, it is not widely known that on June 19, 1967, the Israeli government, at Eban's urging, approved a four-point plan that proposed peace with Egypt and Syria in exchange for a complete withdrawal of Israeli forces from Sinai and the Golan, and sent the plan to Washington. (The West Bank and Jerusalem were left out.) In a speech he gave that same day, Eban expanded on this approach, spelling out, in what would be considered by many to be his finest rhetorical moment, the historical rationale and the necessary steps for a new, post-colonial Middle East:

> For the first time in history, no Mediterranean nation is in subjection. All are endowed with sovereign freedom. The challenge now is to use this freedom for creative growth. There is only one road to that end. It is the road of recognition, of direct contact, of true cooperation. It is the

> road of peaceful co-existence. This road, as the ancient prophets of Israel foretold, leads to Jerusalem....
>
> It may seem that Israel stands alone against numerous and powerful adversaries. But we have faith in the undying forces in our nation's history which have so often given the final victory to spirit over matter, to inner truth over mere quantity. We believe in the vigilance of history which has guarded our steps. The Guardian of Israel neither slumbers nor sleeps.
>
> The Middle East, tired of wars, is ripe for a new emergence of human vitality. Let the opportunity not fall again from our hands.[28]

This was one of the great moments of Israeli public diplomacy, a speech that helped to put Eban in the pantheon of twentieth-century orators the world over. It resonated with leaders and publics across the English-speaking world, having an immense impact on the way the war would be interpreted, especially by America's public and, by extension, its political leaders.

It was also an especially prudent line to take given the continuing Arab rejectionism, backed by the Soviets, in the wake of the war. On September 1, the Arab League issued its infamous Khartoum Resolution that included the "three no's of Khartoum": no peace with Israel, no recognition of Israel, no negotiations with Israel.

The contrast could not be greater. In an era in which the West was unified in its dream of peace and democracy around the world, Israeli diplomats, with Abba Eban foremost among them, struck the perfect notes.

Indeed, the most urgent need for Israeli diplomacy in the aftermath of the Six Day War was to ensure that, unlike in 1956, Israel would be

---

[28] Center for Israel Education, "Abba Eban Speech at Special Assembly of the UN, June 19, 1967," https://israeled.org/resources/documents/abba-eban-speech-at-special-assembly-of-the-un-june-19-1967/ (accessed October 13, 2024).

allowed to hold on to its territorial gains, giving them up only on its own terms, rather than face unbearable pressure to return them immediately and without peace treaties.

But this, too, required intensive diplomatic efforts, especially towards the American public. Indeed, President Johnson said as much, as Eban writes:

> President Johnson had let us know bluntly that the American attitude on withdrawal would be strongly influenced by the reaction of public opinion to Israel's case. If he were to hold firm against pressures for our withdrawal, he could only do so on the foundation of strong public support for Israel. His advisers had told us that it "was up to Israel to win support."[29]

Israel's diplomatic efforts continued throughout the summer and fall of 1967, culminating on November 22 with the passage of UN Security Council Resolution 242, which unambiguously called on the Arab states to recognize Israel and end their state of war, and on Israel to withdraw from "territories occupied in the recent conflict."

That phrase *territories occupied*, without a definite article "the," was the product of an extensive negotiation led by Eban, and later confirmed in its implication by diplomats from the powers that approved it. It deliberately kept ambiguous the question of *which* territories must be withdrawn from—while being exceptionally clear about the demands placed on the Arab states.

The result, in other words, was precisely what Israel was hoping for, and the opposite of the diplomatic debacle that followed Israel's assault on Sinai in 1956: This time, due to its diplomatic efforts, the Jewish state was seen—correctly—as both the victim of genocidal aggression and the legitimate and just victor of the war. In practice, the resolution set the stage for the first-ever peace treaty with an Arab state, Egypt, in 1979.

---

[29] Eban, *Autobiography*, p. 417.

***

The Israeli diplomatic approach before, during, and after the Six Day War produced some incredible advances for the image and position of Israel across the Western World.

But there were some negative diplomatic ramifications as well. For the Soviet Union, 1967 marked a humiliation, since it had backed the losing side. As much as it had opposed Zionism both within its own borders and internationally, it now would dramatically increase its assault on the Jewish state in the international arena. If in the past, denigrating Zionism and Israel was a means to delegitimize Jewish dissidents within, it now became central to its strategy in the Cold War. The Soviet Union and almost all the nations under its umbrella cut their relations with Israel. Suddenly, Israel was seen as a clear pro-Western and therefore anti-Soviet force that had to be stopped.

Although this expressed itself in any number of areas, from military supply and training of Israel's enemies to the support of Arab terrorism, perhaps one of the most lasting assaults was in the sphere of propaganda.

It is little understood just how much of today's global anti-Israel campaign owes its origins to the Soviet Union's campaigns of the 1970s and 1980s. Books, newspaper articles, and entire magazines devoted to smearing both Israel and the Jews began appearing in dozens of languages around the world.

The Soviet Union may be gone, but its legacy lives on, and nowhere more potently than in the content of anti-Israel rhetoric I saw most vividly during my own diplomatic posts in London and at the United Nations, and especially in the demonstrations that filled streets of major cities in the wake of October 7.

It is here that many of the central themes of what today we call the anti-Israel campaign were born: the idea that Israel is a fascist or Nazi state; that Zionism is an extension of Western capitalism, colonialism, and imperialism; that Israel was committing genocide against Palestinians; that Zionism is a modern Western invention disconnected from any previous Jewish history in the land; that the very existence of Israel is somehow illegitimate and criminal; that Israel was guilty of the crime of "apartheid" along the lines of South Africa; that the establishment of voluntary civilian settlements in disputed territory is not merely questionable under international law but the epitome of a war crime, no different in nature from deliberately bombing a schoolhouse.

These messages were repeated over and over again, and found a receptive ear among Western political, cultural, and academic elites who were sympathetic, if not with the Soviet Union itself, then at least with the effort to tarnish Western liberal democracy with whatever tools at their disposal.

In Europe far more than the US, these messages took deep root—in part because the Americans, as leaders in the Cold War for the West, were far more sensitive to the prospect of Soviet Communism seeping into public life. But there was another reason, which we'll explore later: The propaganda interacted, and sometimes dovetailed, with Europeans' own baggage—baggage that began during centuries of Catholic antisemitism, continued with the continental Enlightenment's innate opposition to national movements like Zionism, and reached its peak with the Holocaust and the Europeans' consequent need to expiate their own sins by turning their victims into perpetrators.

The Soviets were effectively saying: If you are angry at America, at the forces of democracy, at the West, at capitalism, then you absolutely must hate Israel, too. They may not have used the term "intersectionality," but by connecting every evil they saw in the West with the evil of Zionism, they certainly seem to have invented it.

But it wasn't just the content of the propaganda that was installed as a fixture of the international diplomatic discourse. The process of creating anti-Israel institutional structures, especially at the UN, which had begun immediately after the War of Independence, was accelerated. The General Assembly passed, in 1975 after a nearly decade-long Soviet-backed campaign, a resolution declaring that "Zionism is racism," which was repealed only in 1991 as the Soviet Union disintegrated. International treaties had clauses inserted into them to target Israel as a condition for Soviet agreement. Certain UN bodies, like the Human Rights Council (UNHRC), have turned Israel into a permanent agenda item for opprobrium. Anti-Zionism, and antisemitism as a matter of course, were woven into the fabric of the international community and international law, much of which remains to this day.

To a surprising degree, Israeli diplomats are still, half a century later, forced to get up each morning and continue fighting on this particular front of the Cold War, often entirely on their own.

***

It took a long time for the diplomatic world to internalize the transformation of geopolitics after World War II. Those of us who remember the Cold War will recall mostly its later years, in a long-bipolar world, in which everything was subordinate to the two great superpowers, the United States and the Soviet Union.

But many of those in positions of leadership in the 1960s had grown up with a completely different soundtrack. A multipolar world that had prevailed for centuries and culminated in two world wars still expressed itself in the leading minds and institutions of the world.

Abba Eban writes in his memoir that in the weeks before the Six Day War, he had gone directly from meeting with French President De Gaulle in Paris to a meeting with President Johnson in Washington. He was surprised at the difference in perception between the two leaders:

> General de Gaulle's belief that there were four powers of roughly equal weight and status, responsible for the future of mankind, did not seem to be shared in other quarters. When I had gone to see President Johnson on May 26, I told him that General de Gaulle had said that "the Four Great Powers ought to get together." The President had given me one of his belligerent looks. "The Four Great Powers? Who the hell are the other two?"[30]

[30] Eban, *Autobiography*, pp. 437–438.

Israelis had long understood, at least since the fiasco of 1956, that it was much better to have the United States on their side than against them. But the penny never really dropped about the necessity for a full alliance with the United States until October 1973.

Most Israelis, even to this day, are reluctant to look at the Yom Kippur War as anything other than a deeply traumatic episode in the decades-long conflict between Israel and the Arab world. At 2 p.m. on Saturday, October 6, 1973, the combined forces of Syria and Egypt launched a massive invasion on two fronts, breaking through Israel's defenses and announcing their intention to bring an end to the Jewish homeland.

It happened during Israel's holiest day of the year, when the majority of the country was quite far along into a twenty-five-hour Yom Kippur fast that began at sundown the day before. It was traditionally considered the ultimate day of judgment, and in an instant, it turned into something like divine retribution, a purification by fire. In an instant, much of the confidence and glory of Israelis in their military power evaporated. In an instant, the possibility of an existential threat—which had been presumably taken off the table since 1967—came roaring back to life.

There was also much death. More than 2,500 Israeli men and women were killed, with more than 7,000 injured. There was no family in Israel that did not know someone who died. During the first week of the war, Israel suffered a major blow on both the Egyptian and Syrian fronts, including immense casualties and the loss of territory. Within a week, however, the Israeli military was able to regroup, and the battle began to turn.

The fundamental question of how and why Israel failed to prevent so large a first strike—so resonant today in the wake of the October 7, 2023, Hamas invasion—has in fact occupied historians for the past half-century. On the face of it, the conditions were not unlike those before 1967: The signs of an impending attack were clear, and Israel had built up its forces and trained for just such a possibility.

There were major differences to 1967, however. Some of the characters were the same—Moshe Dayan was again defense minister, Abba Eban was still foreign minister—but Golda Meir had replaced Levi Eshkol as prime minister. But more important, perhaps, than the *dramatis personae* was the strategic situation: Israel now stood on the bank of the Suez Canal and in possession of the West Bank and Golan Heights—giving it a great deal more strategic depth, more distance between the border and the population centers, and therefore greater flexibility of thinking.

No less important was the fact that 1973 came after 1967: Israel was full of confidence that the Arabs wouldn't dare attack—and indeed, many of the indicators that they were about to do so were dismissed by Israel's top intelligence analysts, on the grounds that they didn't believe the threat to be real. This perception was also bolstered by the fact that Israel's military had grown markedly in strength—especially its air force, which had been refitted with top-of-the line American warplanes to replace the aging French ones that had fought in 1967.

Be that as it may, Israel's failure to launch a preemptive strike similar to that of 1967 was not due to a lack of preparedness. To the contrary, Israel's entire strategy had been built on an updated version of the 1967 strike. But on the eve of the war, Prime Minister Golda Meir took the opposite diplomatic approach from her predecessor: Instead of standing up to the United States and other powers that warned Israel not to strike first, Meir promised U.S. Secretary of State Henry Kissinger that there would be *no* preemptive strike, out of fear of the international isolation that would result. "If we strike first," she said, "we won't get help from anybody."[31]

In the morning hours of October 6, in the same cabinet meeting in which it was concluded that war was imminent, and a full-blown emergency call-up of forces had to take place, Golda Meir gave the order: There would be no preemptive strike. The air force, which had been fully at the ready, was ordered to stand down and to prepare instead a simultaneous counterattack in case of an Arab first strike. Israel would deal with the consequences.

And thus we see how a single moment of hesitation, of buckling to the threat of international sanction and disrepute, deprived Israel of the principal military option it had at its disposal—and made possible what was, until then and for half a century thereafter, the single most cataclysmic event

[31] Abraham Rabinovich, *The Yom Kippur War: The Epic Encounter That Transformed the Middle East* (New York: Schocken, 2004), p. 89.

in Israeli history. Sure, there were other blunders involved, without which the war would have played out differently—beginning with the failure of the IDF's military intelligence to recognize the imminence of the war, and the "concept" embraced by both the IDF and Moshe Dayan according to which Egypt would never attack without weapons that would guarantee its victory.

Indeed, the failure of Yom Kippur was, first and foremost, a failure of intelligence analysis and undue adherence to dogmatic conceptions. However, diplomacy could also have made a substantial contribution at the crucial decision point, by providing Israel the required bandwidth to launch a preemptive strike when needed. The diplomatic sphere should have adhered to the dictum that *Israel will defend itself, by itself* and allowed Israel to exercise that paradigm in real time.

It will always be in the interest of other countries, including our friends and allies, to tie our hands against our chosen path to defend ourselves, and they will always threaten and cajole in order to maintain "stability" or to keep us from striking first. But the threat of a preemptive strike was, at the time, our greatest weapon, and our greatest guarantee that there would not be a catastrophic war. By taking it off the table, Israel's leaders significantly limited their military and diplomatic leverage.

***

Thus it was experienced from Israel's perspective. But from a different perspective, the Yom Kippur War was also a front in the Cold War. The Arab armies were supplied, trained, and in some cases even manned by the Soviets. Israel was helped greatly through previous purchases of American arms and other support. But the Israelis' profound dependence on the United States was brought into relief with what became known as Operation Nickel Grass.

Israel faced an enormous problem as the war progressed: While Egypt and Syria could have their weapons and matériel replenished by the Soviets, Israel's traditional allies—the US and Western European countries—remained committed to a putative "neutrality" in the Middle East and were now unwilling to help. From the Israeli perspective, this was both outrageous and revelatory: Outrageous, because Israel had risked everything, avoiding a preemptive strike and sustaining the most painful military assault since its founding—all on the assumption that if Israel demonstrated its commitment to the civilized world order, the civilized world would return that commitment. And revelatory, because it drove home, more than ever before, the extent to which Israel must always be *solely* responsible for its own security.

Those unwilling to help in Israel's darkest hour included U.S. President Richard Nixon—at least at first. Few Americans understood at the time how American hesitation in 1973 would affect Israeli perceptions of the relationship, and fewer still understand it today, even among Israel's staunchest supporters. For Israelis, American actions at the onset of the Yom Kippur War were a defining moment, an additional trauma of the war, one that would leave a permanent scar on Israel's relationship with the United States. For American governments, support for Israel has always been a cold calculation, and Israelis will never forget it.

A Republican like Eisenhower, embattled by scandal and still grappling with Vietnam, Nixon felt little need to go out of his way to help Israel and potentially trigger a massive Soviet response. He was, however, a committed Cold Warrior, and his mood changed on October 12, the moment the Soviets started intensively resupplying Arab forces. Nixon immediately changed course and ordered that Israel receive armaments as well, including more than a hundred fighter planes and a dozen C-130 transports, as quickly as possible. After constant consultation with Abba Eban and U.S. National Security Adviser Henry Kissinger, Nixon ordered his military to "send everything that can fly."

This order, it turned out, was not so simple to carry out. The war could not wait for delivery of military support by sea. The U.S. needed to load up huge C-5 Galaxy transport planes from various bases in the United States and then find a place for them to refuel on their way to Tel Aviv.

Nobody in Europe was willing to risk the ire of the Arabs and the Soviets by allowing the planes to refuel. Not West Germany, not France, not Britain. The planes took off without any clarity as to where they would land. The wall-to-wall European response, too, would be long remembered in Israel.

After significant diplomatic wrangling over a tense few hours, Portugal finally consented to the use of an airbase in the Azores, islands in the Atlantic Ocean, where the aircraft could refuel before crossing carefully down the middle of the Mediterranean Sea, escorted by American and Israeli fighter jets.

Israel had been able, on its own, to turn the tide on the battlefield on the same day that Operation Nickel Grass began. But the magnitude of the resupply—all told, more than twice the tonnage of what the Soviets gave Syria and Egypt—was what ultimately ensured a decisive Israeli victory, with Israel not just retaking Golan and Sinai but also barreling past the 1967 armistice lines, crossing the Suez Canal, cutting off the entire Egyptian Third Army, and threatening the enemy capitals of Cairo and Damascus. On October 22, the UN Security Council passed Resolution 338, which called for a ceasefire reaffirming the principles of Resolution 242 and the immediate start of peace talks. Two days later, the ceasefire took effect. The Yom Kippur War had ended with Israeli success on both the military and diplomatic fronts.

Yet despite the magnitude of the victory, Israelis for the most part didn't see it that way. For Israel, the Yom Kippur War was a moment of shattered myths, of shock at the catastrophic intelligence failures that allowed the Arab forces to gain the element of surprise and resulted in the deaths of thousands of young Israeli soldiers, of a harsh reality check after the pristine and almost messianic success of 1967. In a dynamic that would echo sharply in the aftermath of the Hamas attacks of October 7, the Yom Kippur War, despite being a substantive victory at the end of the day, taught the Israelis lessons that were no less harsh than those learned by the Egyptians.

First, Israelis lost the myth not only of their own infallibility in war, but also of the political leadership of the Labor party. Yom Kippur was also seen through a Westernized lens that drew much from the American experience in Vietnam: a younger generation, disillusioned by leaders in the context of a major military debacle that brought death to thousands of their peers.

But from a diplomatic perspective, Yom Kippur taught Israelis two more crucial lessons. One was that no matter how much the world promises to the contrary, Israel will never gain true favor and respect by sacrificing its central strategic advantages—in this case, the possibility of a preemptive strike. We must never play Samson to the world's Delilah, cutting off our hair at the crucial moment, lest we meet our end in a Philistine dungeon.

The second lesson concerns the reality of both European and American positions towards Israel. At the moment of truth, when Israel was in the most dire straits—a moment which Moshe Dayan, our most renowned former general and minister of defense during the war, described as an existential threat to the "Third Temple"—when the chips were down, our European "friends" were nowhere to be found.

For its part, the United States was the only major power that proved able and willing to help. But even the Americans did not help due to a heartfelt commitment to Israel. The fact is, they held back until it was clear that the Soviets were pouring in weapons for the other side—until, that is, it became an American problem rather than just an Israeli one.

Much has changed for the better in the relationship between Israel and the United States since then. In the decades that followed, a deep mutual commitment, based on both shared values and especially shared interests, would express itself through the rest of the Cold War and continue to deepen long after. Over time and in fundamental ways, the mouse and the elephant grew to depend on one another—a mutual dependence that increased as Israel grew in economic and military strength. The United States today works together with Israel on countless levels, from intelligence and military technology to broad areas of commercial investment and tourism. Throughout the years, Israel received sophisticated weaponry and cutting-edge technology, and the two countries shared intelligence, which is unique and defines the special strategic relationship between the two countries. (It is important to point out, however, that many of these exchanges were made only after Israel had first shown that it was on the verge of acquiring independent capabilities of its own.)

This relationship has not been without its points of sharp and sometimes public disagreement, especially where Israel's perceived core strategic needs are concerned. Despite the alarmist statements of many people, both inside and outside the pro-Israel community, such disagreements have never altered the fundamental calculus of the relationship. When push comes to shove, both countries realize that Israeli leaders will, at times, be willing to disagree with Washington, even defying its commands when Israel's vital national security interests are on the line. This dynamic, I will argue, has made the relationship stronger rather than weaker.

***

The relationship between Israel and the United States is a sprawling, complex creature that comprises interests, sentiment, domestic American politics, and mutual benefit. It is important to understand the specific circumstances of its origins—which I explore more deeply in the next chapter—for they are rather different from what is commonly believed in both countries, and this difference is crucial in understanding the dynamics that continue to live at the core of the relationship.

It begins with the realities of international relations—and it begins significantly later than Harry Truman's unforgettable words about "the old doctor" Chaim Weizmann.

Again, for the first two decades of Israel's existence, the United States refrained from supporting Israel in the area where the Jewish state most desperately needed help: in supplying the weaponry needed to not merely defend against, but to deter, the overwhelming aggression of the Arab world. This, despite the fact that Israel's enemies were supplied by the Soviet Union.

And so, Israel scrambled and hustled. In its earliest years, before the Soviets turned frontally against the Jewish state, Israel got its weapons from Czechoslovakia. That source quickly dried up, however, and under the leadership of a young, creative, and ambitious director-general of the defense ministry by the name of Shimon Peres, Israel managed to develop a warm relationship with France. It was the French, not the Americans, who supplied Israel with the main weapons used in 1956 and 1967. It was also the French who supplied Israel with the crucial elements of its nuclear facility in Dimona, allowing Israel, according to foreign sources, to enter the "nuclear club" long before anyone expected—much to the dismay of President John F. Kennedy.

When Lyndon Johnson ascended to the presidency in 1963 in the wake of the Kennedy assassination, Israel had a true friend in the White House, a man who had led the Democrats' charge on Capitol Hill to prevent President Eisenhower from unleashing his wrath on Israel after the Sinai Campaign. And indeed, it was only under Johnson that Israel began purchasing advanced fighter craft—especially the A-4 Skyhawks and F-4 Phantoms—to replace its aging Mirages and Mystères. But few remember that even this sudden and dramatic shift took place only *after* the 1967 Six Day War. Why?

The reason is rather straightforward. It was only then, after 1967, that Israel emerged as a genuine power in the Middle East, and as a potential bulwark against the Soviet empire's reach in the region. Washington dropped its official posture of neutrality in the Middle East only when it became a clear American interest to do so.

This fundamental link between American support for Israel and the perception of America's interest was made painfully clear, of course, during the Yom Kippur War. Israel had blundered its way into an existential fight for its survival and was begging for immediate military support. Nixon and Kissinger agreed—but only after the Soviets started heavily resupplying the Arab side. Their calculus may have been perfectly understandable; they didn't want to trigger a global conflict with the Soviets. But that does not change the revelatory quality of the moment: Israel would be supported in its most desperate hour of need only to the extent that American interest dictated it must be so.

Indeed, when turning to the decade and a half that followed the Yom Kippur War, one discovers that it was only after the true foundations of the relationship between the two nations were laid—grounded squarely in shared interests—that the relationship really began to take off and, over time, to assume many of the central characteristics it has today.

CHAPTER 4

THE EMERGENCE OF THE NEW ISRAEL, 1975–1992

In the nearly two-decade period from the aftermath of the Yom Kippur War through the 1980s to the end of Prime Minister Yitzhak Shamir's premiership in 1992, the Jewish state was transformed.

Politically, it saw the fall of the Labor party, which had ruled since the country's establishment, and with the 1977 elections, the rise of Likud, which became the dominant political force of the next generation. Economically, Israel fell into an acute crisis in the mid-1980s, including hyperinflation, the collapse of the banking system, and currency devaluation. As a result, Israel's leaders instituted deep reforms. They repudiated longstanding policies that had favored a centralized command economy and transitioned toward a more modern, market-based approach that would in time make Israel the vibrant "start up nation" of today.

Israel's position on the international stage also changed dramatically. Few imagined in 1973 that the Yom Kippur War would be the last in which the country's very survival was truly on the line. (Even the no-less-traumatic events of October 7, 2023, do not, from a military standpoint, rise to that level.) Israel's national life, after the 1973 war, seemed to be no less precarious than it had been twenty years earlier. The scandal and malaise that followed, including an official tribunal that investigated its leadership, called Israel's future into question in the thinking of many of its own citizens and observers abroad.

Israel's apparent fragility seemed to be confirmed, in 1975, by the UN General Assembly's adoption of a Soviet-sponsored resolution equating Zionism with racism. Today, Israelis have grown accustomed to outrageous declarations emanating from the bowels of Turtle Bay. At the time, however, many Israelis still recalled the UN's central role in the Jewish state's progress toward independence and saw the UN as an authoritative voice of world opinion and a source of hope for peace. The sight of Israel's UN Ambassador Chaim Herzog standing before the General Assembly and tearing the document in two was powerful and gratifying, but it didn't make Israelis feel any less vulnerable.

In the next two decades, however, Israel transcended the feeling that it was hanging by a thread. A country that began this period surrounded by hostile, powerful armies, dependent on Washington to save it from annihilation, facing diplomatic indifference from Europe and outright hostility, including severed relations, from half the nations on Earth stretching from Africa and the Arab world across Eastern Europe and the Soviet Union—Israel would emerge by the early 1990s as a strong and stable nation, and a more valuable ally to the United States than ever before.

Indeed, by the early 1990s, Israel had made peace with its most feared enemy (Egypt), a second major enemy (Iraq) would have its military decimated by a U.S.-led coalition, and the Soviet Union, which had spent decades supplying and supporting its enemies, would collapse, unleashing a huge wave of Jewish immigrants to Israel and allowing the Jewish state to establish diplomatic relations with numerous new countries in its wake.

This extraordinary transformation in a fairly short period needs to be understood, for it helps to explain Israel's standing in the world today. The transformation involved three main elements: (1) changed relations between Israel and the Arab states, (2) the development of the U.S.-Israeli alliance, and (3) the focus on the Palestinians, especially the PLO, as central to the conflict. A fourth element—Israel's economic transformation from stagnant and centralized to market-driven and stable—also had a major impact on Israel's diplomatic position across the board.

***

Again, the wall-to-wall belligerence, boycotts, non-recognition, and war that Israel, since its inception, had faced from the entire Arab world was encapsulated in the notorious Khartoum Resolution made by the Arab League when it met in Sudan in September 1967: no peace with Israel, no recognition of Israel, no negotiations with Israel.

In its bellicosity towards Israel, the Arab world's leader was Egypt.

Although Israel had been indirectly exchanging messages with Cairo about the possibility of a peace deal involving an Israeli withdrawal from the Sinai Peninsula for years, the first direct and serious peace diplomacy did not occur until after May 1977, when Israel's Labor party lost the national election for the first time to Likud, headed by Menachem Begin, who had led the Irgun underground during the British Mandate.

Begin came to power on a wave of anger against the Labor establishment, which Israelis blamed for failing to wage war well, to bring peace, or to deliver a broad-based prosperity. In particular, Israel's Mizrahi immigrants, most of whom had come from Arab lands and Iran in the 1950s and 1960s, resented not sharing in Israel's successes and viewed Labor as the party of the Ashkenazi elite.

Although Begin was known as a passionate nationalist who embodied Jabotinsky's hawkishness and the traditional Jewish longing for the Land of Israel, he was more complex. In the immediate aftermath of the 1967 war, he had endorsed the government memorandum, shared with the U.S., that approved the idea of trading land for peace with Egypt.

Begin did not view Sinai as part of the ancient Jewish birthright. The special Jewish connection to the West Bank and Jerusalem, which Israel had conquered from Jordan in 1967, did not, in his view, extend to the territories conquered from Egypt in the same war.

After Begin became prime minister in 1977, Israel began holding secret talks in Morocco with Egyptian officials. Soon Moshe Dayan, the former IDF general and defense minister who had now returned to politics as Israel's foreign minister, met with Egyptian Deputy Prime Minister

Hassan Tuhami, and made it clear that a full withdrawal from Sinai in exchange for full peace was on the table. The Egyptians were impressed.

To make peace with Israel, Egyptian President Anwar Sadat would have to abandon the ideal of pan-Arab unity, to which his predecessor had been committed. Sadat would also have to disconnect Egypt's diplomacy from the Palestinians. He could not serve Egypt's interests, as he saw them, if he allowed Palestinian leaders, in effect, to veto his policies.

The most important thing to know about the peace accords signed between Israel and Egypt in 1978 and 1979, however, was that they happened despite, not because of, years of diplomatic efforts to reach a comprehensive resolution of the Arab-Israeli conflict.

It should be obvious that when it comes to Middle East peace, despite all the rhetoric to the contrary, American and Israeli interests are not, in fact, always aligned. Sure, both sides want the conflict to end. But for Americans the issue is a matter of interest; for Israelis it is a matter of life and death. This is not a fine distinction. For an American administration, the cost of failed diplomacy reflects itself mainly in depleted political capital and global standing. For an Israeli government, however, signing a bad agreement can result in bloodletting and even war; it can endanger the very existence of the state.

For many years, the predominant view of U.S. officials was that the only peace worth pursuing was a comprehensive, region-wide accord that resolved all claims and ended the conflict. This made sense from an American perspective: Comprehensive peace was a prize big enough to justify the U.S. president's personal involvement. The effort to achieve it would be considered worthy even it failed. No American leader, it should be stressed, has ever been penalized politically for failing to resolve the Arab-Israeli conflict.

From Israel's perspective, however, the pursuit of a comprehensive peace was at best a waste of time, and at worst a recipe for disaster. Israel was a country fighting for its survival against a broad alliance of belligerents demanding its annihilation. Outside powers pushing for a comprehensive accord could be expected to call Israel a warmonger if it refused to give up assets crucial to its security. This risk for Israel would be exacerbated in a large multinational forum, such as the one President Jimmy Carter had been pushing, where Israel would have to stand alone against a large array of adversaries acting in lockstep. No resulting deal could be a good one.

By contrast, Israel could gain significantly from bilateral agreements, if and when they became possible. For Israel, any peace, even with less-influential countries, would bring immediate benefits. Bilateral accords are necessarily easier to achieve: not just because the calculus of interest and compromise is simpler, but also because the details can be kept secret until it is a *fait accompli*. Disparaging a bilateral peace agreement—as Carter did when Egypt and Israel began moving in that direction—in favor of an unachievable "comprehensive" deal was viewed as a grave error by Israeli leaders on the Left and Right.

For years prior to Camp David, the United States pushed for multilateral negotiations to end the conflict. During the Nixon administration, in 1969, Secretary of State William Rogers revealed a ten-point plan for Middle East peace without coordinating with the parties. It went nowhere. Rogers was replaced by Kissinger, who invested in "shuttle diplomacy," going back and forth to different Middle East capitals as secretary of state under Presidents Nixon and Ford, with more modest goals in mind. He produced a few minor agreements, but did not move the parties much towards peace. Carter, who took office in January 1977, pushed for a grand Geneva Peace Conference that included Israel, the Arab states, and Palestinian representation to aim for a complete resolution of the conflict. This, too, went nowhere.

Israel and Egypt, it turned out, had other plans. After months of secret talks, on November 9, 1977, Sadat announced that he would "go to Jerusalem" to speak to the Knesset and lay out his vision of peace. To please the Americans and others, he gave lip service to the idea of a comprehensive peace, including resolution of the Palestinian issue, and claimed he would not seek a separate peace with Israel. Key Israeli leaders, however, understood that Sadat's main interest was a bilateral deal to retrieve the Sinai Peninsula. Israel was eager to pursue peace on this basis; within days, the Knesset extended a formal invitation. On November 20, 1977, Sadat was on a plane to Israel.

My father, Uri Prosor, was among the dignitaries who waited for the Egyptian leader on the tarmac at Ben-Gurion Airport in Tel Aviv. He always spoke about that day as one of the most powerful moments of his career, in which everyone held their breath, knowing history was about to turn. A moment bursting with possibility, but also with peril.

No one in Israel knew for sure what would happen when Sadat's plane landed. Many doubted the Egyptian president's intentions. In fact, until the last minute, Israeli security officials had contingency plans in place, just in case the people who disembarked were armed terrorists rather than the Egyptian leader. Sadat, after all, was the man who had pulled off the Yom Kippur sneak attack against Israel only four years before.

When Sadat did speak before the Knesset, it was not all reassuring. Yes, he called for peace, and yes, Prime Minister Begin spoke of "no more war…no more bloodshed." This was promising.

But even though the two leaders were open to exchanging a full Israeli withdrawal from the Sinai for a full peace treaty, both leaders operated under constraints. Sadat had concerns about being seen as betraying the Arab world, and especially the Palestinian cause. He said there would be no separate peace, and that any agreement on Sinai would have to be accompanied by an agreement on the West Bank and Jerusalem. Begin was interested in decoupling the issues: The West Bank was the Jewish historical heartland, and Begin wanted it settled by Jews. Jerusalem was even more sensitive: It would never be on the table, as far as he was concerned. Sadat, as it turned out, proved far more open in private to the decoupling than his public statements suggested. Indeed, in retrospect, we see that one of Sadat's strategic goals was to free Egypt from the veto of other Arab leaders. He was especially intent on liberating Egypt from the shackles that connected it to the Palestinian cause.

After Sadat's dramatic visit to Jerusalem in 1977, Israeli and Egyptian talks continued. There was a great deal of resistance, resentment, and internal politics for both sides to overcome. A follow-up summit meeting in Ismailia, Egypt, in December 1977 came up empty.

American officials at first declared open opposition to a separate Egyptian-Israeli peace deal. In time, however, Carter recognized that he had no choice but to embrace the momentum and proposed a three-way summit at Camp David, Maryland, in September 1978. There, the first of two major peace accords between Egypt and Israel were concluded, followed in March 1979 by the signing of the Egyptian-Israeli peace treaty on the White House lawn.

The peace between Israel and Egypt radically changed Israel's strategic position. No longer would Israel need to maintain a vast and constant military mobilization against a united and powerful Arab world. The threat of annihilation was suddenly removed—and would not return until some of its enemies (first Iraq, then Iran, then Libya, then Syria) began working on nuclear weapons. One could even argue that it was not until 1979 that Israel was finally established, once and for all, as a secure fixture of the Middle East, and therefore of the international community.

The negotiations were tense and nearly broke down on more than one occasion. Both parties were driving a hard bargain: Israel wanted at least some assets or rights to remain in Sinai, such as the use of airstrips, and wanted to discuss only bilateral issues. Sadat would settle for nothing less than a complete withdrawal, and said he wanted Israeli concessions on the Palestinian issue as well. Through no small amount of work by the American hosts, a compromise was eventually reached: There would be a full withdrawal. Two different memoranda would be signed—one outlining bilateral peace between Israel and Egypt, and one offering general statements about the Palestinians, but without any mention of the fate of settlements or Jerusalem.

It is an interesting question whether the net effect of American involvement in the negotiations was positive or negative: Did it make the treaty easier or harder to achieve? The Americans had not started the talks, they had not convinced the parties that peace was possible. On the contrary, all of America's prior efforts to foster a negotiated solution to the Arab-Israeli conflict had proved futile. But there were plenty of moments when either side could have abandoned the talks, and didn't. Was that the result of American pressure, or of the will of both sides to end the state of war?

***

The most important of the lessons of Camp David is that peace begins not with diplomacy, or with international pressure, but with a decision by leaders to move their nations to agreement. American efforts spanning almost a decade had come to nothing. Only Sadat's decision to come to Jerusalem, and Israel's positive response, created the opportunity to make peace.

After more than two decades as a senior diplomat, I am still baffled by the refusal of international leaders and diplomats to internalize this lesson. The amounts of time, money, and energy wasted on premature international conferences, peace envoys, and coercive summits in order to create "dialogue" where the will to peace is not yet there, are enormous.

I am not suggesting there is no value to the manifold quiet discussions that are the true bread and butter of diplomacy—whether in the form of secret negotiations, "track-two" informal discussions, or any number of forums where the details of a possible deal can be brainstormed, critiqued, and exchanged away from the public eye. These are often highly useful, because peace is not just hard to agree on, it is also hard to implement: A great deal of creativity and nuanced detail are necessary, and quiet diplomacy plays a crucial role.

Less helpful, however, are the grand public gestures of international peacemaking—the multilateral conferences and formal frameworks imposed from without, such as the ill-fated Madrid peace conference of 1991, or the framework of the "Quartet" of the U.S., EU, UN, and Russia. It's almost inevitable that such gestures are tailored not to achieve the goal of actual agreement, but rather to advance the interests of the international actors themselves. By design, they create not actual pressure on the parties to reach agreement, but merely the *appearance* of pressure—an appearance that frequently achieves the opposite of the desired effect, forcing the parties to harden their positions. In effect, such efforts are more likely to create new obstacles than solutions.

Every agreement comprises two core components: will and way. The mutual will to agree, and the pathway for that agreement to overcome innumerable hurdles. Both of these components are necessary. And while international actors can have an impact on whether a leader wants to make peace, the last place where that is likely to happen is on a global stage.

Where there *is* a will, however, the reverse is true: Diplomacy, including that facilitated by third-party countries, can help to produce a deal and sustain it.

There is a second lesson from the peace with Egypt. On October 6, 1981, Anwar Sadat was assassinated by Islamists during a military parade. Over the decades that followed, under the presidency of his successor Hosni Mubarak and certainly under the brief reign of Mohammad Morsi and the Muslim Brotherhood in 2012 and 2013, the peace between Egypt and Israel never really went anywhere beyond the formal cessation of hostilities and security cooperation. Again, the potential that treaty enthusiasts saw in 1979 was never realized. Not in cultural exchange, not in tourism, not in business investment, not in joint ventures. It was a formal peace, but not a people-to-people peace.

This is no small matter. International relations are ultimately underpinned by commercial and interpersonal ties between peoples. It is impossible to maintain a durable and meaningful peace, I believe, without cultivating open people-to-people ties. Contacts between intelligence agencies and security forces alone cannot create peaceful sentiment between states, and it is a grave mistake to think that they can.

Israel has no territorial disputes with Egypt—nor with Jordan, with which it concluded a peace treaty in 1994. These peace accords are still in force, and Israel has a strong interest in preserving them. Yet in practice, they have not produced great popular mutual acceptance. The past decades have been an enormous missed opportunity with respect to both Egypt and Jordan—a gap that has only grown wider since October 7, 2023.

Instead of building meaningful people-to-people relations, Jordanians and Egyptians are exposed daily to anti-Israel and antisemitic propaganda in their schools, newspapers, and popular culture. Israel's relationship with Egypt and Jordan is often called a "cold peace," but it does not amount even to a non-aggression pact, given that Egyptian and Jordanian officials wage diplomatic warfare against Israel at the United Nations and other forums.

This question—what sort of peace are we talking about?—became central to Israelis' thinking when we began developing relations with the Gulf states in the 1990s. I was deeply involved in these efforts when I served as director-general of the Foreign Ministry in the 2000s, efforts that would one day culminate in the Abraham Accords of 2020. We were conscious of the lessons from Egypt and Jordan when we started deepening relations with the Gulf states, but we hoped that economic interests would prevail and lead our counterparts to prefer deeper and more extensive ties. My basic working assumption was that without publicly deepening our people-to-people contacts, these relationships would never get off the ground.

Nonetheless, one should not discount the benefits of the peace, such as it was, achieved with Egypt in 1979. For decades since Israel's founding, the Arab world as a whole rejected Israel unequivocally, violently, and with the full backing of the Soviet Union. Egypt proved that peace with Israel was possible, setting a precedent that would be repeated with other countries. The treaty meant, above all, that Israel's most fearsome enemy was no longer an enemy. And it bolstered Israel's image as a permanent part of the region's political map, not just a passing phenomenon, thereby deterring efforts to destroy it by force.

***

The 1979 accords had repercussions beyond the peace between Israel and Egypt, however. Though the agreement might have happened without American intervention, the decision to place it under American auspices fundamentally altered Israel's relationship with Washington, setting it on a course that has come to resemble a permanent alliance.

In the decade after the 1967 Six Day War, the U.S. supported Israel intermittently, selling it weapons (such as advanced fighter planes), largely to serve American Cold War interests. Whatever sentiments they felt towards Israel as a Jewish state and post-Holocaust refuge, Presidents

Johnson, Nixon, and Ford viewed the country above all as a strategic asset that helped to contain the Soviets.

In the early 1970s, President Sadat showed interest in breaking with Nasser's approach and ending Soviet influence over his country. He evicted Soviet military advisers in 1972. He wanted to make Egypt part of the Western world and understood that it would require ending the conflict with Israel.

It was Sadat who persuaded Washington to support the Camp David Accords with significant American money. Billions of dollars began to flow annually to both Egypt and Israel, and each country began receiving more U.S. taxpayer dollars than any other foreign recipient.

There is a common misconception that in exchange for this aid, Israel acts as an American proxy. Those who believe it also often suppose that Israel is therefore utterly dependent for its continued survival on the good graces of Uncle Sam.

The reality is much more complicated. Not only is Israel *not* an American puppet, it's also not in America's interest that it be one. America benefits much more from Israel's strength as an independent state that fiercely pursues its own interests than it would from a vassal. And the proof that this is the case lies in the simple fact that despite numerous disagreements and moments of misaligned interest, the relationship has only deepened with time.

The aid that began flowing to Israel in 1979 did not come from sentiment. President Carter was known to possess relatively little love for the Jewish state. But more importantly, the agreement also began a pattern of large-scale foreign aid to Egypt, a nation which, for all its evident graces, enjoys no special attachment from almost any significant American voting constituency. To this day, Egypt is the second-largest recipient of American foreign aid after Israel—yet nobody argues this is the result of irrational popular support for Egypt or an out-of-control "Egypt lobby" in Washington. Indeed, the ties that America enjoys with Egypt pale in comparison to those it has with Israel. The funding for Israel and Egypt, together, began as a price that America was happy to pay for the first-ever peace treaty in the Middle East, and the stability and Cold War influence that came with it.

Today the aid the US government provides to Israel, between $3.5 billion and $4 billion a year (not including the special allocations since October 7), is not what it was in the 1970s. It has been reduced not just by inflation—losing about two-thirds of its value in real terms—but much more so by real economic growth: Today it constitutes a much smaller percentage of each country's budget than it was back then. It is also strictly military in nature: The aid procures American military hardware and funds joint projects in which Israeli innovation helps both nations to improve their defense systems. The Iron Dome anti-missile system is the most famous example. While the defense industry in Israel is small compared to that of the United States, it has grown dramatically in recent years. The U.S. now buys and benefits from Israeli drones, missile defense, defense- and cyber-related software, and more—all of which exist because Israelis see themselves as profoundly responsible for their own security.

This cooperation has also led to the development of an unparalleled missile-defense system known as the Arrow 3. This state-of-the-art system, the result of a U.S.-Israeli joint effort, was successfully used in combat for the first time on November 9, 2023, when it shot down a Houthi ballistic missile launched at Israel from Yemen, and then again during the Iranian missile assault on Israel on April 14, 2024. It's now helping to defend the UAE and Saudi Arabia from Iran, and will hopefully help to defend European countries from Russian aggression, as well: In November 2023, Germany finalized the purchase of the Arrow 3 in the largest defense export contract in Israel's history.

No less important than technology and hardware is the intelligence that Israel shares with the U.S., intelligence based on a far more robust Israeli human intelligence (HUMINT) operation—that is, espionage—across the region that takes full advantage of the widespread Israeli fluency in Arabic and Persian. The U.S., for its part, shares intelligence that is based on a far more developed signals intelligence (SIGINT) capability—especially through employment of satellites. This combination of Israeli HUMINT and American SIGINT has created an unimaginably powerful intelligence capability for both nations, especially where the Middle East is concerned.

Israelis are also grateful for America's involvement in encouraging certain reforms of Israel's economy, especially beginning in the mid-1980s. This was a period of severe economic turmoil for the Jewish state—one that resulted not only in major reforms, but also in a powerful deepening of ties with the United States at a level that was not just related to defense and peace.

When Shimon Peres entered the office of prime minister in September 1984, after an inconclusive election resulted in a national unity government with Likud, Israel's economy was in an unprecedented tailspin. Growth had stalled out and turned negative, while inflation was skyrocketing, reaching triple digits and projected to reach quadruple digits. Bank stocks had collapsed. Catastrophe loomed.

Peres offered an economic stabilization plan that would require reforms to a degree that is hard to grasp. It included severe price controls, the reopening of collective-bargaining agreements and unlinking of salaries from inflation, sharply devaluing the shekel, slashing government subsidies, and across-the-board large budget cuts, selling off government-owned industries, deregulation, monetary controls, and on and on. It was so comprehensive, and so successful, that it became one of the world's most important case studies in the economic transformation of a nation in severe distress.

But it also hinged on an important act of diplomacy. For alongside his incredible political challenge of convincing all the different parties to accept a complete overhaul of the economy, it was Peres who negotiated a deal with the United States to receive billions of dollars in loans to effectively underwrite the endeavor. Without that, it is doubtful whether the competing parties inside Israel—politicians, business leaders, and labor unions—would have ever agreed. As with the peace between Egypt and Israel, here, too, America used dollars to create invaluable stability, advancing interests of Israel and itself.

The liberalization of Israel's economy in the wake of the 1985 stabilization plan began a process of reform that would carry through subsequent governments, and especially accelerate during the 2000s and 2010s, when Benjamin Netanyahu, a firm believer in free markets, was in the role of finance minister and then prime minister. This process, which began in the mid-1980s, unleashed the tremendous creative potential of Israeli innovators and entrepreneurs, and made it possible for international corporations to invest heavily in Israel. By the 1990s, major companies like Cisco, Intel, IBM, and others were using Israel as a crucial center for research and development. By the 2000s, Israeli start-ups were announcing major exits. By the 2010s, new Israeli companies like WeWork, Waze, and Wix became household names around the world. Billions of dollars were flowing into the Israeli economy.

Much of Israel's success has come from investments pouring in from abroad, with American investors taking by far the largest role. This is encouraged and supported through a highly developed system of connections with American officials—not only with the federal government, but also at the state and local levels.

Israel has emerged from its economic adolescence in the 1970s and 1980s and is well into adulthood. And, Israel's economic strength serves the common interests of both America and Israel.

America benefits more from an ally like Israel that is strong, independent, and powerful, even though it will sometimes chart its own course, than from an ally that is compliant because it is weak and not independently capable.

A natural outcome of such a reality, however, is that there will be moments when Israeli and American interests clash. There will often be "daylight" between the two governments, and there is no harm in saying so. On the contrary—it is a natural part of a healthy, vibrant U.S.-Israel relationship.

***

The fact that Israeli and American interests, while largely overlapping, do not always line up, is not fully understood because in most cases the differences are resolved behind closed doors. But sometimes they burst into the open. And when Israel's most vital security interests have been at stake, Israeli leaders have refused to bend to American demands much more often than is usually understood. Again, it is not a cause for panic—it is, rather, a natural part of the relationship.

A few examples may illustrate the point. We have already seen how, after the 1956 Sinai Campaign infuriated President Eisenhower, Israel took its time withdrawing from Egyptian territory, making sure to exact assurances of the security of its shipping through the Straits of Tiran and the demilitarization of Sinai—and also exerted as much power as it could through its supporters in Congress to keep the president's fury at bay. We also saw how Israel decided, despite the opposition of President Johnson, to launch a pre-emptive strike in June 1967 after Egypt's blockade of the Straits of Tiran. In both cases, Israel faced potential catastrophe, and there was simply no way that an Israeli government could accommodate American demands. In neither case did it cause real damage to the relationship: Eisenhower shifted his disposition towards Israel soon after, whereas Johnson started supplying Israel with advanced weaponry after the Six Day War.

There are plenty of other examples. There is Israel's rejection of the 1969 Rogers Plan—which Israeli Prime Minister Golda Meir dismissed out of hand, calling it "an attempt to appease the Arabs at the expense of Israel." In 1975, the United States was eager to bring Egypt under the American umbrella and put immense pressure on Israel to withdraw from strategic parts of Sinai, even without a peace treaty. Israel, however, was in no mood to make concessions—especially since the Sinai was also producing significant oil for the Jewish state, but also because it saw the Egyptian presence in Sinai as a massive strategic vulnerability that had enabled Egypt to go to war in the first place. President Gerald Ford was so angry that he withheld the sale of F-15 fighters and ordered a "reassessment" of US relations with Israel. Prime Minister Yitzhak Rabin, however, didn't budge.

Another example is 1981, when Israel, under Prime Minister Menachem Begin, destroyed a nuclear reactor being built in Osirak, Iraq, and then, a few months later, extended Israeli law to the Golan Heights.

Generally speaking, throughout the Cold War, the United States opposed *any* Israeli military actions against Arab states that were seen as risking a wider conflagration. Iraq was viewed as friendly by US officials because of its ongoing war against the Islamic Republic of Iran. But from Israel's perspective, the development of an Iraqi nuclear capability was an existential threat that had to be eliminated. The Osirak reactor would soon go online, and Israel needed to strike before it did.

After Israeli warplanes destroyed Osirak on June 7, 1981, much of the world condemned Israel. The United States supported the UN Security Council condemnation. President Ronald Reagan wrote in his diary, "I swear I believe Armageddon is near." Washington suspended strategic cooperation between the two countries, and later cancelled the sale of F-15 fighter planes.

But Israel defended its action, insisting on its right as a sovereign state to act in its own defense. On December 20, Begin summoned the U.S. ambassador and issued a statement of protest, which was reprinted in *The New York Times* and included the following words:

> Over the last six months, the United States Government has punished Israel three times.... What kind of talk is this, "punishing Israel"? Are we a vassal state of yours? Are we a banana republic? Are we 14-year-olds who, if we misbehave, we get our wrists slapped?
>
> Let me tell you whom this Cabinet comprises. It is composed of people whose lives were marked by resistance, fighting and suffering. You will not frighten us with punishments. He who threatens us will fund us deaf to his threats.[32]

[32] "Transcript of Prime Minister Begin's Statement to the U.S. Envoy to Israel," *The New York Times*, December 21, 1981, Sec. A, p. 20, https://www.nytimes.com/1981/12/21/world/transcript-of-prime-minister-begin-s-statement-to-the-us-envoy-to-israel.html (accessed October 19, 2024).

A decade later, in 1991, the United States went to war against Iraq—and then, again, twelve years after that in 2003. It was clear to everyone by that point that Israel had done the right thing. As *New York Times* columnist Nicholas Kristof put it in 2002, if not for the Israeli strike at Osirak, "Iraq would have gained nuclear weapons in the 1980s, it might now have a province called Kuwait and a chunk of Iran, and the region might have suffered nuclear devastation."

Begin's successor, Yitzhak Shamir, was also willing to disagree with the United States when he felt that Israel's vital interests were at stake. During the First Gulf War in 1991, President George H. W. Bush, who staunchly opposed Shamir's settlement policies, withheld $10 billion in loan guarantees that Israel had requested in order to absorb a million immigrants from the Soviet Union. It became a crisis in relations that did not end until Shamir left office the following year. In Shamir's view, however, settling the West Bank was a national-security imperative and was based on historic rights of the Jewish people. Whatever one's view of the policy of settlements, it is noteworthy that the Israeli government was willing to clash head to head with the United States on a matter it saw as vitally important.

Such clashes have occurred frequently enough, and under so many different presidents and prime ministers, that they can be considered a standard feature of the relationship. They have not weakened the relationship: On the contrary, it seems clear that they have only strengthened it, by showing that it can survive and surmount disagreements. They have shown that U.S.-Israeli relations are not built on humiliating subordination but mutual respect for the policy differences that inevitably arise between sovereign states, even when those states are strongly attached to each other as strategic allies.

In 2007, Israel discovered that Syria was building a nuclear reactor and sent its jets to destroy it—and I had a front-row seat as coordinator of the U.S.-Israeli strategic dialogue. Israel's prime minister at the time was Ehud Olmert, an impressive manager who did not hesitate to make tough decisions. He sent the head of Mossad, Meir Dagan, to Washington with intelligence proving that Syria was building a nuclear reactor with

North Korean assistance. Israel felt obliged to notify the White House and convey a clear message that Israel could not live with a nuclear reactor in Syria and was determined to take it out. The timing of the attack was open to debate, but action was necessary before the reactor went online, which would make an attack impossible.

Dagan flew twice to the United States, bringing the proof that the Americans requested. But even after Israel eliminated all reasonable doubt that Syria, in violation of US red lines and nonproliferation policy, was about to go nuclear, President George W. Bush informed Olmert that he had ruled out any military action—by either the U.S. or Israel—against the facility, and instead looked for diplomatic alternatives.

Secretary of State Condoleezza Rice proposed a few ways to handle the emerging "Syrian problem." The first was to complain to the UN Security Council and to warn Syrian President Bashar al-Assad, who had no idea at this point that anyone knew about his secret nuclear program, to halt work at the reactor. The problem was that the moment such an action was taken, Israel would lose the element of surprise in any strike, and Assad would feel obligated to retaliate if a strike took place, and to complete the reactor as soon as possible if it didn't. Then Rice had another, even less promising idea: to report Syria's activities to the International Atomic Energy Agency (IAEA) in Vienna—the same IAEA that had done nothing about Iraq's nuclear reactor in the 1980s. Israeli officials were astonished that Rice thought she could solve this real and grave problem by, in effect, wagging her finger at the cameras. It was wildly unrealistic to think that the UN or the IAEA could bring about the dismantling of Syria's nuclear reactor.

Olmert spoke to President Bush directly and made it clear to him that Israel could not and would not live with a nuclear threat on its border, and would not agree to diplomatic moves that would make it public. Assad, he argued, would likely not retaliate if both the program and the strike could be kept secret even after the fact. Israel respected the administration's concerns, he told the president, but would nonetheless act in accordance with its national security interests and destroy the facility at a time of its choosing. After President Bush hung up, he reportedly turned to his astonished advisors, and said: "That guy has guts."[33]

On September 7, 2007, just after midnight, Israeli jets bombed the Syrian nuclear reactor. Olmert recounts the conversation he had with President Bush in the hours that followed:

> I arrived back at my office in IDF headquarters at 3:30 am. I contacted the White House and was told that Bush, who was in Australia, would get back to me within the hour. When he called, I was careful with my words, even though I was sure he was on a secure line.
>
> "Hey buddy," he said in his Texan drawl. "What's up?" I told him I was sorry for interrupting his trip but I wanted to let him know that the "thing" in Syria had been taken care of.
>
> "That's great!" he enthused. He asked if I was expecting a response. I said that it was still too early to say for sure, but it seemed unlikely.
>
> "If there are any problems, I want you to know that the United States will do everything to help you," he added.
>
> I knew I would sleep well that night.[34]

The Syrians never did retaliate. No less important, however, was the president's response to Olmert's so-called "insubordination." Israel does not take orders from anyone, including Washington, when it comes to the key elements of its security. Neither does the United States usually

---

[33] Elliott Abrams, "Bombing the Syrian Reactor: The Untold Story," *Commentary*, February 2013, https://www.commentary.org/articles/elliott-abrams/bombing-the-syrian-reactor-the-untold-story/ (accessed October 19, 2024).

[34] Ehud Olmert, *Searching for Peace: A Memoir of Israel* (Washington, DC: Brookings Institution Press, 2022), p. 258.

hold it against us after the fact. If anything, it creates a relationship of mutual respect.

This disagreement, of course, was not a public one, and would not be disclosed until years later, after both leaders were out of office. But other clashes, such as those that involved Rabin, Begin, and Shamir, were widely discussed in real time.

Among the most dramatic examples was when Prime Minister Benjamin Netanyahu appeared before a Joint Session of Congress in March 2015 and delivered a long speech attacking the emerging nuclear deal with Iran. From Israel's perspective, the nuclear agreement would inevitably result in, rather than prevent, an Iranian nuclear bomb, and it crossed a clear red line in terms of Israel's vital interests.

People who did not like the substance of Netanyahu's position on the Iran nuclear deal often criticized the prime minister on procedural grounds: that he failed to coordinate properly with the White House, publicly disagreed with a sitting president, and instead accepted an invitation from House Speaker John Boehner and Senate Majority Leader Mitch McConnell, both Republicans. But the real issue was a matter of substance. Netanyahu, with good reason, believed that the Iran deal threatened not only Israel's national-security interests, but its very survival. He concluded that he had to do everything in his power to block the deal, even at the cost of an open dispute with President Obama. Even though Obama resented it, Israel's interests required spelling out the dangers of the deal to Congress—because Congress, it was believed, had the power to stop it.

Despite the criticism of Netanyahu's move—both in the U.S. and in Israel—professional integrity compels me to say that if an Israeli prime minister is convinced that there is an existential threat to Israel, he or she must do everything in his or her power to protect the country. Even if the leader of Israel's most important ally disagreed, the case against the nuclear deal had to be heard. The path for achieving this goal could have been more diplomatic and sensitive, perhaps, but it is important to distinguish between the path and the essence of the matter.

***

Every time there is an open policy dispute between Israel and the United States, friends of Israel become fearful. They voice their horror that Israel is hanging by a thread, that only American support is what saves it, and that Israeli defiance of the U.S. is endangering that support. But in real life, the fact that Israel stands on its national security interests only works to its benefit in the long run. Americans respect those who stand their ground, and they respect Israel's unique position in a particularly challenging neighborhood. That is a large part of the reason why the U.S.-Israeli relationship has always been able to overcome the occasional sharp disagreements about policy.

Will this always be the case? Not necessarily. Bipartisan support for Israel in Congress, which has long acted as a check on presidents antagonized by one Israeli action or another, remains broad but will not necessarily stay that way forever. It is wise for Israel to work to preserve and deepen popular affection on both sides of the aisle in America. This is harder to do now than in the past, because America is more polarized than ever.

Of course, there have been plenty of cases when Israel did give in to American pressure. During the Gulf War in 1991, Prime Minister Yitzhak Shamir chose, despite the advice of most of his cabinet, not to respond militarily to Iraq's launching of Scud missiles at Tel Aviv. He instead deferred to American concerns that Israel's involvement in the war would ruin the carefully constructed coalition that the U.S. had built, which included Arab states hostile to Israel.

And in 2000, Israel backed out of the sale of sophisticated Phalcon intelligence aircraft to China—even though it was an entirely Israeli-made military product, and even though the sale was initially undertaken with American knowledge, and the contract had been signed years earlier and payment had already been made. But Washington had changed its mind, growing increasingly concerned that the technology might endanger U.S. forces in the Pacific rim. Israel agreed to renege on its deal—and suffered hundreds of millions of dollars in penalties, as well as damage to its relationship with China that has never fully healed.

More recently, in the early morning hours of April 14, 2024, Iran launched hundreds of cruise missiles and ballistic missiles as well as armed unmanned aerial vehicles (UAVs) at Israel. Between Israel's missile defense, Israeli Air Force (IAF) fighter jets intercepting, and the support of U.S., British, French, Saudi, and Jordanian forces, almost none of the missiles reached Israel, and none caused significant damage or loss of life. Israel had every right to retaliate with full force, as many in the cabinet wanted, but instead chose to accept the American recommendation that it instead go with a very symbolic, but physically minimal, response hitting a small number of sensitive military targets inside Iran.

In none of these cases, however, did Israel accept an unreasonable risk. Saddam Hussein's Iraq was about to be defeated by the overwhelming coalition forces, and an Israeli military response would be at most a symbolic gesture. The sale of Phalcon to China was, at bottom, a business deal. When Washington made sure that the cost to Israel would be far higher than the profit, it made perfect sense to cancel it, even at risk to relations with China. And, in the case of Iran, the revelation of an *ad hoc* coalition that helped to defend Israel—including Jordan and Saudi Arabia—brought far more benefit to Israeli deterrence than whatever price there may have been in a limited response.

Israel has always understood America's importance in the world. Since the 1970s, America has become Israel's main weapons supplier, diplomatic partner, and ally. The United States meanwhile understands that Israel will defend its interests, and, on vital security matters, will not buckle to pressure.

Israel's relations with America have deepened as Israel has grown stronger, economically and militarily. Today it brings more to the table than at any time in the past.

Begin was right: Israel is *not* a vassal to Washington, and both sides have understood this quite well. It is, rather, a smart, loyal, and highly capable American ally.

***

The third major transformation during the 1980s and early 1990s related to Israeli-Palestinian relations. Once peace had been sealed with Egypt, the threat of major wars faded, and the issue of the Palestinians took on an increasingly central role in the conflict.

Prior to that period, the Palestine Liberation Organization (PLO) was widely shunned around the world as a terror organization. The Jordanians were seen as the only respectable guarantor of Palestinian rights. But by the early 1990s, the Jordanians had relinquished their claims to the West Bank, and the PLO had been given the central and exclusive stage in representing the Palestinian cause.

This period, in other words, also saw a transformation of the conflict itself, from a broader David-and-Goliath battle pitting tiny Israel against the vast Arab world, to something focused much more narrowly on the Palestinians.

This was useful for both the anti-Israel cause and Arab state leaders. It allowed Mubarak's Egypt, for example, to preserve its treaty with Israel while seeking common ground with other Arab states by supporting Palestinian grievances against Israel. It allowed the Arab world to invert the David-and-Goliath narrative: Instead of little Israel facing the vast Arab world, Israel was recast as the oppressor, and the Palestinians as the underdog.

With the decline and fall of the Soviet Union, and America remaining as the sole superpower, the entire idea of destroying Israel by conventional military assault became more of a fantasy than an operational plan. Israel's enemies worked creatively to reframe the conflict to make ideological warfare and terrorist attacks more effective. They argued that the cause of the Palestinians' rights—with the PLO as their "sole legitimate representative"—was the essence of the conflict.

Israeli leaders were ill prepared for this reframing of the conflict. Again, the West Bank, where the majority of Palestinians live, plays a completely different role in the Zionist worldview than did Sinai: While Menachem Begin had, as early as 1967, assented to the idea of a complete return of the land to Egypt in exchange for a full peace treaty, he was absolutely opposed to compromise on the territories conquered from Jordan: The Old City of Jerusalem had been the focus of Jewish longing since time immemorial, and the West Bank (or Judea and Samaria, as the area was long called before 1949) was the birthplace of ancient Israel, the setting for countless biblical tales.

No Israeli leader of either Left or Right in the late 1970s or 1980s spoke about a "two-state solution." Israelis across the political spectrum saw the PLO as a terrorist group, not as responsible national leaders, and rejected the suggestion that the conflict could be resolved by creating a PLO "mini-state" in the West Bank and Gaza. The term "ministate" was used with scorn by Yitzhak Rabin and Shimon Peres. Israeli proponents of a peace deal involving the West Bank and Gaza thought it could be made either with Jordan or with the local Palestinian communities; none said that such a deal should create a new, fully independent Palestinian state. And Jerusalem, again, was completely off the table. Indeed, a last-minute effort by Carter to include mention of Jerusalem as a future issue for negotiation nearly blew up the 1978 Camp David talks. ("Give me ten minutes," Begin is said to have responded. "Because that's how long it will take me to pack my bags.")

Opposition to recognizing the PLO was grounded in years of painful experience. The group had been founded in 1964 as a terror organization and, together with its various spinoffs, had launched the most horrific attacks, including airplane hijackings, the killing of Israel's Munich Olympics athletes in 1972, and murderous cross-border raids against Israeli civilians.

By the late 1970s, the PLO had built a vast base of operations in southern Lebanon, from which it launched frequent attacks on northern Israeli communities. In 1982, Israel sent its army into Lebanon to eliminate the PLO in what became known as the First Lebanon War. The war morphed into an effort to install a new government in Lebanon that would make peace with Israel and permanently pacify the border.

This war succeeded in removing the PLO from the border but failed in its broader political aims. The PLO's base in Lebanon was eviscerated, but, due to American pressure, its leadership was allowed to remove itself to Tunis. The war entailed a few major controversies: Israeli officials initially declared that the army would not go more than forty kilometers into Lebanon, but that promise was broken—and it remains an open question whether Begin was in on a secret plan to move beyond the declared limit, or whether his defense minister, Ariel Sharon, deceived him on the matter. Either way, Israeli leaders looked bad, not least to their own public. A massacre carried out by Lebanese Phalangists at the Sabra and Shatila refugee camps was blamed largely on Sharon, damaging Israel's international standing. After a commission of inquiry blamed him for allowing it to happen, Sharon found himself in the political wilderness. And the power vacuum created by Israel's expulsion of the PLO from southern Lebanon was filled not by the Lebanese army, but by Hezbollah, an Iranian-backed Shiite terror group. That set the stage for further conflict, the 2006 Second Lebanon War, and a heavily armed, Iran-backed military foothold on Israel's northern border. As I write these words in the summer of 2024, Hezbollah has been assaulting Israeli communities since October 7, 2023, tens of thousands of Israelis are unable to return to their homes, and the prospects of a Third Lebanon War appear higher than ever.

Washington had used diplomacy and the dispatch of U.S. armed forces to Lebanon to save the PLO from destruction. This helped to kill the chances for a non-PLO, non-terrorist, responsible Palestinian political leadership to arise.

In the fall of 1987, a violent uprising known as the "intifada" began in Gaza and the West Bank. It began as a grassroots action, but PLO leaders quickly moved to embrace and expand it. They saw it as advancing the PLO's strategy of trying to demoralize Israelis through violence against civilians. Terror attacks involved mainly Molotov cocktails, stabbings, and rock-throwing, rather than guns, but the intifada was intensely violent. Its goals were destructive, not diplomatic.

A final effort to negotiate a "Jordanian option" was undertaken by Shimon Peres, in his capacity as foreign minister under the unity government in April 1987. Peres launched secret talks with Jordan's King Hussein in London, which ended in an agreement to host a peace conference that would explore the possibility of solving the Palestinian issue by extending Jordanian sovereignty in the West Bank.

But Prime Minister Yitzhak Shamir, Begin's successor as leader of Likud, was famously unmovable when it came to the West Bank. From his perspective, Judea and Samaria, as he called it, were part and parcel of the ancient Jewish homeland, and his primary concern was settling Jews throughout that homeland—just as it had been before statehood. The Palestinian Arabs as such had never been a sovereign nation, and he believed that giving them control over a state would strengthen the international campaign to destroy Israel. Shamir rejected the Peres-Hussein agreement out of hand.

The Jordanian option was finally laid to rest when, in July 1988, Jordan relinquished all claims to the West Bank. Recall that Jordan had rejected the 1947 UN partition plan and, upon the British withdrawal of forces, launched a war in 1948 to kill the infant State of Israel. In that war, Jordan conquered the West Bank and eastern Jerusalem. Jordan then claimed to annex those territories and, despite virtually no international support, continued to assert ownership even after it lost those territories to Israel in 1967. Now, in 1988, Jordan's relinquishment of its claims meant that there could be no Jordanian option. And the first intifada effectively precluded diplomatic progress with non-PLO Palestinians.

The PLO had shown zero interest in peace with the Jewish state, but key Western nations and an increasing number of Israelis were arguing that it was Israel's only possible peace partner.

The 1980s, in other words, were a period in which Israel's image—both internationally and internally—transformed. Peace with Egypt, the collapse of the Soviet Union, and the Lebanon war as well as the strike on Osirak—all of these gave rise to the conclusion that Israel was now a strong power. The idea gained currency that Israel could have "peace now" simply by changing its own policies. People both in and outside of Israel were pleased to argue that the problem in the Middle East was not Arab hostility to Israel and rejection of Israel's right to exist, but Israel's unwillingness to recognize the rights of beleaguered, stateless Palestinian Arabs.

Many Israelis failed to see what was actually happening: They were losing an international war of narratives, images, and ideologies. The PLO did realize it, however, and began to take major diplomatic initiatives accordingly. In November 1988, it issued a "declaration of independence" at a meeting of its legislative council in Algeria. There was, back then, nothing even resembling a Palestinian government in the West Bank and Gaza. There was, in reality, no Palestinian state, independent or otherwise. But the PLO declaration won recognition from a number of states—a symbolic gesture aimed at delegitimatizing Israel.

As part of a deal to win diplomatic recognition from the United States, the PLO announced in December 1988 that it accepted UN Resolutions 242 and 338, which recognized Israel's existence. This announcement was as empty as its declaration of independence. The PLO continued to launch terrorist attacks against Israel and continued to preach hatred of Israel and rejection of Israel's right to exist. The announcement, however, paved the way eventually for the UN General Assembly to invite PLO chairman Yasser Arafat to speak and to give formal recognition of "Palestine" in UN bodies as a non-voting member. Meanwhile, the Reagan administration, in its final days, shocked Israel by granting the PLO official recognition and allowing it to open an office in Washington.

These were the developments that led to Israel's engagement of the PLO, which reached a climax with the Oslo I, Oslo II, and Wye River Accords in the 1990s. The PLO had benefited in the 1980s from the growing belief around the world that the Palestinian issue was the heart of the Middle East problem. But the PLO was hurt by other diplomatic and political developments—including its support for Iraq's Saddam Hussein in the Gulf War of 1991 against a vast coalition led by Washington and joined by much of the Arab world. The administration of President George H. W. Bush was infuriated. The PLO was also set back by the disintegration of the Soviet Union, its superpower sponsor.

In October 1991, the United States launched an international Middle East peace conference in Madrid, which enjoyed the co-sponsorship of the dying Soviet Union just weeks before it formally disintegrated. Israel felt obligated to abandon its long-held insistence on restricting negotiations to bilateral talks, in part because of the tensions that had developed with the United States over the loan guarantees affair. But because the Israelis under Shamir would not sit in the same room as the PLO, a joint Palestinian-Jordanian delegation participated, along with representatives from Lebanon, Syria, and other Arab nations.

Rarely has a diplomatic conference had so little chance of success—and that's saying a lot. Proposals made to the Palestinians were sent by fax to PLO headquarters in Tunis for response. It was a charade, and naturally nothing came of it. Because where a party to a conflict has no will to make peace, there is no way. Shamir understood this and spent most of the conference sitting morosely in his chair.

Israel was ready to talk to Palestinians, but not to the PLO, which it did not see as a good-faith actor. The PLO, it should be recalled, was founded not in response to Israel's conquest of the West Bank in 1967, but in 1964—that is, three years before Israelis were even in the West Bank. So, when PLO officials spoke of "occupation" or "liberation," they were talking not of the West Bank and Gaza, but all of Israel. From its inception, the PLO aimed to use violence to undo the events of 1948 that gave birth to Israel—in other words, to destroy the Jewish state. Its aim was always more than an independent Palestinian state in the West Bank, Gaza, and East Jerusalem; if anything, the latter was merely a way station to the same maximalist goals the Arabs had embraced from the beginning. PLO officials were masters of confusing rhetoric and shamelessly used different, inconsistent words for different audiences, but Israelis who paid attention grasped that, as a matter of sincere, deeply held principle, the PLO had zero interest in a two-state solution if one of those states were Israel.

Agreeing with that assessment of the PLO meant, as a practical matter, that there was no diplomatic way forward to make peace, so American officials simply ignored the merits of Shamir's view of the PLO. Shamir had rejected the Jordanian option out of hand and was not about to go with something even more unthinkable, like embracing the PLO as peacemakers. The differences between the Israeli and American positions were sharp and intractable, and likely would have continued that way had Likud not lost the 1992 Knesset elections.

Obviously, dialogue is a necessary condition for negotiated agreement. But it is rarely a sufficient one. Every conflict has its own inherent dynamic, its inner politics on both sides, its logic that can flow from economics, the military reality on the ground, historical grievances, and the actual and perceived interests of both sides—everything from land and oil to honor and history. And every ounce of external pressure placed on a party to concede its core interests risks a backlash that makes agreement harder to attain in the future.

On July 23, 1992, Israelis went to the polls. For the first time in more than a decade, the election resulted in a decisive victory for one side, rather than a national unity government. The Labor Alignment, led by Yitzhak Rabin and Shimon Peres, took over the nation's leadership, and set about to alter fundamentally the course of Israeli history.

CHAPTER 5

THE RISE AND FALL OF THE OSLO ACCORDS

For decades, the Palestinian issue was just one of many parts of the broader conflict with the Arab world. It was not the most pressing of Israel's problems. The violent rejectionism on the part of Palestinian residents of the West Bank was simply an extension of the overall violent rejectionism from the Arab world, and it was not nearly as dangerous to Israel as the tank divisions and fighter planes of the combined armies of Egypt, Syria, and the other Arab states.

But after Egypt made peace with Israel and the Soviet Union collapsed, what was once the "Arab-Israeli" conflict looked increasingly like a Palestinian-Israeli conflict. This also was true inside Israel. The new perspective deepened the divide between citizens who believed that Israel, by softening its own policies, could have "peace now," and those who feared that territorial concessions to the Palestinians would be exploited by Israel's enemies to facilitate terrorism and otherwise weaken the Jewish state. Each side in this debate within Israel came to see the other as leading the country to ruin.

Later, I will explore the ways that the Oslo Accords marked a major strategic shift in the ongoing war launched by Israel's perpetual enemies, who wanted nothing other than to bring the Zionist enterprise to ruin. From the Israeli perspective, however, this period was experienced very differently—as a time of tremendous hope, alongside fierce internal debate.

When Labor won the 1992 elections, there was already a sizeable part of the Israeli public who believed—as did many outside Israel—that the Israeli-Palestinian problem could be solved relatively swiftly by dividing the land between the Jordan River and the Mediterranean Sea. According to that view, the key to peace was Israel's willingness to relinquish control over some land, so the Palestinians could fulfill their national aspirations by establishing a sovereign state—and the sooner, the better.

This view rested on a few assumptions, however. First, that the Palestinians' ambitions were now limited to creating a small state of their own (in other words, those ambitions no longer included "liberating" all of Palestine west of the Jordan River, that is, destroying Israel); second, that Palestinian leaders were ready for diplomacy in good faith to bring about a land-for-peace deal; and third, that those leaders were prepared both to abandon terrorism and to control Palestinian extremists who remained intent on inciting and perpetrating anti-Israel terrorism.

Labor's 1992 victory made Yitzhak Rabin prime minister. He had soothed voters' fears with his tough-talking, general-in-command attitude and nostalgia for the Labor of bygone years. Shimon Peres, however, was the main force behind the diplomacy that produced the 1993 Oslo Accords. Peres, the new foreign minister, was a visionary of a Middle East without walls, a benign and enlightened region of open markets and the free exchange of goods, services, tourism, and investment.

For that dream to be realized, Peres believed, there had to be peace throughout the region. Otherwise, Israel and its potential trading partners and investors would continue to be distracted and discouraged by violence and uncertainty. And region-wide peace required first solving the conflict with the Palestinians.

These were the airy notions that in the early 1990s caused a new wind to blow through Israeli diplomacy. Israel encouraged the world to think differently about Middle East peace and to discard old ideas of Israel as an island of Western democracy in a benighted region, a state that had to defend itself against extremists and terrorists committed to its destruction and hostile to the West in general.

In his best-selling 1993 book *The New Middle East*, Peres made the case that with the signing of the 1993 Oslo Accords, a new era was dawning across the region.

He called for replacing the hard borders of the Middle East with "soft" ones that would allow for general demilitarization and the free exchange of people, goods, and services. He called for dismantling standard nation-states in favor of confederated democratic states and common economic markets. He believed the Middle East was ready in general for mutual recognition, demilitarization, and real peace. This would include a "Jordanian-Palestinian confederation for political matters, and a Jordanian-Palestinian-Israeli 'Benelux' arrangement for economic affairs" as well as a "regional security system" that would supplant existing national militaries in a period of trans-national terror, missiles, and nuclear weapons.[35]

Peres embraced far-reaching utopian ideas about the transformation not only of international politics, but of human nature itself, using the loftiest of tones. As he put it:

> People tend to remember more and think less. Our memories are familiar, affectionate, nostalgic. Our thoughts, which concentrate on the unfamiliar, are less welcoming. However, we must focus on this new Middle East reality, with its new dimensions and different nature of security, and not wander among memories of victories in long-gone wars—wars that will never be fought again.

He concludes:

> We can wash this blood-soaked land of conflict with living water, we can grow flowers on the battlefields of the past and bring smiles to Jewish and Arab children—indeed, to

[35] Shimon Peres, *The New Middle East* (New York: Henry Holt, 1993), pp. 174, and 80–83.

> all our children, who will inherit our land and live there in happiness and peace.[36]

Today it is easy to dismiss such ideas as fantastical—especially in the wake of October 7 and the overwhelming support that Palestinians have expressed for Hamas's atrocities. Back then, an Israeli's reaction to Peres's dream, which was usually either to dismiss it angrily or embrace it hungrily, became the touchstone of "Right" and "Left" in the country for the next decade and a half.

To many of us back in the early 1990s, in other words, Peres's dream didn't seem so farfetched. The collapse of the Soviet Union, the end of the Cold War, the democratization of Eastern Europe and Latin America, the establishment of the European Union, the Oslo Accords themselves, and the emergence of the internet—all of it felt like history was propelling us into a new era. Those of us who supported Oslo may be forgiven for hoping at that moment that perhaps the long history of wars, tyranny, and the violent struggle among nations, to evoke Francis Fukuyama's best-selling 1992 book *The End of History and the Last Man*, had reached its end.

Peres's vision, put simply, rode a wave of geopolitical optimism that carried many of us with it. I was stationed in Bonn when Oslo was signed in 1993. Germany had just reunified. The Berlin Wall had fallen before my eyes. The West had won the Cold War. It was a magical moment when anything, it seemed, was possible.

Nor was Peres the first Zionist leader to articulate such a dream. Indeed, a similar vision of regional comity driven by shared economic interests was central to Herzl's fantastic story in *Altneuland*. It was always embedded in the DNA of Zionism. As early as 1952, just four years after independence, Abba Eban was trying to establish Israel as a seeker of regional peace in a speech before the United Nations. As he describes it, he

> proposed a detailed agenda for a negotiation involving a transition from armistice to peace; the negotiation of final boundaries; a regional plan for the absorption and

[36] Peres, *The New Middle East*, pp. 85 and 194.

> resettlement of refugees; and a system of cooperation creating an "open region" in which there would be a concerted attempt to bring about an economic renaissance in the Middle East. I called for free ports, mutual access to air and sea communications, and an intensive process of human exchange.[37]

But Herzl was writing in 1902, and Eban was speaking in 1952, when a fledgling Jewish state had just extracted victory from the jaws of a still-ferocious Arab world. By 1993, what had seemed for Herzl to be a futuristic fantasy, and for Eban a theatrical diplomatic tactic, now seemed to have a bit more to it: Egypt had already made peace, Jordan would soon do the same, and a deal with the Palestinians was at hand. As foreign minister of a Jewish state that was firmly established and four and a half decades old, Peres produced his bold vision at a time when it seemed, to many, to be possible.

Peres's vision translated into practice with the signing of the Oslo Accords on September 13, 1993, in which Israel formally recognized the PLO and allowed it to rule, in the first stage, over the Gaza Strip and the West Bank city of Jericho in exchange for renunciation of terror and recognition of Israel. In subsequent agreements under Prime Ministers Rabin and Netanyahu, Israel withdrew from the West Bank's main population centers ("Area A"), while maintaining overall security control and civilian control over the areas most heavily populated by Israelis ("Area C"). The new Palestinian Authority, run by officials of the PLO, was created with its capital in Ramallah, with its own parliament and police force.

A year and a half after Oslo, the government of Rabin and Peres signed a peace treaty with Jordan, which shares Israel's longest border. Suddenly, Israel was a key player promoting world peace. We were actively ushering in the new era that Peres, with messianic fervor, had told Israelis was available to us if we only reached out and grabbed it.

It is relatively easy, with hindsight, to understand why Oslo failed. The PLO was—and, alas, remains—a revolutionary terrorist organization.

---

37 Eban, *Autobiography*, p. 169.

It long ago declared itself to be the "sole legitimate representative" of the Palestinian cause, but did little to improve the well-being of ordinary Palestinians, preferring instead to organize terrorist attacks against Israeli civilians and preach hatred of Israel and Jews. Its leaders proved mostly corrupt and dishonest, little more than mob bosses using violence to maintain their power and to further their destructive goals. To this day, they routinely deliver contradictory messages to different audiences and make promises they brazenly violate. They talk vaguely of peace in English, but continue to offer both honor and financial incentives to terrorists who kill and maim Jewish civilians in schools, coffee shops, and discotheques. The PLO leadership has never been willing to commit to ending the conflict once and for all and to live permanently with a sovereign Jewish state in any part of what it considers to be Palestinian land—which includes all of Israel.

At the time, however, we allowed our optimism, determination, and perhaps a modicum of wishful thinking to prevail. It is both the strength and weakness of grand visions of the future: Once embraced, they tend to drown out whatever objections and doubts that may arise. We dismissed the robust protest movement that arose, led by Likud, as pure politics and naysaying. When your own greatest aspirations receive the warm backing of the leaders of the world's greatest nations, it is hard to keep a sober assessment of what is actually possible.

Today we know that Yasser Arafat, who led the PLO for thirty-five years, and the Palestinian Authority for a decade, and who signed the Oslo Accords, never intended to make peace with Israel. From the moment he left his exile in Tunis and established himself and his cronies as the ruling regime in the West Bank and Gaza, he devoted himself to preparing for the next round of conflict. He did this to increase his leverage in negotiations and also to further his goals of "liberation" and "resistance." His diplomacy, including the talks in which I participated directly, never allowed the conclusion of an agreement that would include an end to the conflict.

As soon as Israel granted him power in the West Bank and Gaza, he turned the territories into staging areas for violence, not the foundation for peace.

In the summer of 2000, Arafat caused the collapse of the Camp David II talks that he had conducted with Prime Minister Ehud Barak and President Bill Clinton. He then launched a large-scale terror war against Israel, which he labeled the second intifada and sustained until he died in November 2004. This intifada killed more than a thousand Israelis. After it ended, Israel, in 2005, unilaterally withdrew from Gaza, evacuating twenty-one settlements as well as army bases. Israel handed the territory over to the Palestinian Authority. Then, in early 2006, the terrorist group Hamas violently expelled Palestinian Authority officials from Gaza and took control. In the decade and a half that followed, Hamas time and again launched rockets, underground infiltrations, balloon bombs, and other attacks against Israeli civilians. Israel retaliated to stop the attacks and attempted to restore deterrence. After some time, Hamas would attack again. Much as it took Israel by surprise, the terror assault of October 7, 2023, it now seems, was a logical progression from seventeen years of Hamas belligerence, deception, arming up, and brutal entrenchment in Gaza—all aiming to prove that it, rather than the PLO, was the true "resistance" to the evil of Zionism.

In 2008, months before he resigned in the wake of his indictment on corruption charges, Prime Minister Ehud Olmert took one final stab at reaching a conflict-ending peace deal with the Palestinian Authority. He had developed an ongoing rapport with Arafat's successor, Mahmoud Abbas, and spent nearly two years negotiating a comprehensive agreement. Finally, on September 18, Olmert and Abbas hammered out the contours of a deal that would cover the hardest issues including borders, demilitarization, refugees, and the status of Jerusalem. Abbas said he needed a few days to consult and think before offering a final approval. But he never returned an answer. As Olmert recounts:

> Thirteen years have passed, and Abbas still hasn't gotten back to us.... We were inches away. I was within a hair's breadth of fulfilling the dreams of millions of Israelis who

> longed for peace. I had seen the promised land, but was not allowed to enter.[38]

Many of Israel's critics allege that we have failed to make serious peace offers to Palestinians. These arguments intensified during the recent war with Hamas, as many sought to blame Israelis themselves for the savage and bloody attacks against their citizens. History shows that the onus falls on the Palestinians themselves. If they do not have a state of their own after seventy-five years, it is not for lack of good-faith efforts on Israel's part.

Not only did Peres's vision of a new Middle East fail to materialize in the wake of Oslo, what ended up happening was very much its opposite. And as we will see later, when, more than a quarter-century after Oslo, Israel signed the Abraham Accords with the UAE and other Arab states, heralding something that did begin to offer the promise of real peace in the region, it took a path that completely repudiated the logic of Oslo—peace without any resolution to the Palestinian conflict.

How did Oslo happen? As problematic as its outcomes were, it is nonetheless instructive to look at the diplomacy that brought it about. For it still stands as an instructive milestone in a century of Zionist diplomacy.

***

Like many successful diplomatic initiatives, Oslo began informally and in secret. In the early 1990s, Ron Pundak and Yair Hirschfeld, both scholars and private individuals, began participating in back-channel conversations with members of the PLO, as well as the Norwegian diplomat Terje Rød-Larsen—and with the full knowledge of the deputy foreign minister under Peres, Yossi Beilin.

Peres had by this point come to the conclusion that if peace were to be achieved, Israel had no choice but to negotiate directly with the PLO. The PLO had acted for decades as a terrorist organization. Its support among Palestinians was impossible to gauge because it routinely used violence

[38] Ehud Olmert, *Searching for Peace: A Memoir of Israel* (Washington, DC: Brookings Institution Press, 2022), pp. 297298.

against its political opponents. It claimed, however, to be the Palestinian people's "sole legitimate representative," and many people around the world, including in Israel, credited this claim. Over the years, efforts by Israel to engage in political talks with non-PLO Palestinian representatives, sometimes with support from the United States, had invariably failed.

These semi-official Norwegian-sponsored Israeli-PLO talks appeared to be fruitful, however. By early 1993, a close aide of Arafat's, Ahmed Qurei, also known as Abu Alaa, started participating. Soon after, Peres himself started flying to Oslo for secret meetings. By August, negotiators from both sides had put their initials on a Declaration of Principles, and all that remained was for Israel and the PLO formally to approve it.

Most of us remember the Oslo Accords as having been signed on the White House lawn in the presence of President Clinton on September 13, 1993. But the truth is, the Americans were scarcely involved in the process. They knew that, in addition to the official talks taking place in Washington with a joint Jordanian-Palestinian delegation, something was brewing in Oslo. But it was only once the Declaration of Principles was signed in August 1993 that the Americans were brought in.

This was almost certainly a good thing. US administrations often tried to pressure Israel to reach agreements—as if to suggest that, somehow, we weren't sufficiently creative or interested in peace to achieve it on our own. The result was that Israeli politicians felt less inclined to make such deals, rather than more so. One reason was that they did not want to be seen by the public as giving in to foreign pressure on the most vital interests of the country. In a head-to-head battle between domestic politics and foreign pressure, a politician's political survival usually wins.

In the case of Oslo, there was no pressure at all. The Americans welcomed the peace and gave their blessing, but did not twist arms to make it happen. This made it easier for Rabin to convince the Israeli public that he was operating in what he truly believed was Israel's national interest.

This is an important lesson about Zionist diplomacy—and perhaps diplomacy in general. Israelis do not want to feel pressured into making concessions on what they believe are vital interests, and Israeli political leaders who forget this inevitably end up losing elections, or worse.

On November 4, 1995, a right-wing extremist named Yigal Amir assassinated Prime Minister Rabin after a pro-Oslo rally at Kings of Israel Square in Tel Aviv. Such an assassination in Israel was unprecedented. It sent shock waves through the country on both sides of the political divide. Peres became acting prime minister and leader of the Labor party. In the 1996 election, Benjamin Netanyahu defeated him to begin a period of nearly uninterrupted rule by parties of the Israeli Right, or their ideological spinoffs, that continues to this day. Notably, despite his fierce opposition to the Oslo Accords, Netanyahu did not tear them up. He made new agreements and implemented them within the Oslo framework.

During the late 1990s, my own role as a diplomat grew dramatically. In 1998, I was invited to join Prime Minister Netanyahu in talks that resulted in the Wye River Memorandum, which further expanded the territory under Palestinian control. In 2000 and 2001, Prime Minister Ehud Barak entered into two separate rounds of failed negotiations with Arafat—first at Camp David, which I personally attended, and the failure of which triggered the second intifada; and then in Taba, Egypt, just weeks before he left office.

***

I sat in the second of two golf carts heading out from the remote Israeli pavilion at the Aspen Institute's picturesque Wye River Conference Center in Maryland. We were on our way to meet US Secretary of State Madeleine Albright. Sitting in the lead cart was Foreign Minister Ariel Sharon, the representative of the Likud's right flank in the first Netanyahu government, with his spokesman and a security officer. In the second cart were Sharon's chief of staff Tomer Orni and me, in my role as the political counselor in Washington. Sharon, who had been a famous battlefield general, trusted no one and arrived at the summit armed with maps of the territories under negotiation, insisting on entering every meeting with his own maps. It was October 1998.

At one point, among the winding paths, Orni and I lost sight of the first cart, and realized we were going to be late for the meeting with

Albright. "We're on time for every meeting with every foreign minister of every other country, but we have to be late for Albright?" Orni grumbled, clutching the maps that Sharon needed to begin the meeting. Eventually we burst into the conference room, puffing and panting. We were late.

Sharon grabbed the maps, unfurled them on the table, and gave Albright a look that said: Now let's get down to business. Albright knew what she was up against. The Americans regarded Sharon as the most stubborn and difficult figure in the Israeli government. When he spread out the maps and started lecturing her about the different neighborhoods of Hebron and which forces would patrol where, she indulged him by going into the fine print. She wanted to have a genuine dialogue with him, hoping to allay his suspicions and mollify his opposition to the summit—a last-ditch effort to save the dying Oslo Accords.

Since the deal to grant the Palestinians partial autonomy in the West Bank and Gaza Strip was signed in 1993, Prime Minister Yitzhak Rabin had been assassinated, the initiative's godfather Shimon Peres had been ousted from office, and Benjamin Netanyahu had been elected prime minister on a wave of disappointment about Arafat and opposition to further territorial concessions. Despite numerous Palestinian suicide bombings, the Americans were determined to keep the peace process alive and pressured Israel to go ahead with further "redeployments"—the diplomatic euphemism for withdrawals. Sharon had already made his attitude clear, not least by refusing to shake the hand of Yasser Arafat, despite strenuous attempts to persuade him—including by President Bill Clinton.

Halfway through his second term, Clinton had invited Netanyahu and Arafat for ten days of intense negotiations and demanded that they come to an agreement to continue implementing the Oslo Accords, including additional transfers of territory in the West Bank to the newly established Palestinian Authority. Hoping to eliminate the background noise that might make it difficult for the leaders to make decisions, the Americans chose to host the delegations at the isolated site of the old Wye River Plantation near the eastern shore of Chesapeake Bay. The Americans did the best they could to prevent leaks. They jammed cell phone service, limited the access of aides and spokespeople in and out of the retreat, and hermetically sealed the perimeter, as only the Americans know how. They were determined to lock the Israelis and Palestinians in a room, as it were, until a deal was struck.

The Israeli delegation included not just Netanyahu and Sharon but also Defense Minister Yitzhak Mordechai and Trade and Industry Minister Natan Sharansky, whom the Americans admired as the embodiment of Soviet Jewry's fight for liberation. The high-ranking Israeli presence was an indication of the summit's importance. We had unprecedented access to Clinton and Vice President Al Gore. They mingled with us for the whole summit in jeans and sweatshirts, as if on vacation. They joined us for meals, walks through the woods and gardens, and conversations out on the grounds as they tried to bridge the gap between the sides. This was the Americans' way of bringing their pressure to bear. The pastoral setting and friendly atmosphere were the velvet glove for America's diplomatic fist. The Americans wanted Israel to make major concessions.

There were three separate compounds at Wye River: Israeli, Palestinian, and American. Each delegation spent most of its time holding internal consultations at its own compound. This was normally also where we ate. Occasionally, two or three members of the Israeli delegation set out for another delegation's compound in a golf cart for a brief discussion about a certain item on the agenda and then came straight back. The advantage of this hands-off approach was that it did not force either side into a formal and confrontational encounter, but rather created a setting in which each side could engage seriously on weighty issues, take its time, and do so without active mediation.

In such negotiations, issues are rarely settled in three-way meetings attended by everyone. The thorniest issues are normally resolved in one-on-one meetings between leaders. Everyone else is supposed to talk to their counterparts in the other delegations, work out the lay of the land, understand what the other side is thinking and feeling, and sound out what their red lines and core issues are and where they might compromise. Their job is to lay the foundations for the meetings between the leaders themselves, who will make the most critical decisions.

Arafat was at the peak of his power as the leader of the Palestinian Authority. He often made a point of thrusting his trembling hands into the air and waving them vigorously to show who was boss. But his dramatic hand gestures were unnecessary, because he already had all his aides in a hammerlock.

The Israeli delegation, in contrast, had none of that authoritarian discipline. Its members did not share opinions on the key issues. In fact, some lacked basic mutual respect. Netanyahu showed more antagonism toward Mordechai and Sharon than toward Arafat.

As a career diplomat, I knew that when Israeli politicians sit opposite their Palestinian counterparts, they usually are thinking about the voters back home. Netanyahu's supporters opposed any additional concessions to the Palestinians. Netanyahu understood, however, that Israel should not appear to be negative and unconstructive. He was genuinely attentive to the Americans' expectations. He managed to maintain a dialogue with Arafat and show that he was interested in a breakthrough. But at the same time, Netanyahu had to reassure his political base in Israel. At the summit, Sharon effectively represented that political base. He limited Netanyahu's freedom of maneuver with Arafat. Nevertheless, the Israelis arrived with plenty of good will to test whether Arafat had become interested in peace. What was lacking was cooperation from the Palestinian side.

The Americans were determined to relieve the tension, settle disputes, and nudge the parties toward an agreement. Netanyahu agreed that in Hebron, Israelis and Palestinians would be monitored by a body known as the Temporary International Presence in Hebron (TIPH). It ended up serving no useful purpose, monitoring only one side—Israel. It was "temporarily" deployed for twenty-three years, until Israel put it out of its misery in 2019.

Despite Netanyahu's criticisms of Oslo, he effectively revived the moribund process by agreeing to the 1997 Protocol Concerning the Redeployment in Hebron and allowing further Israeli withdrawals. He complained about Palestinian violations of the peace agreements, but did not insist that they be remedied before Israel made additional concessions. Knowing that those concessions would outrage the Israeli Right,

Netanyahu asked President Clinton for a compensating favor: the release from prison of Jonathan Pollard, the American-Jewish U.S. Navy intelligence analyst convicted of spying for Israel in 1987 and sentenced to life imprisonment. The case had become a *cause célèbre* for the Israeli Right.

Clinton promised to pardon Pollard, and the Israeli delegation was elated, But, at the last minute, Clinton backtracked, and his staffers then depicted Netanyahu as a liar by claiming that no promise had been made to release Pollard.

I was there. Netanyahu had clearly been relying on Clinton's promise.

Clinton, as it turned out, had his own reasons for reneging: U.S. media reported that CIA Director George Tenet had threatened to resign if Pollard were released. For the U.S. intelligence community, Pollard remained an open wound. He was neither forgiven nor forgotten. Dennis Ross, the U.S. special Middle East envoy, later revealed that Clinton had asked him whether Pollard's release was important for Israel. Ross said that yes, many Israelis viewed Pollard as they viewed Israeli soldiers, someone they should never abandon in captivity. Ross, however, advised Clinton to keep Pollard as a means of pressuring Israel in the future.

Clueless about the drama, Pollard languished in jail for another seventeen years until he was paroled in 2015. In 2020, he completed his parole and, aged and ailing, relocated to Jerusalem.

***

The Wye River summit was my first serious experience of direct, top-level peace negotiations.

Israel returned to the negotiating table two years later, in July 2000, this time at Camp David. President Clinton invited Yasser Arafat and Israel's new prime minister, Ehud Barak, to the Maryland retreat in the hopes of brokering a permanent Israeli-Palestinian peace accord. Camp David II, as it is often called, was the first time, to the best of my knowledge, that Israel agreed to put Jerusalem on the table. The Israeli delegation made an extremely generous proposal, including sweeping territorial concessions, even in Jerusalem. Barak summoned Reuven Merhav, a former Mossad operative and director-general of the Foreign Ministry, to consult on the capital's fate. They opened up maps of Jerusalem and for the first time ever divided the city in pencil: Israeli neighborhoods to the west, Arab neighborhoods to the east.

Shimon Peres, the minister of regional cooperation at the time, happened to be in the United States on other business. One morning, his aide Avi Gil phoned me and offered me to take his place joining Peres for his morning walk. I jumped at the opportunity to have a private conversation with a statesman I greatly admired.

Peres and I went for a stroll. He spoke in his characteristically soft and self-assured manner and shared with me his perspective on the negotiations with the Palestinians. To my great surprise, he believed that Barak was making a terrible mistake by agreeing to put Jerusalem on the table. "The question of Jerusalem is going to blow up in his face," he said. "Better to push it off to the end and try to agree on all the other issues first." I suspected that he was speaking from a place of political jealousy, because Barak was in charge now, and Peres was a former prime minister in a junior role.

The next day proved Peres partially right. The talks did not stumble on the question of Jerusalem specifically, but because the Palestinians were unwilling to declare an end to the conflict despite Israel's extremely generous offers for territorial concessions. Arafat insisted, moreover, that Israel accept an influx of large numbers of Palestinian refugees and their descendants—effectively bringing an end to Israel as a Jewish-majority state. In other words, Arafat said he would make peace only if Israel agreed to commit suicide.

Barak would later claim that he had "revealed the true face of the Palestinians," deliberately exposing the insincerity of their commitment to peace. While it was true that Camp David exposed their true intentions, this had never been Barak's plan. He actually thought he could close a final peace deal.

With Camp David II, the peace process hit a brick wall, and the prognosis was grim. Shortly after blowing up the negotiations, Arafat ordered Palestinian security forces to launch a terrorist war that included the bombing of Israeli buses, nightclubs, and cafés. It lasted four years and destroyed not only the Oslo process but also the political standing of the Israeli Left. It became known as the second intifada.

***

The Wye River and Camp David summits, and the intifada that followed, shocked me and transformed my thinking about the conflict—and not just mine. When my colleagues and I arrived at Wye River, we had genuinely believed there was a peace partner on the other side, ready to make concessions and end the conflict. We ignored all the warning signs to the contrary, including the considerable difference among the messages conveyed by Palestinian leaders in different languages. In English, for Israeli and Western ears, they spoke like liberals about peace, while in Arabic, to their own people, they spoke the language of grievance, resentment, uncompromising nationalism, religious extremism, and violent vengeance.

Hopeful Israelis like me, craving diplomatic progress, failed to pay proper attention to the fork-tongued nature of Palestinian public discourse. Until then I had believed, naïvely, that Israel had it within its own power to move the conflict toward resolution simply by showing greater generosity to the Palestinians. I had assumed that the moment Israel stuck its neck out and signaled its openness to major concessions, the Palestinians would reciprocate.

The Palestinian refusal to make peace at Camp David II had a similar effect on a great many Israelis, good people who strongly supported peace diplomacy and had been optimistic about its prospects. One of the most interesting examples was Shlomo Ben-Ami, a historian who served as foreign minister in the Barak government and devoted much of his brief political career to advocating for peace, because he believed in the sincerity of Palestinian intentions and the importance of a negotiated resolution of the conflict. Ben-Ami has since changed his attitude. "The Palestinians have failed," he told me, "and led us with them to the black hole where we are." He then pointed out that Arafat did not even recognize the fact that the Temple Mount was a holy place for Jews. This gap, between the deep importance that Israel attaches to Jerusalem and the Temple Mount, and the Arab unwillingness to understand or respect this point of view, is profound and real, and might be unbridgeable.

We Israelis want to be optimistic. We want to believe that we control our own fate and can have "peace now" if we truly desire it and are willing to accept risks to achieve it. But what if the Palestinian side is not ready to acknowledge even minimal Jewish national rights? The Palestinians "do not want their own state, they want to condemn our state," Ben-Ami concluded painfully in another interview. "They do not want to compromise. The process for them is not of reconciliation, but of revenge, of redress of injustice, of undermining the existence of the Jewish state."[39]

An old cliché, frequently quoted by Israeli peacemakers, holds that "peace is made with enemies." Wrong. Peace can be made only with *former* enemies. You make peace with people who have decided that violence is not worthwhile and have concluded that it is in their interest to reach an agreement. You can make peace with people who have given up on their intention to destroy you, but not with people who cannot even bring themselves to pretend that you have a right to live.

It is not a good sign if your potential peace partner glorifies terrorist murderers and dedicates new public squares in their names. It is bad news if your potential peace partner teaches kids in its schools that Arab rights to all Israeli land are absolute and not subject to compromise. Israelis by and large have come to realize that there's a difference between peace diplomacy with enemies and with former enemies. The latter may work. But, as I came somewhat reluctantly to see, offering risky concessions to people who remain your mortal enemies is not only fruitless, but terribly unwise.

At Wye and Camp David, the atmospherics and what diplomats call "modalities" were ideal for peacemaking. The U.S. president's generosity with his time, the obvious sincerity of the Americans, their collegiality and gracious hospitality, the commodious accommodations, the care taken

[39] *Makor Rishon*, June 27, 2019, https://www.makorrishon.co.il/opinion/149945/ (accessed November 25, 2024).

to protect the parties from outside interference—all deserve grateful and admiring mention.

It was wise that other Arab representatives—from Egypt, for example—were invited to join the proceedings. The conferences amounted to clean laboratory tests of whether the Palestinians were willing to make peace. What we learned was unambiguous: They were not. They refused to agree to *any* language that violated their commitment someday to "liberate" the whole of Palestine. To eliminate Israel.

I know that domestic politics affect Israel's peace diplomacy. Israeli leaders have political and personal considerations that influence their thinking about what should be offered in international negotiations. Those considerations sometimes conflict with what I believe is in Israel's national interest. But precisely because I got to see the negotiations up close and was so involved in the details, I believe I know why those talks failed. Netanyahu did not achieve peace; nor did Barak. It neither case was it due to the inability or unwillingness of Israeli leaders to make generous, reassuring concessions.

Those talks failed because the Palestinian side was unwilling to end the conflict permanently—or even to promise to do so. It was more interested in preserving the principle of exclusive Palestinian national rights throughout Palestine than in signing a peace deal. What was remarkable about Arafat was his hostility to Israel, his dishonesty, but also the sincerity of his nationalist and religious principles.

The Camp David II fiasco helped General Anthony Zinni, President Clinton's special envoy to the Middle East, to see Arafat more clearly. Having visited the region soon thereafter, Zinni commented to a mutual friend of ours that Arafat was behaving like the infamous New York crime boss Carlo Gambino and was a pathological liar who could not be trusted. I reported Zinni's view of Arafat in a top-secret cable, marked "for your eyes only" and delivered straight to Foreign Minister Silvan Shalom and Prime Minister Sharon. Somehow it was leaked to Israeli journalists, who did not hesitate to report its contents.

Watching the Palestinians reject Barak's extraordinary peace offer at Camp David, I started to question my own assumptions about their willingness to conclude peace with Israel—doubts that grew stronger with each passing year. The Palestinian Authority's reflexive dismissal of President Trump's 2020 peace initiative and its refusal to stop paying pensions to the families of terrorists are just two of the more glaring recent examples. Its refusal to condemn Hamas's unthinkably brutal assault against Israeli civilians on October 7 is another.

***

For decades, the Israeli Right had opposed talks with the PLO. Their claim was that the Palestinians were uninterested in peace and would use any Israeli territorial concessions to stage terrorism against Israel. They cited Arafat's infamous "Phased Plan," announced in 1974. Arafat said then that the PLO was willing to engage in diplomacy, not just armed struggle, and would establish itself in any territory that Israel relinquished. It would then use that land for the eventual "liberation of all Palestinian territory"—that is, the destruction of Israel.

Many of us Israelis knew of the Phased Plan but assigned it little importance. We were in denial. The Oslo Accords encouraged such denial. Peace seemed imminent. The signing ceremony on the White House lawn and the Nobel prizes were thrilling and delightful for most Israelis, and especially for us professional diplomats. Seemingly overnight, doors opened to representatives of Israel: We could give interviews to Arab media outlets, we could negotiate new cooperative agreements across Europe and around the world. The peace train had left the station, and we were on board.

But the arguments of skeptics registered with me. I did not credit them fully, but I did wonder: What if this is all an elaborate ruse?

I told myself that the answer is not necessarily either-or. It is possible for a leader like Arafat to move towards peace while keeping his powder dry, leaving his options open and waiting to see if the Israelis prove reliable. Arafat had to concern himself with Palestinian politics, the ebb and flow of his own grip on his rule, the standing of rival Palestinian forces arrayed against him—especially Hamas.

I expected the Palestinians to generate international pressure on Israel. That's not necessarily inconsistent with peacemaking. It can be a negotiation tactic. I rationalized: If I were them, I would do the same. Up to a point.

What I came to realize was that the propaganda efforts of PLO leaders went far beyond negotiation hardball. Their attacks were designed not just to pressure Israel, but to delegitimize it; not just to push Israel towards greater flexibility, but to persuade the world that Israel should not exist. They portrayed the Jewish state as an illegitimate occupier—not just in the West Bank and Gaza, but in every inch of Israeli land. They offered no mitigating statements, no "if only" options for peace, no semblance of pragmatism. They were not remotely aiming to bring negotiations to a soft landing, a hard landing, or any landing at all. They were simply at war with us—the same war of absolute rejection they had embarked on from the moment Ben-Gurion declared independence in 1948.

To this day, I hope, pray, and believe that a consensual resolution of the Palestinian-Israeli conflict can one day be found. Today it seems harder than ever to imagine. But despite October 7 and the Gaza war, it is still the case that Israelis have no desire to control Palestinians. The Palestinians have no desire to live under occupation.

Israeli efforts to negotiate a peace deal have been earnest, generous, and sincere. We have dealt with the Palestinians through direct occupation. We have tried negotiating with local Palestinians, as at Madrid in 1991; negotiating with the PLO, as in the Oslo process; and unilateral withdrawal from Gaza. Now that we are in the thick of a new Gaza war and, most likely, a lengthy reoccupation, we must still ask ourselves how peace may one day be achieved. What other options remain?

I will return to this crucial question later.

***

In the meantime, there are some clear lessons from the rise and fall of the Oslo Accords.

Individuals matter. The Oslo process began as a private initiative. That initiative, over time, attracted the participation of increasingly high-level officials. It evolved into secret talks at the highest levels. My point here is not that the initiative was wise; we now know it was not. My point is that private individuals can sometimes bring about great changes in international relations. Private-citizen diplomacy—known as "track-two" negotiations—sometimes can be highly beneficial, the example of Oslo notwithstanding.

The meaning of Oslo's failure has still not been grasped by many people in and outside Israel. Diplomats in particular should ponder what went wrong. We allowed old peace-process bromides to become a substitute for serious thought about the conflict. Among these falsehoods: (a) The conflict can be resolved whenever Palestinians and Israelis sit down, negotiate, and agree on dividing the land into two states, mainly along the lines of the pre-1967 boundary (a "two-state solution"); (b) the lack of peace is the fault of Israel (or Israel and the Palestinians); (c) international mediators, such as the Quartet, are required to push the parties to see past their religious, nationalistic, or ego-driven (that is to say—their *irrational*) concerns and to appreciate the practical benefits of ending war, occupation, and terrorism; and (d) the Palestinian issue is the key to regional peace, and if we do not solve it, the whole region will have to wallow in instability and mutual hostility.

All of these notions continue to be embraced widely among diplomats in Washington, London, Paris, Brussels, and at the UN in New York—even after October 7. It seems that no amount of disproof ever discredits them. They are the core of a conventional wisdom that is longstanding because it is convenient for many officials, journalists, and others despite its evident falsity.

That conventional wisdom ignores that too many Palestinian leaders emphatically rejected Zionism, denying that the Jewish people had a right to a national home, long before there was a Jewish state. British officials heard these points and read them in formal Palestinian resolutions and memoranda from the moment Britain conquered the Near East from Turkey in World War I. Palestinian Arabs violently opposed Zionist efforts to establish a Jewish homeland in the Jews' ancestral land. The Arabs resorted to rioting, murders of Jewish civilians, and recruitment of the Arab states. The issue was not the size or shape of the boundaries of a Jewish state; it was the principle that there should not be a Jewish state at all in what the Arabs considered to be their land exclusively. The Arabs were not willing to share the land with the Jews, despite the ancient historical connection of the Jews with the land and despite the Jews' urgent need for a national home and refuge.

The conventional wisdom ignores, moreover, that the PLO was established and committed to Israel's destruction in 1964, years before Israel acquired control over the West Bank and Gaza. PLO leaders over time came to see the benefits of diplomacy and a pretended willingness to make some kind of peace, but they have never been willing actually to end the conflict or even to promise to allow a Jewish state to live permanently at peace on what they consider to be Arab land.

The conventional wisdom also tends to belittle the importance of Israel's peace agreements with Egypt and Jordan, and the normalization agreements more recently with the UAE, Bahrain, and Morocco, known collectively as the Abraham Accords. These agreements, concluded in 2020, were a product of a smart and efficient international pressure, but first and foremost of bilateral talks, often in secret, in which parties could reach agreement when the moment was right. What should be clear is that Israel is more than willing to make peace whenever a genuine peace—one that does not require national suicide as an opening condition—is offered.

The notion that the Palestinian issue lies at the heart of regional conflict is clearly not correct. The major upheavals—the "Arab spring," the Syrian and Yemeni civil wars and Iran's aggressions against the Gulf Arabs—have nothing to do with the Palestinian issue. And the belief that the Quartet or other multilateral initiatives are needed to end conflict in the region is not correct either, as the Abraham Accords made clear.

I do believe that peace may be achieved one day, ending more than a century of bloodshed and grief and bringing huge benefits to Israelis and Palestinians alike. But it will require new thinking.

The young ambassador with his parents, Uri and Nechama, in Genoa. His father, Uri, was deeply dedicated to the mission of bringing Jews to Israel.

The Ambassador and his wife, Hadas, during his days as a battery commander in the Artillery Corps, on a jeep trip to the Golan Heights in 1979. This jeep became famous for its frequent brake failures during hikes and vacations.

In 2004, the Ambassador embarked on a discreet and groundbreaking journey to the Gulf, navigating the complexities of a delicate democracy. The visit included enigmatic stops in Dubai and Abu Dhabi, shrouded in diplomacy and quiet significance.
Credit: Shlomo Shalom, Yedioth Archive

The Ambassador alongside the then-Minister of Foreign Affairs, Silvan Shalom, during a discussion at the UN General Assembly.
Credit: Shahar Azran

The Ambassador presenting President Shimon Peres with a symbolic gift of a backpack upon his retirement, marking the end of his term. The backpack, often associated with young Israelis embarking on post-army journeys, was chosen to represent the beginning of a new phase in life—a journey into uncharted territories and new adventures.

The Ambassador with President Ezer Weizman during the first-ever official visit of an Israeli president to the United Kingdom, marking Israel's 50th Independence Day.
Credit: John Rifkin

The Ambassador and his wife, Hadas, at the reception hosted by Queen Elizabeth II for President Ezer Weizman at Spencer House, during his time serving as the embassy's spokesperson.
Credit: John Rifkin

The Ambassador, alongside Prime Minister Benjamin Netanyahu and Ron Dermer, huddled in intense deliberation, refining the final touches of the Prime Minister's pivotal speech before the UN General Assembly—a moment charged with anticipation and significance.
Credit: Shahar Azran

The Ambassador briefing Prime Minister Benjamin Netanyahu, ensuring preparation for the engagement.
Credit: Shahar Azran

The Ambassador with Elie Wiesel, a man who dedicated his life to teaching the lessons of the Holocaust to future generations.
Credit: Shahar Azran

At the Independence Day reception at the UN with
Henry Kissinger and Samantha Power.
Credit: Shahar Azran

The Ambassador speaking at the UN.
Credit: Shahar Azran

The Ambassador at the UN.
Credit: Shahar Azran

A meeting at the UN with Tony Blair, former Prime Minister of the United Kingdom, a year after concluding his term as Israel's ambassador to the UK.
Credit: Shahar Azran

The Ambassador, during his tenure as Israel's ambassador to the UK, with his wife Hadas at one of London's dazzling events in 2009. The Brits are unrivaled champions when it comes to ceremonies and protocol. Credit: John Rifkin

The Ambassador at the United Nations with his late father, Uri, and his mother, Nechama, may she live a long life. He deeply misses his father, whose presence and influence remain a profound part of his life.

The Ambassador with his wife, Hadas, and their three children—sons Lior and Tomer, and daughter Oren—celebrating his 60th birthday in Jerusalem. Credit: Nir Buxenbaum

PART II

THROUGH MY OWN EYES

CHAPTER 6

MR. PROSOR GOES TO WASHINGTON

The funny thing is, it was never my dream to work in Washington. In fact, I nearly missed the opportunity of a lifetime to witness some of the most formative events in Israel's diplomatic history of the past half-century.

On a beautiful morning in June 1998, my wife Hadas and I were driving together to work at the embassy in London, where Hadas worked in the consular department. I was in my last few weeks as the spokesman at our embassy and was excited to begin what I believed was my next diplomatic assignment, as deputy ambassador at the embassy in Berlin. We were looking forward to returning to Germany, some seven years after I finished my first posting in Bonn. Exactly halfway between the suburb of Golders Green and the embassy in central London, my cell phone rang. "It must be the moving company," I said.

But the voice on the line spoke Hebrew. "I'm calling from the personnel department at the Israeli Foreign Ministry," said the unidentified male at the other end. "The Foreign Ministry's appointments committee has made a decision. Congratulations, you've been appointed political counselor in Washington."

I pulled over and laughed, surprised. "Check again, you must have the wrong number. You've reached Ron Prosor in London," I said. "I didn't even apply for a position in Washington."

"No, there's no mistake," said the caller after an uncomfortable pause. "You've been appointed political counselor in Washington. Now, let me give you some personal advice: Nobody ever says no to this job."

We drove the rest of the way in a baffled silence, and I entered the embassy in a fury. Moshe Raviv, the ambassador, saw me and asked, "What happened, Prosor?"

"Moshe, you won't believe it," I said. "I've been appointed, with neither my knowledge nor my consent, political counselor in Washington. I was meant to be the *deputy ambassador* in Germany—a higher-ranking position, one that I was looking forward to and which fits my qualifications."

Raviv, one of Israel's most seasoned ambassadors, eyed me up and down and then started laughing. "Look at this guy!" he said, gesturing toward an invisible audience. "He followed a rainbow and is disappointed by the pot of gold! What are you talking about? I served in that exact role for six years. It's one of the most important jobs in the foreign service." For a moment, it sounded like he was receiving a commission from the personnel department. "You've landed a position that will change your career. There's no comparison. This position in Washington is far more important for Israel than deputy ambassador in Germany."

As with any large hierarchical organization, the Israeli foreign service has a career ladder. The lowest rank on the diplomatic food chain, straight after the cadet course, is second secretary; the highest rank is ambassador. In between, from bottom to top, are first secretary, counselor, minister counselor, and minister—the rank that deputy ambassadors hold. I had my heart set on the job in Germany, which, I believed, represented a significant step up.

What I failed to understand, however, was that rank was not always the most important thing on a diplomat's résumé. Sometimes the specific country or city where one serves is of far greater importance. Because of their importance to Israel's national security interests, Israel considers its embassies in certain countries—"core countries" in the professional jargon—to be the elite commando force of the foreign service. It funds them more generously and sends its most qualified personnel.

At the top of the list is the United States, followed at some distance by Great Britain and the other permanent members of the UN Security Council—Russia, China, and France—as well as Germany, India, Japan, and Brazil. These are Israel's most important foreign relations. The Arab countries, especially Egypt and Jordan, would belong to the same list, were it not for the Israeli security services' near-absolute monopoly over bilateral relations with those countries.

Israeli diplomats in core countries have a hand in critical decisions on issues of national importance on a daily basis, and this involvement brings them into unmediated contact with Israel's top decision-makers. As the political counselor in Washington, I would end up negotiating the details of multibillion-dollar aid packages with the White House, State Department, and the chairs of the House Budget Committee and the Senate Appropriations Committee, Foreign Relations Committee, Intelligence Committee, and others. I participated in closed-door peace talks and meetings between Israeli prime ministers and U.S. presidents, who got down to business right in front of me. There could be no better vantage point, and no more meaningful service, for any Israeli diplomat.

Washington proved an absolutely fascinating tour of duty. It was there that I first saw the front lines of Israeli and global diplomacy. I handled critical issues on the U.S.-Israeli strategic agenda. I beheld the whole world through a rare, panoramic lens, from within the beating heart of a superpower whose influence goes well beyond the confines of planet Earth—as dawned on me when I visited the headquarters of the U.S. Space Command in Colorado.

The Roman Empire of the modern era left a profound impression on me. Washington is a gripping, exciting, muscle-flexing, multilayered cosmopolitan city. I enjoyed learning to navigate its mazes. There is no other capital in the world where Israel enjoys so much support as a trustworthy ally, and therefore where Israeli diplomats enjoy such an attentive ear. As a diplomat, Washington was my boot camp and officer's course rolled into one, over four tempestuous and enriching years.

Later, when I served in more senior roles, I made tough demands of my subordinates and told them that only their professionalism would pave the way to future successes. What I always had in mind was the role of political counselor in Washington, which required me to get up to speed extremely quickly on issues that people often spend their lives studying, in areas as diverse as the theory and practice of politics, diplomacy, international relations, security, strategy, decision-making, arms control, and nonproliferation.

I watched from up close as America shook off the debris of 9/11. I took part in the peace talks at Wye River in October 1998, as well as those at Camp David in July 2000. And I sat in the room as Israel delivered unprecedented evidence that Iran was trying to build a nuclear bomb.

My years in Washington gave me the most important skills of my career and served me later on. There I learned which levers of influence Israel has in the world, and how to move the needle of strategic change from the concept stage to the execution point. In Washington, I learned how the flutter of a butterfly's wings in one place leads to a great storm in another; how a single meeting at the Pentagon can determine whether a military event takes place in our region—and whether Israeli lives are saved or lost.

In Washington, I also got to know American society through its impressive representatives in Congress. It is said that Washington and New York are not the real United States. This is true, in a sense. But in Washington, the interests of real Americans are put on the table every day without hesitation, and their representatives work to promote them tirelessly. A member of Congress sees a mission in picking up the phone to the Israeli ambassador to complain about the treatment that one of his or her constituents received at Ben Gurion Airport.

In Washington, I learned about American power, whether in economics and security, military affairs and diplomacy, or business and technology.

And most important, in Washington, I learned how irreplaceable an ally the United States is for Israel—and Israel for the United States.

***

Relations with the United States are the cornerstone of Israel's foreign and defense strategy, and this is true regardless of which party is in power in either country. Jerusalem and Washington enjoy significant ties at practically every level: from security to international relations, commerce, research and development, economics, and civil society. This relationship had been built over decades on the basis of the two nations' common interests. It is far from being a friendship between equals, of course, because Israel is a much smaller country—though energetic—while the United States is a giant.

From Israel's perspective, the challenge is always to identify those areas where it can offer the United States unique added value. Being a source of groundbreaking technological innovation, an important brother in arms in the fight against terrorism, an effective and extremely diligent intelligence partner—all these are part of Israel's comparative advantages in the relations between the countries, and it is important not to forget them. At the end of the day, the best predictor of longevity and fertility of a relationship, between countries just as between individuals, is the feeling that both sides are benefiting from it.

Since the Reagan administration in the 1980s, the U.S. has committed itself to maintaining Israel's qualitative military edge (QME) in the region, a recognition that whatever Israel lacks in manpower and territorial depth must be made up through superior weaponry. Beginning in 2008, this expressed itself in U.S. law as well—a commitment that has held firm even in the most difficult periods in the U.S.-Israel relationship. In addition, the United States has consistently acted to disrupt or stop hostile anti-Israel UN resolutions of consequence, including the (mostly) reliable use of its veto power at the Security Council.

The golden age of the bilateral relationship was the Clinton-Rabin era of the early 1990s. President Bill Clinton and Prime Minister Yitzhak Rabin developed a warm personal friendship, thanks to which Israel received almost anything it asked for. Clinton's relations with two of Rabin's successors, Shimon Peres and Ehud Barak, were also marked by mutual personal fondness, resulting in a great deal of understanding towards Israel during the waves of terror that followed the Oslo Accords in the late 1990s, as well as the failure of the Camp David II talks and the subsequent launch of the second intifada in September 2000.

The relationship between President George W. Bush and Prime Minister Ariel Sharon in the early 2000s took a while to ripen: It started with mutual suspicion, given Sharon's hardline image and the U.S. government's fraught history with him when he was defense minister during the First Lebanon War. But Bush and Sharon soon developed a warm friendship. A major factor, it seems, was the severe crisis of trust that developed between Bush and Palestinian leader Yasser Arafat, which reached its climax with Arafat's bold-faced lies over the *Karine A* arms ship affair, when Israel caught the Palestinians trying to smuggle fifty tons of weaponry from Iran in January 2002, at the height of the second intifada. Bush understood that Sharon had been true to his word. Sharon was a tough negotiator, but the minute he agreed to do something, he kept his word, even under extreme political pressure.

Ehud Olmert, who succeeded Sharon as prime minister in 2006, maintained a warm working relationship with Bush and cordial personal ties with the administration. This relationship paid off in the almost unlimited "line of credit" the United States extended to Israel during the Second Lebanon War in 2006, and when Bush reacted favorably to Israel's decision to destroy the nuclear reactor being built in Syria in 2007.

The warm ties between Prime Minister Benjamin Netanyahu and President Donald Trump were perhaps the most intimate the two nations have ever known. The two leaders built a working relationship based on a confluence of political, personal, and ideological affinities, bringing Israel some of its most significant diplomatic achievements in its history: the relocation of the U.S. embassy to Jerusalem and recognition of the city as Israel's capital, recognition of Israeli sovereignty over the Golan Heights, and the 2020 Abraham Accords. One can disagree with both leaders' policies, direction, style, or timing, but the personal connection that underpinned these developments was undeniable.

With the election of Joe Biden as president in 2020, and of Naftali Bennett as prime minister in 2021, as well as Yair Lapid who replaced him in 2022, the close and fruitful ties between the two countries continued much as in the past. When the Biden administration restarted nuclear talks with Iran, Israel's concerns were heard and, perhaps to a certain degree, taken into account. When Lapid, as foreign minister, wanted to pull together a regional summit with the Abraham Accords countries along with Egypt on extremely short notice in March 2022, his first call was to Secretary of State Antony Blinken, who helped to make it happen. The Negev Summit, which took place on March 27 and 28, 2022, at Sde Boker, the kibbutz where David Ben-Gurion called home in his last years, was a remarkable feat of Zionist diplomacy: For the first time, foreign ministers of the UAE, Bahrain, Morocco, Egypt, Israel, and the United States gathered to deepen their ties and create the framework for an increasingly important new alliance in the region.

The fact is that despite the immense historical significance of the Abraham Accords, contributing to the stability of the Middle East, their import was never properly internalized in the U.S., nor in Europe. There are many reasons for this failure; but it is hard to shake the feeling that much of it has to do with the specific identity of the leaders who brought the accords into being, especially President Trump.

The U.S.-Israel relationship, built on a decades-old foundation of mutual interest, respect, and trust, is not without its hiccups, as we have seen. The relationship between Netanyahu and President Barack Obama was a difficult one. With Netanyahu's return to power in January 2023, relations with the Biden administration remained fundamentally on keel, despite bumps in the road, including the internal Israeli controversy surrounding the government's proposed legislation to revamp Israel's judiciary, as well as a public dispute over the withheld delivery of certain munitions during the Gaza war. But when Israel most desperately needed American military assistance, both in the immediate aftermath of October 7 and when Iran launched hundreds of missiles and armed UAVs at Israel in April 2024, the U.S. did not hesitate to offer its support.

Keeping the relationship on solid ground has required a constant investment on Israel's part that, as Abba Eban pointed out, is far more complicated than anything Israel has undertaken for any other country on Earth.

It has also required, as I discovered in Washington, no small degree of creativity, genuine empathy, and a willingness to shoot straight.

***

Benjamin Disraeli, who became Great Britain's first Jewish prime minister in 1868, once said: "There is no gambling like politics." I took one of my political gambles in the late 1990s in Washington. The United States was riding high on the successes of President Clinton, who had extricated the nation from an economic crisis and reaped the fruits of the world economy in an era of ever-greater globalization. Vice President Al Gore was the runaway favorite to win the 2000 presidential election, and we in Israel expected another four years of working with a Democratic administration led by the same coterie of officials we had gotten used to over the previous eight years.

Nevertheless, we had a vital interest in maintaining bipartisan support for Israel in Washington, so I made it my mission to beef up Israel's ties with the Republicans. I was no fortune teller, just aware of American political history and the need to think ahead. The United States is rightly proud of its political pendulum, and the party that controls the White House usually changes every four or eight years. Yet at the Israeli embassy, we had almost no acquaintance with the people being lined up to fill the cabinet in case Al Gore lost.

We turned our focus to the Republican Party and mapped out the likely key figures in a future Republican administration, from cabinet secretaries, assistant secretaries, under secretaries, special envoys to advisors, aides, and other senior officials. My calendar filled up. The Republicans were surprised by my interest and delighted to meet with an official representative of Israel, which was a lively topic on their professional agenda.

Languishing in the wilderness of Washington's think tanks and research institutes, they had free time in abundance.

One of my first meetings was with John Bolton, a Yale-educated lawyer who specialized in U.S. foreign policy. Bolton was (and still is) a true friend of Israel and the Jewish people, who identified with Israel as a democracy and the values it represents. Bolton understood the threats that Israel faced in the Middle East and believed that Iraq and Iran were a menace to Middle East stability and global security. He was a fascinating conversationalist with a comprehensive worldview and a rigorous understanding of geopolitics. Two years after we first met, shortly after George W. Bush was sworn in as president, Bolton was appointed under secretary of state for arms control and international security. His door was always open to me, and this access bore plenty of fruit for Israel. Bush would later name him UN ambassador, and he would serve as national security adviser under President Trump.

Robert Frost once said that "a diplomat is a man who always remembers a woman's birthday but never remembers her age." In diplomacy, like many other professions, personal connections are everything and can open doors—even locked ones. It is often said that in Washington people don't have friends, only interests, and if you want a friend, get a dog. Nevertheless, I found genuine friends. John Hannah and Lewis "Scooter" Libby, who would go on to be Vice President Dick Cheney's senior advisor and chief of staff, respectively, became close friends of mine, and we used to have Shabbat dinners together. With Hadas by my side, and wine, challah, hummus, and schnitzel on the table, we enjoyed long conversations about the bond between our countries. Douglas Feith, the under secretary of defense for policy, came over for dinner with his family, and we were received warmly in theirs. Our children studied together at the Jewish day school.

In the four years I spent in Washington, under two different administrations, we saw our bipartisan diplomatic investments bear fruit in countless ways—whether in providing opportunities for Israel to show its profound support in the wake of 9/11, or in fostering American understanding that the Palestinians were the ones responsible for the failure of peace talks and the eruption of the second intifada. We had a number of rare opportunities to share intelligence, technology, empathy, and even life wisdom.

The power of that bond was expressed most powerfully, and most tragically, in the fall of 2001. Less than eight months into Bush's first term, my new friends in the administration would have to face an unprecedented horror that was both national and personal, and the relationships I had cultivated suddenly took on a much deeper character—the kind that comes only from shared trauma.

***

September in Washington is delightful. The leaves haven't yet turned, and the unpleasant chill of late autumn—similar to winter in Jerusalem—has not yet arrived. Yet by September the seemingly endless swamp-heat of the D.C. summer has finally begun to dissipate. It is an optimistic time: like spring, but without the allergies.

One especially crisp September morning, Hadas and I got our kids ready and waved them goodbye as they boarded the bus from our home on Magic Mountain Drive in the affluent suburb of Rockville, Maryland, to their Jewish day school. The day was awash with sunlight, and the skies were especially clear.

I drove to the embassy as I did every morning, winding through pastoral roads to the political capital of the world. As every morning, I began the day reading classified reports from the Foreign Ministry research department in Jerusalem. The morning TV talk shows provided the office's regular background noise.

Suddenly I noticed that the monotonous chit-chat had given way to breaking news, and images appeared of a plane crashing into the north tower of the World Trade Center in New York. I wish I could say that I understood at once that the world had changed before my eyes, but the reality was more prosaic. Like many, I assumed that there had been a terrible accident, and I went about my business. I finished writing a cable to the Foreign Ministry about an unrelated matter and sent it off.

When the second plane hit the south tower at 9:03 a.m., I understood.

I ran toward the office of the Israeli ambassador, David Ivry, a former commander of the Israeli Air Force and deputy IDF chief of staff. He was already on his feet, totally focused, and ordered the immediate and total evacuation of the embassy compound. He had received information that terrorists had hijacked even more planes, and he feared that one of them, cruising toward Washington, might nosedive into the Israeli embassy. We abandoned our desks in a frenzy and were packed into vehicles and whisked off to the ambassador's residence for an emergency briefing.

Also arriving at the residence were several members of the Knesset on a visit to Washington. They had been on their way to the Pentagon when the third plane crashed into the beating heart of the U.S. defense establishment. More than anything, we were disoriented, shocked, and speechless.

In the days after the attacks, Washington was gripped with sorrow, grief, panic, and rage, yet above all there prevailed a strong feeling of uncertainty. We at the embassy felt not just empathy with the Americans but a sense of common destiny. Israel, we felt, was one of the few countries that truly identified with the United States in its darkest hour, and who understood the significance of the atrocities. On the spot, we decided to help our friends cope with the disaster by any means possible and at every level, from treating the injured to sharing intelligence.

The catastrophe caused a dramatic change in the thinking and behavior of Americans both in and out of government. When President Bush had taken the oath of office the previous January, our working assumption had been that his Texan origins and family's business background meant that he would be particularly attuned to oil and energy interests—including a sympathy for the Arab states. But 9/11 challenged this paradigm. Bush understood that the United States was not off-limits to terrorists, and that it would have to take forceful action against them, their backers, and their state sponsors, even at the expense of short-term economic interests.

On a profound level, something changed in America's relationship with Israel, as well. The attacks occurred almost a year into the second intifada. For months, people across the world had witnessed the awful carnage of Islamic terrorism. Suicide bombings of buses, cafés, and nightclubs, terror attacks that had come after similar ones in the mid-1990s.

But before 9/11, it was always "over there," across the world, relegated to things that happen in foreign countries and reported on in the news; 9/11 created a deep understanding, not just among Americans as a whole, but especially among those in positions of leadership, people who had to make decisions daily about how to prevent and how to respond. They knew that *we* knew that it wasn't enough to view 9/11 as simply a tragedy and a crime. The nation had been attacked and was now at war.

It is not a coincidence, for example, that the first foreign dignitary to come to Ground Zero after the attacks was Ehud Olmert, at the time mayor of Jerusalem. He had developed a strong bond with New York Mayor Rudolph Giuliani after the 1996 Number 18 bus bombings in Jerusalem, when Giuliani made a point of flying to Israel and riding the same bus route with Olmert. Now, Olmert came to the still-smoldering ruins of the World Trade Center.

At the federal level, a new era of intelligence and defense cooperation between Israel and the United States began. Washington discovered that in its hour of need, it had a devoted and loyal friend. Israel was already the undisputed world leader in airport security, and its fearsome intelligence agency, Mossad, had a foothold in several places of strategic importance for U.S. intelligence. Many more Israeli security-related companies started working with the Americans than before, drawing up operational instructions for tightening their security, training personnel, and equipping the biggest airports in the United States with new technologies.

Israel's knowledge, experience, unique methods, and equipment became highly sought commodities in the administration, and we worked to supply whatever our American friends needed. The flow of intelligence between Israel and the United States reached an all-time high, and Israel proved its mettle in coordinating multiple levels of activity in terms of intelligence gathering, analysis, and military and covert operations. The Americans were particularly interested in improving their interagency cooperation, because one of the failures that allowed 9/11 to happen was the lack of coordination among the United States' various intelligence and security agencies. Israel served as a role model for how security forces should coordinate.

The robust bond with the United States is Israel's international calling card. In the diplomatic world, where a high profile is a valuable commodity, Israel builds on its strong ties with the United States to promote relations and interests with other countries. The latter understand that the world's preeminent superpower wants to put Israel on a pedestal, and hope that strong relations with Israel will help them curry favor in Washington.

Since the 1950s, when Abba Eban served as Israel's ambassador to both Washington and the UN, Zionist diplomacy has understood the multiple fronts that Israel must engage in the United States: Simultaneously, it must cultivate its friends in the administration, in Congress, and among the American public, especially the American-Jewish and evangelical communities. And, as I discovered, it also means investing not only in those currently in power, but also in relationships with key people in the party *out* of power—the next administration waiting in the wings.

But sometimes, no matter how hard you try, maintaining a fully bilateral embrace is exceptionally difficult.

Of all the issues we worked on together with the Americans during my tenure in Washington, perhaps none was as grave, enduring, and potentially divisive as the question of Iran's attempts to develop a nuclear weapon. This generation-long saga, which puts Israel's very survival on the table, which caused a very public rift in the U.S.-Israel relationship in 2015, and which continues to weigh on our relations to this day as talks between Iran and the West have started, stopped, and ground to a halt after 10/7—all began with a single top-secret meeting I attended in 1998, three years before the events of 9/11.

***

A standard-looking manila envelope was opened at a conference table in the office of the National Security Council, buried deep in the Executive Office Building adjacent to the White House. The American officials were intrigued by the material they found inside and took a long, hard look at their Israeli guests on the other side of the table.

Maps, top-secret reports, blueprints, and a few seemingly unremarkable photographs of desert landscapes were pulled out of the file. But nothing about these documents was straightforward. Their contents attested to the lethal intentions of a hostile regime and its efforts to develop nuclear weapons. The Americans passed the documents among themselves and pored over them. It was clear that they did not entirely understand what they were looking at.

"Take your time," I said softly.

"A lot of work has been put into this," added Major General Amos Gilead, chief of the IDF Military Intelligence Research Directorate—one of the most brilliant minds in Israeli intelligence and a man blessed with sublime strategic foresight, who never recoiled from telling the highest-ranking leaders exactly what he thought. He had landed in Washington on a stifling summer's day in 1998, heading a delegation of IDF intelligence officers and Mossad spymasters.

The windowless conference room was packed. We Israeli diplomats and security officials sat at one end. Opposite us were representatives of the Pentagon, State Department, Department of Energy, CIA, and of course the National Security Council.

In the months before, the lights at the Israeli embassy had stayed on well into the night as we prepared for this meeting. Our mission: to show the Americans conclusive proof that the Islamic Republic of Iran had begun a secret race to build nuclear weapons. The desert photographs depicted the nuclear facility the Iranians had already started building. The dossiers were the fruit of months of rigorous work by Israel's various intelligence agencies.

Nevertheless, the Americans' first response was to stare at us in disbelief. *Oh boy*, I could hear them thinking, *it's the Israelis making mountains out of molehills again.*

The IDF intelligence officers fidgeted in their seats. They had traveled halfway around the world to present their top-notch intelligence material about Iran, but the Americans had a hard time believing that the fundamentalist regime in Tehran was truly determined to build a nuclear weapon. Gilead, who had been leading the presentation, shot me a look that said: *You take over*.

What we were asking for was not easy. The Americans understood that if the pictures on the table were real, it was the end of the Middle East as they knew it. They would have to dedicate resources and heightened attention to an issue that had not been on their radar. It was no simple matter to reverse the course of a behemoth, such as the U.S. government, and this was, again, in the pre-9/11 days, before America changed the way it saw Islamist terror.

The key to persuading the Americans, I felt, was to help them to understand that taking action against the Iranian nuclear project was a core U.S. interest, not a favor to Israel.

"Friends, we understand that you can't believe your eyes," I said. "We also found this hard to believe—and even harder to get our hands on. There's a wide range of intelligence here. It took us many months to compile this information, at great risk to human life. We can see that the Iranians are starting to develop nuclear capabilities that will have far-reaching consequences for the stability of the Middle East and will threaten U.S. interests in the region.

"Israel is not the only country that will suffer," I continued. "U.S. allies, Sunni Muslim states, will come within the range of Iran's nuclear missiles and will fall hostage to the extremists in Tehran. The Middle East is fissile enough as it is without an impending nuclear arms race, which would truly turn the region into a new but much more dangerous Middle East. You have a unique opportunity here to start investigating, at relatively little cost, whether there isn't a major threat growing right under your noses. If I were you, I'd invest the little time and resources you will require to corroborate the veracity of this information before the matter becomes more urgent."

That meeting in Washington fired the opening shot of the ongoing global preoccupation with the Iranian nuclear threat. We drowned the Americans in documents, photographs, and other proof of the Iranian nuclear program, until they understood the severity of the situation and started asking for more material and clarifications. Israel and the United

States started cooperating on obtaining fresh intelligence about Iran's efforts to break out towards a nuclear bomb.

Despite our many efforts, events over the next decade prevented the United States from focusing on Iran—from 9/11 and the burst of the dot-com bubble to the wars in Afghanistan and Iraq and the 2008 financial crisis that heralded the Great Recession.

One of the more surprising obstacles concerned the American experience with North Korea. The Clinton administration had signed an "Agreed Framework" with North Korea in 1994 with a view to keeping the Korean Peninsula free from nuclear weapons. When we shared with a senior American official involved in the negotiations our concerns that North Korea might export its nuclear expertise to the Middle East, the official answered, "Israel has nothing to worry about, North Korea will never get nuclear weapons."

The future begged to differ. Not only did North Korea get the bomb, conducting its first test in 2006, but our often-voiced fears about the North Korean regime spreading nuclear knowhow to our own doorstep would come true in 2007, when it helped the Assad regime in Syria to build a covert nuclear reactor.

The West's negotiations with North Korea were an abysmal failure. The North Koreans crossed red line after red line because they knew that there was no threat of military action. In the late 1990s, Washington treated Pyongyang almost nonchalantly. The Clinton administration's policy was all about inclusion and dialogue, and North Korea exploited it to violate every single one of the understandings. Four consecutive administrations—Clinton, Bush, Obama, and Trump—came up empty. So far, the Biden administration has followed the same pattern.

The Americans did not learn from their mistakes with North Korea, and they repeated them with Iran. Their problematic approach became brutally evident in 2007, when the U.S. Intelligence Community published a national intelligence estimate. The report, written by CIA, State Department, and Pentagon officials to advise U.S. policymakers, concluded that the Iranians had *abandoned* their secret nuclear weapons program in 2003. The danger, claimed the report, had passed.

What happened in 2003 to make the Iranians suspend their nuclear weapons program? The United States invaded Iraq, Iran's immediate neighbor to the west, toppling Saddam Hussein, and also launched a military campaign that ended the rule of the Taliban regime in Afghanistan, Iran's immediate neighbor to the east.

Seeing American wrath unleashed across two of their borders, the Iranians understood they might be next. Terrified, they hit the pause button. But what the 2007 report failed to mention was that by the time it came out—as subsequent revelations from a recent trove of top-secret documents smuggled by Mossad out of Iran proved—Tehran had already sensed that the threat had passed and restarted the program.

Israel's leaders had picked up on the Iranians' sensitivity to threats of force. Years later, Prime Minister Benjamin Netanyahu and Defense Minister Ehud Barak concluded that only a credible military option combined with crushing economic sanctions would make the Iranians think twice about accelerating their nuclear program. History proved them right. A few years later, sanctions imposed unilaterally by the Trump administration, without the initial support of the international community, were effective above and beyond the expectations of many in the world and proved that pressure achieves results.

But the gap between the U.S. intelligence assessment and the reality on the ground was probably less a failure of intelligence-gathering than an intrusion of politics into intelligence-assessment. Some have claimed that the report's authors crafted it deliberately to deter the Bush administration from threatening Iran with military force over its nuclear program.

If so, they succeeded: The report tied Bush's hands. Once it became clear that Saddam Hussein did not actually possess weapons of mass destruction (WMDs), which had been the official justification for the invasion, Bush was not willing to consider another military mission—and even tried to dissuade Prime Minister Olmert from attacking the Syrian nuclear reactor in 2007. This is another example, perhaps, of how a political and bureaucratic power play can change the course of international history on matters of cardinal importance, and how if you fail at something, it is harder to win political support to try something similar elsewhere.

The intelligence failures leading to the Iraq War changed the rules of the global geopolitical game. Until 2003, there had been a regular exchange of high-quality intelligence between Israel and the United States, but the fiasco over Iraq's WMD capabilities made intelligence agencies all around the world—including in the United States—much more suspicious. From that point on, every snippet of information passed between intelligence agencies around the world was examined under a magnifying glass and corroborated with independent sources.

The two-way flow of information between Israel and the United States was dealt a terrible blow, because it started to take ages for intelligence to reach decision-makers' desks. The post-Iraq War interruption to the bilateral information traffic remains one of the most serious challenges impeding U.S.-Israeli intelligence cooperation.

***

As different as they may be in size, Israel and the United States have a great deal in common. They are both Western democracies with a strong sense of responsibility for the welfare of their citizens and an unwillingness to let others dictate their fate. In this sense, our two nations have more in common than either of us do, say, with European states: The latter, traumatized by the world wars of the twentieth century, have for decades been deeply suspicious of national sovereignty and identity, as well as of the military might required to safeguard them. As a result, the Europeans effectively subcontracted their defense to America and diluted their sense of national self through the instrument of the European Union. It took the 2022 Russian invasion of Ukraine, it seems, to begin the process of changing their approach—a process that accelerated with the pro-Hamas riots across Europe in the wake of October 7.

There is something else Israel has long had in common with the United States: We often have the same enemies. This was true during much of the Cold War, when the Soviet Union invested massively in the militaries of Israel's enemies and in a global propaganda campaign to discredit Zionism and the Jewish state. And it has been true in the case of political Islam, which generally vows to destroy the United States and Israel in the same breath. It doesn't matter whether we are talking about Sunni fundamentalism (Hamas, ISIS, al-Qaeda, the Muslim Brotherhood) or Shi'ite fundamentalism (Iran, Hezbollah, the Houthis)—both kinds are equally committed, equally destructive, often cooperate with each other, and equally willing to put Israel and the United States in the same box when it suits them.

What all these commonalities have meant is that in the large scheme of things, Israel and the United States will march together, if not always in lockstep. Problems that arise will inevitably come and go, whereas a powerful gravitational force will always bring our nations together. Both nations, however, have their own internal politics and changing of the guard, dynamics that can create short-term friction but also bring restoration—as we saw in the less-than-warm relationship between President George H. W. Bush and Prime Minister Yitzhak Shamir, or between Benjamin Netanyahu and Barack Obama. In both countries, leaders come and go, but interests remain.

One of the things that has made this relationship work is the understanding that, just as American leaders hew to their national interests—so do Israel's. As much as we respect and are grateful for America's support, we will always have separate calculations of interest and evaluations of risk. There will also be lines that both sides are unwilling to cross. And it is understood that it's the responsibility of Israel's leaders to express such disagreement, usually but not always behind closed doors.

It is through this lens that one may best understand the way the fight against Iran has influenced U.S.-Israel relations.

In 2006 and 2007, between finishing my tenure as the director-general of the Foreign Ministry and arriving in London as ambassador, the Israeli government put me in charge of coordinating the strategic dialogue with the United States.

During this period, as advanced intelligence streamed in, Iran became a global hot potato. The world started to digest the meaning of Iran's actions, and even Europe could no longer bury its head in the sand. Iranian President Mahmoud Ahmadinejad's grotesque rhetoric, including his threat to wipe Israel "off the face of the Earth" and rampant Holocaust denial, left no doubt as to Tehran's intentions.

Besides the dialogue with the United States, which contained its fair share of disagreements over how to proceed, we conducted a parallel operation of dialogue and information-sharing with France and Great Britain. We spoke to each country in its own language—the language of national interests.

The British, for example, were not going to stick their necks out against Iran out of fondness for Israel, but we found a soft spot to rally them to action: the Persian Gulf, one of Britain's top global interests. When we showed the British the dossiers about Iran, we stressed that the biggest threat Iran posed was to the Gulf states. "Israel can defend itself from Iran," we said, "but what can the UAE and Bahrain do against the Iranian menace?" When speaking to the French, we focused on their close ties with Saudi Arabia, due in part to the dependence of the French petroleum corporation Total on Saudi oil. The French became much more interested once they could imagine billions of euros' worth of petroleum going up in flames in a potential Saudi-Iranian war.

By the time Barack Obama defeated John McCain in the 2008 presidential election, I was already in London. It would not take long before Israel began to sense a troubling change of winds from Washington with respect to Iran.

***

Frederick the Great, the eighteenth-century king of Prussia, once said that "diplomacy without arms is like music without instruments." Negotiations cannot be conducted in a vacuum, but only in a broader context, in which the military option remains on the table.

Certain political players persuade themselves that they have the power to make hostility go away by talking with the hostile party. That gives them the comforting feeling that they can control their fate. But in many cases, the hostile party may not be subject to persuasion. Hostility may itself be, in their eyes, a core interest. And that means that you simply have to defend yourself, perhaps forever. As a political message in a democratic country, the idea of having to fight forever is unbearable, so some leaders tell their people that by changing their own policies, they can have "peace now." Unfortunately, that's not always true.

So, while Iran enriched uranium, Israel conducted military maneuvers to signal that the military option was alive and well. Israel operated on the assumption that only a concrete threat to Iranian interests, whether in the form of economic damage or military action, would force Tehran to change course. Whatever people say about the Iranian regime, the ayatollahs are responsive to the mood on the street and alert to the people's pain, and this pain only intensified when economic and military threats became credible.

Israel sent signals not only to Tehran but to Washington as well. We undertook a series of actions, both overt and clandestine, to make clear that unless practical steps were taken to eliminate the threat of a nuclear Iran, Israel would have no choice but to activate the military option by itself, as it did with the Syrian nuclear reactor in 2007. In the world of geopolitics, shaping perceptions is one of the most powerful ways of shaping reality. The fear in the international community that Israel was prepared to attack Iran by itself forced other actors to do everything they could to prevent an escalation.

Israel's pressure paid off: The Obama administration pushed the UN Security Council to impose crushing, painful, and effective global sanctions on Iran, and the European states voted in favor. Most experts tend to agree that the new sanctions regime, which was far tougher on Iran than what came before, helped to force Iran's hand and brought it to the negotiating table with the "P5+1": the five permanent members of the UN Security Council plus Germany.

Israel should not carry the burden of fighting the Iranian nuclear threat alone. Preventing Iran from going nuclear is a global interest, and therefore every country should play its part. If the ayatollahs' regime were to acquire nuclear weapons, it would pose a clear and present danger to the entire world, not just the Middle East. Israel's role in this international struggle is to open the world's eyes to the dangers, to keep the issue on the agenda, and to supply information that the international community often prefers to disregard.

Our campaign against the Iranian nuclear project was an all-hands-on-deck affair. It began in Washington, took us to major world capitals, the UN Security Council, and Iran's secret nuclear archive. It is still ongoing. Not even the 2015 Iran nuclear deal, known formally as the Joint Comprehensive Plan of Action (JCPOA), ended the battle; it only moved it into a new phase.

***

It would be inaccurate to describe President Obama as hostile to Israel. It is not difficult, for example, to point to the fact that, over its eight years in office, the Obama administration did a great deal for Israel in terms of military, defense, and intelligence cooperation, increasing to $30 billion the U.S. ten-year military aid package to Israel.

Nevertheless, two factors made the eight years of Obama's presidency into a particularly difficult time for U.S.-Israel relations. First, the personalities of Obama and Netanyahu—who was Israel's prime minister for almost the entire eight-year period—did not click. The two men did not trust each other from the outset. Each saw the other as presumptuous, unwise, and driven by less than noble motives. They also embraced highly divergent views not just about the Middle East, but about more profound questions of power and the rationality of political actors. And, as we have seen, just as good chemistry at the highest levels can have an enormous impact on relations among nations, so can bad chemistry.

No less important was a strategic decision made by President Obama early in his first term to take a softer approach towards Iran, even when he was imposing tough sanctions. It expressed itself in the speech he gave at Cairo University in 2009 in which he tried to encourage a new era in U.S.-Iran relations. "Rather than remain trapped in the past," he declared, "I have made it clear to Iran's leaders and people that my country is prepared to move forward. The question, now, is not what Iran is against, but rather what future it wants to build."

It expressed itself, we would later learn, in a series of secret letters Obama sent to Iranian leader Ali Khamenei. It expressed itself in his constant refusal to include Iran-backed Hezbollah or the Houthis in Yemen whenever he described the Islamic terror groups he saw as America's enemies, something that happened a lot during the war against ISIS. It was expressed in the lengths to which he was willing to protect Iranian interests—like his inexplicable decision to give Syria a pass after it used chemical weapons against its own citizens, despite have previously declared it a red line.[40]

And, it ultimately expressed itself in his determination to reach a deal with the regime over its nuclear program—and to do so in the face of severe criticism not only from Israel, but also from the Arab states. Obama saw in such a deal with Iran not only a way to prevent it from acquiring nuclear weapons, he said, but also "the basis for us trying to improve relations over time," and the means through which Iran could become "a very successful regional power."[41]

In so doing, Obama overturned the applecart of commonalities in the U.S.-Israel relationship. Iran is, again, Israel's number one strategic threat, an implacable enemy regime dedicated to Israel's destruction and actively seeking the means to realize that vision. It has made little effort to hide its intentions—and has sacrificed the welfare of its own people to further those goals. We see it not only in its nuclear and ballistic missile programs, but in its constant efforts to spread its influence by insinuating itself into weak Arab states—Iraq, Syria, Lebanon, and Yemen—supporting independent militias and terror attacks against both Americans and Israelis

---

40 According to Frederic Hof, Obama's representative in Syria who resigned in protest, that decision was made for the sole purpose of keeping Iran, which sees the Assad regime as its lackey, at the table for the nuclear deal. Frederic C. Hof, "Beating the Blob and Disentangling from Partners," The Atlantic Council, May 9, 2016, https://www.atlanticcouncil.org/blogs/syriasource/beating-the-blob-and-disentangling-from-partners/ (accessed October 20, 2024).

41 "An End to Iran's Containment?" *The Washington Post*, March 12, 2015, https://www.washingtonpost.com/opinions/an-end-to-irans-containment/2015/03/12/8ada87d6-c680-11e4-b2a1-bed1aaea2816_story.html (accessed October 20, 2024).

through them. It supports Hamas and is the main backer of Hezbollah and Palestinian Islamic Jihad—the three terror organizations responsible for *all* of Israel's military conflicts over the past two decades. The idea of turning this regime into a "very successful regional power" through a deal that removed sanctions and addressed only its nuclear program, but effectively bolstered the rest of its nefarious activities, was as highly problematic a move from the perspective of Israel's core interests as one could imagine the United States ever undertaking.

The basic premise of Obama's policy on Iran was, from Israel's perspective, exceptionally difficult to swallow: that Iran's hostility to the West could be defused by reducing the West's hostility to Iran. That Iran, in essence, could be appeased through the carrot rather than the stick.

And so, when it became clear that the administration had gone "all in" on reaching a deal with Iran, and that such a deal would clearly be harmful to Israeli interests, the entirety of Israel's diplomatic community—along with Israeli political and defense leaders, allies in Congress, and other friends around the world—got to work attempting to prevent such a deal from happening.

***

We failed, of course. Not even an impassioned public plea by the prime minister of Israel before a joint session of Congress was able to dissuade the Americans. This deal was, it turned out, more important to the president than any other policy effort at the time—what his confidant Ben Rhodes called "Obamacare for the second term."

Why exactly that was the case remains something of a mystery.

I was Israel's ambassador at the United Nations when the P5+1 completed the Iranian nuclear deal in July 2015, and I can say with confidence that the world should and could have pushed for a better deal. Secretary of State John Kerry, who led the lackadaisical negotiations with the Iranians, was determined to secure a win after nearly four years of foreign policy failure in the Middle East.

Kerry was willing to reach an agreement even at the cost of conceding items of critical global importance.

Among other things, the JCPOA included a "sunset clause" that would legalize Iran's nuclear activities despite standing in full violation of international treaties and would effectively enable Iran to develop nuclear weapons as of 2025, under the umbrella of international legitimacy. In addition, the agreement—which was never a signed agreement, merely an agreed "plan of action"—placed no limits on Iran's ballistic missile program and contained significant loopholes in the international inspections regime, leaving certain areas and facilities off limits to the prying eyes of the IAEA inspectors. It also ignored Iran's deep involvement in global terror, giving Iran legitimacy to destabilize the region and its pragmatic regimes—and the resources to continue arming and funding Hamas.

Even after the United States' justified withdrawal from the nuclear deal under President Trump, Israel's role in the struggle to stop Iran from going nuclear is far from over. Throughout the restarted negotiations in Vienna in 2022, Israeli officials were in constant contact with their American counterparts and were being briefed on the talks to a degree far beyond anything we enjoyed during the original negotiations.

Israel must wage a two-pronged battle, continuing to beef up its intelligence and military preparedness while also waging a diplomatic offensive, integrating these two complementary strategies until Iran abandons its nuclear ambitions, or at least until the world establishes a proper inspection and nonproliferation regime to contain it and thwart Iran's ballistic missile program and international terror apparatus—which, in the wake of October 7, has revealed itself as a danger to the whole world.

***

It is no secret that the relationship between Netanyahu and Obama was less than ideal. I cannot say with certainty that the personal animus between the two leaders was behind the decision of the administration, in its final days of December 2016, to make an unprecedented move against the interests of Israel at the United Nations Security Council. But I'm sure it didn't help.

Prior to 2016, it was a longstanding tradition that, during the lame-duck period between a presidential election in November and the inauguration of a new president the following January, the incoming and outgoing administrations endeavored to speak in one voice and refrain from criticizing each other, especially on foreign policy.

The Obama administration broke with this tradition. Instead of passing the baton to the incoming Trump administration as was the tradition, Obama instructed UN Ambassador Samantha Power not to veto Security Council Resolution 2334, which proclaimed Israeli settlements in "the occupied Palestinian territory" of the West Bank and East Jerusalem, captured by Israel in 1967, to be illegal. This was in stark contrast to the longstanding policy to protect Israel at the UN, where Israel is delegitimized and attacked on a daily basis, a clear position of not only the incoming administration but of past presidents. The goal of this move, which shocked not only Israel but many Americans, was to remind Israel of its dependence on America, to hamstring us diplomatically, and probably also to create problems for the incoming administration.

Resolution 2334 was adopted on December 23, 2016. Among other things, the resolution cites a precedent-setting opinion of the International Criminal Court (ICC), which sharply criticizes Israel in relation to the security fence and its settlements policy as a "flagrant violation of international law." This, despite the fact that neither the U.S. nor Israel are parties to the treaty that recognizes the ICC.

Settlements aside, the question of the security fence cuts to the bone, especially for any Israeli traumatized by the waves of terror attacks during the second intifada—and which Israeli wasn't traumatized? The fence, it will be recalled, was built as a security measure to prevent the infiltration of terrorists from the West Bank in the wake of the endless waves of bus bombings and coffee shop bombings, months and years of heart-wrenching carnage between 2000 and 2003. By all expert accounts, the fence saved countless lives of Israeli civilians. Now we were being told that the very act of protecting our lives—putting up a damned *fence*—was a "flagrant violation of international law."

An additional element created by Resolution 2334 was the determination that the settlements, including fully developed, half-century-old predominantly Jewish neighborhoods in Jerusalem, have no legal basis and constitute a blatant violation of international law, and Israel must immediately and completely freeze all construction activity in them.[42] The decision does not distinguish between isolated settlements, settlement blocs that are well within the consensus as remaining part of Israel in any future peace agreement, or the post-1967 neighborhoods of Israel's capital Jerusalem, all of which have equal injustice in its eyes. Neither does it distinguish between construction on private land and construction on land owned by the State of Israel. Instead, it defines the Western Wall—the holiest site of prayer for world Jewry—as "occupied Palestinian territory"; so, too, does it define the centuries-old Jewish Quarter of the Old City of Jerusalem; so, too, does it define the campus of Hebrew University on Mount Scopus in Jerusalem, which was founded in 1925, well before the nation was founded and anything called "the occupation" had even begun.

Again, this perversion of international law stands in contradiction to both logic and the existing international agreements on which international law is supposed to be based. Logically, because no sovereign entity called Palestine exists as of yet, and if aspiration is sufficient to determine right, then Israeli aspirations ought to have as much a claim as Palestinian ones. And this "law" goes flatly against the Oslo Accords, which pose no restriction to Israeli construction in the areas under its control, and which is a binding signed agreement, which is supposed to be the core of international law.

Much ink has been spilled trying to justify Obama's last-minute diplomatic punch. There was a *lot* of bad blood between him and Netanyahu. And Israel, to be fair, was not blameless. It takes two to tango, and in this dance, it is obvious that we stepped on each other's toes.

The behavior of the U.S. administration in the last days of the Obama presidency stained the U.S.-Israel bilateral relationship. Intimacy between

---

[42] Section 2 of the resolution.

the Israeli government and the White House is an essential component of *both* countries' national security doctrines and of the active cooperation between them on a range of issues, from Iran to Ukraine to the Abraham Accords.

Israel's supreme interest lies in the strength of its bipartisan support in Washington—support that was demonstrated a few weeks later, in early January 2017, when the U.S. House of Representatives passed a resolution, by a large bipartisan vote of 342 to 80, condemning Resolution 2334 and calling on the administration to continue vetoing any subsequent anti-Israel decisions. A similar resolution, with 78 co-sponsors in a body with only a hundred members, was submitted in the Senate as well.

But as with all administrations, Obama's came to an end. On January 20, 2017, Donald J. Trump, a world-famous real estate mogul with a strongly pro-Israel voter base, would take American Mideast policy in a completely different direction.

The pendulum had again swung, this time quite violently.

***

In today's climate in the United States, it is exceptionally difficult for a non-American to say anything about the Trump administration without the risk of distortion or worse. Trump was, and continues to be, a controversial and polarizing figure. His decisions as a politician after the November 2020 election, and especially on January 6, 2021, have become the subject of so much public attention, including a criminal investigation, that it is difficult to express an evaluation of any aspect of his presidency without being immediately associated with one or another camp of American politics—and this is something that would be both unfair and inaccurate to do in my case.

As a representative of the State of Israel, as an Israeli whose analysis and perspectives lie solely within the scope of the interests of my own country, I may be forgiven for speaking about President Trump neither as a savior nor as a villain, but simply as a foreign leader whose decisions affected, and will continue to affect, the fate of my country.

Therefore, nothing I say here should be construed as an evaluation of his first term as president, other than in the narrow confines of Israel and the Middle East. In that limited context, however, I will say, in no uncertain terms, that the period of the first Trump administration, from January 2017 to January 2021, was exceptionally positive for Israel.

It was the Trump administration that unequivocally restored the U.S. commitment to vetoing hostile resolutions at the UN Security Council in the wake of Resolution 2334 and prevented it from setting a precedent. And it was Trump who withdrew from the Obama-era Iran deal.

But these actions, as important as they were, were minor compared to other actions taken by the administration in support of Israel. Let's begin with the most obvious one: The Trump administration recognized Jerusalem as the capital of Israel and relocated the U.S. embassy to our capital city.

This is no trivial matter. Israel declared Jerusalem as its capital immediately after independence in 1948 and moved the central institutions of government—the Knesset, the Supreme Court, and the prime minister's office—as soon as was practically feasible. Yet in an unprecedent repudiation of Israeli sovereignty, Israel's choice for its capital went unrecognized, due mainly to the original aspiration, as expressed in the UN Partition plan of 1947, that Jerusalem would remain under an international "condominium."

For Israelis, this lack of recognition stood as a permanent slap in the face, a daily reminder that even as an equal member of the family of nations, the Jews were still somehow less equal than others. In 1995, the U.S. Congress passed a law mandating the recognition of Jerusalem as Israel's capital, and it was only because of a waiver clause in the law that allowed presidents to put off recognition every six months on "national security" grounds, that it took as long as it did. For more than two decades, through the administrations of Clinton, Bush, and Obama, the waiver was renewed—perpetuating the affront to Jewish and Israeli honor that the law was supposed to remove. It was only President Trump who defied all the warnings of an imminent conflagration that would surely result from recognition, and formally recognized what every Jew has known in his heart for thousands of years: that we have one capital city, and it isn't Tel Aviv.

On May 14, 2018, the seventieth anniversary of Israel's independence, the U.S. opened its embassy in Jerusalem for the first time. All the dire warnings of an international uproar proved empty. Nothing happened.

Of similar magnitude is the U.S. recognition of Israeli sovereignty on the Golan Heights in 2019. Again, Israel captured the Golan in response to successive, unprovoked violent assaults from the Syrian regime against Israeli civilians, which reached their peak in the 1967 Six Day War.

The Golan Heights are unquestionably a part of the ancient Jewish settlement of the land dating back thousands of years—as countless archeological findings, including more than thirty ancient synagogues as well as the ancient Jewish towns of Gamla and Katzrin, have confirmed.

But no less important, it has become, over more than half a century, an integral part of Israel. Generations have built communities and lives there. Unlike Judea and Samaria, which Israel has never annexed, the Golan Heights were incorporated into Israel in 1981, more than four decades ago, its Arab and Druze residents offered full equality and citizenship just like the in the rest of Israel.

Meanwhile, Syria, which has claimed that territory since its own independence from France in 1936, has disintegrated into a brutal civil war, and is in essence a failed state, with entire sections controlled by Sunni and Kurdish opposition forces, and Russian, American, Iranian, Lebanese Hezbollah, and Turkish forces waltzing through its borders. At a time when the powers of the world were openly discussing Syria's future, considering redrawing its borders because Syria, as a single coherent sovereign entity, had more or less ceased to exist, the idea of refusing to recognize Israel's exceptionally stable and constructive sovereignty over that piece of territory has long been both silly and unjust.

Israel's northern borders prior to 1967 were the product of the arbitrary decisions of Britain and France in the wake of World War I, first outlined in the Sykes-Picot agreement and confirmed in the League of Nations mandate. There is nothing ancient or historical in Syria's claims to the Golan—unlike Israel's claims. Syria, itself a product of colonialism, owned the Golan for thirty-one years, during which it subjected its residents to the same brutal, barren authoritarian rule that exists through much of the Arab world. By comparison, Israel had, by the time of U.S. recognition, been in the Golan for fifty-two years. During that time, Israel has built towns, schools, roads, factories, farms, and shopping centers to the benefit of Jewish and non-Jewish citizens alike. And unlike Judea and Samaria, Israel's ownership of the Golan is a matter of wall-to-wall consensus within Israel.

While the Trump administration's recognition of Jerusalem and the Golan Heights were, for me, perhaps the most significant developments that benefited the Jewish state, righting historic wrongs that consistently undermined relations between the U.S. and Israel, equally historic was the signing of normalization agreements with major states in the Arab world including the UAE, Bahrain, and Morocco, collectively known as the Abraham Accords. I will discuss this in greater depth later, but suffice to say here that despite endless griping by opponents and their claims that the accords were largely meaningless, confirming relations that had been developing for decades, the reality proved otherwise: Since they were signed in 2020, billions of dollars of additional trade, investment, and tourism have been exchanged, especially with the UAE, whose airlines now offer six nonstop daily flights between Tel Aviv and Dubai. Unlike the peace with Jordan and Egypt, the Abraham Accords proved to be an instantly warm peace, and has even withstood the turmoil of the Gaza war. It is the beginning of an important relationship that looks more like an alliance, especially with respect to Iran.

Nor were these the only positive developments that resulted from the Trump administration's unconventional approach. For decades, the U.S. has been locked into a construct for peace between Israel and the Palestinians based on an old formula of the "two-state solution": an independent Palestinian state, more or less within the pre-1967 borders that Jordan occupied in 1948, with complex solutions for the fate of Jerusalem, settlements, demilitarization, refugees, and so on. For many years, Israel made attempts, at America's urging, to reach agreement on this basis.

Yet by the time the Oslo Accords had collapsed, it became clear that in any such arrangement, the Palestinians' minimal requirements for ending the conflict—assuming they ever wanted to do that at all—were far beyond Israel's minimal requirements for protecting the security of its citizens. It didn't help that throughout the process, the Palestinians maintained a broad terror infrastructure that was constantly planning and attempting attacks. They continue, even today, to incentivize terror by giving stipends for life to the families of terrorists arrested or killed.

But for the U.S., the two-state solution was the only possible resolution—even after October 7—and the only question was how hard to push it. And because the Palestinians appear impervious to American pressure, pushing harder inevitably meant putting pressure on Israel, which inevitably triggered an Israeli backlash.

It also artificially inflated the settlements in the West Bank as the *key* problem that needs solving—which is an absurd distortion of reality. There were no West Bank settlements when the Arab world began its policy of absolute rejectionism of Israel, nor when the PLO began its crusade of "liberating" all of Palestine by destroying the Jewish state. Today, the blanket term "settlements" no longer fits with a far more complex reality on the ground: Some areas (such as the cities of Ariel and Ma'aleh Adumim, or the Etzion Bloc) are highly developed and growing communities with tens of thousands of residents, many of whom were born there. Though Israel proved it was capable of uprooting tiny communities when it withdrew from Gaza, it is neither reasonable nor possible to imagine a 100 percent withdrawal from the Israeli cities of post-1967 Judea and Samaria.

The Trump administration was the first to disabuse itself of the classic two-state paradigm and, with the help of the Abraham Accords, to attempt to offer a different approach. The Trump peace plan, published in 2020, didn't go anywhere—the Palestinians declared it "dead on arrival"—but that wasn't necessarily the most important part. The key was that *any* resolution will need new, out-of-the-box thinking based on an acute understanding of the actual power relations both among the Palestinians, whether in the West Bank or Gaza, and across the region, and a refusal to embrace the kinds of dangerous illusions that produced the Oslo Accords. That happened for the first time under the Trump administration.

***

The administration of President Joe Biden was a period of crisis and extremes for the United States, seemingly from beginning to end: from COVID-19 to economic convulsion, the war in Ukraine, social unrest, dramatic Supreme Court rulings, the unprecedented indictment and trial of former President Trump, the beginnings of what may become a new Cold War with China, and more. With the eruption of another major Middle East war, the Biden administration, on the whole, stood by Israel in its strategic challenges—not only against Hamas but also against Hezbollah and Iran. Here, too, there is complexity—especially during an American election year—and here, too, the disagreements are mere distractions in a relationship that appears to be as solid it has ever been.

What emerges from the long history of U.S.-Israel relations, especially from the many different ways I was personally engaged in it over the past two and a half decades, is this: The United States and Israel have always had bumps in the road—but these, inevitably, eventually give way to the overwhelming commonality of interest, core values, and global challenges. Supporters of Israel will panic at any hint of crisis between the two governments, but the panic is almost always unwarranted, even if it takes time to work itself out.

This is for one simple, overwhelming reason: The interests our two nations share are just far too great to be overcome by the shifting winds of ideologies, personalities, or specific policies. And those interests grow stronger with each passing day.

***

This dynamic was perhaps made clearest in the initial months of the Russian invasion of Ukraine in February 2022. Suddenly, and rather unexpectedly, Israel found itself under a blast of scrutiny from the American media—fueled, it seems, by some fairly high-up decision-makers—for its alleged failure to fully take the side of Ukraine.

This accusation was both false and bizarre. False, because despite its own unusual strategic situation—Israel does not benefit from the protections of NATO, yet had a large force of Russians across its border in Syria, and depended on coordination with Russia to enable it to freely execute operations against Iran in Syria—Israel nonetheless issued repeated condemnations and sent significant humanitarian aid to Ukraine, including the first foreign field hospital set up within its borders. And bizarre, because Israel was not the only country weighing its own interests and risk assessment to make its own decisions about the precise kind and quantity of aid to the Ukrainian cause. The United States declared early on that it would not put American soldiers in harm's way. Israel, which had soldiers and pilots engaged in Syria on an ongoing basis, made a decision that was not very different.

But this, too, came and went. Prime Minister Naftali Bennett, coordinating fully with the Americans, as well as the French and Germans, dispensed with the criticism when he undertook to mediate personally between Kyiv and Moscow at the request of Ukrainian President Volodymyr Zelenskyy. It didn't materialize into an end to hostilities—such efforts very rarely do—but it successfully changed the narrative about Israel's involvement in the conflict. Indeed, the image of an Israeli prime minister acting as mediator in the world's greatest conflict in a generation was one of the greatest indicators of the new role that Israel has begun to play on the world stage, and the respect given to Zionist diplomacy.

The impact of the Ukraine war on Israel's global standing did not, it should be noted, end with Bennett's fledgling mediation efforts. Russia's invasion has proven to be a once-in-a-generation seismic event, shattering European conceptions of their own strategic and military needs. Across Europe, demand has risen dramatically not only for conventional arms like tanks and fighter planes, but also for advanced anti-missile defense systems, cyber-defense and cyber-intelligence, and drone warfare capabilities—all of which are areas in which Israel has excelled. European states have also been reminded of the sanctity of their sovereign territory and the need to defend it by force of arms—and the degree to which nations that do not respect it threaten their own worlds. In their eyes, Israel has seen it all before and knows all too well the needs of a liberal democracy facing genuine strategic threats from without.

Much of this has become clearest to me in the two years since I took up my most recent post, as Israel's ambassador in Berlin. I have watched from up close as Europe has changed profoundly, and I have seen attitudes towards Israel shifting as well during this time. In September 2023, Germany signed a deal procuring Israel's most advanced long-range anti-ballistic system, the Arrow 3, for an estimated $3 billion—before it had even been proven on the battlefield during the Gaza war. And when Finland formally joined NATO on April 6, 2023, the very next day the Finnish Ministry of Defense announced plans to purchase Israel's David's Sling air defense system for $345 million.

There is something deeply moving, and also philosophically mind-boggling, to have reached this point in our history. Seventy-five years after Israel was founded in the shadow of the Holocaust, when Jews around the world were desperate to recover a sense of control over their own destiny, in the wake of thousands of years of exile that culminated in their utter devastation on European soil—now it was the sovereign Jewish state, strong and prosperous, providing Europeans with the means to control their own destiny.

***

But while the United States is Israel's vital superpower ally, and will continue to be its most important diplomatic priority for the foreseeable future, there is more to a nation's life than security and defense. Economically, culturally, and in a wide range of other areas, Israel is no less dependent on good ties with Europe than with the United States—perhaps even more so.

Here, too, there is a great deal of complexity, as Israeli diplomats must navigate the policies, needs, and concerns of many different national governments, which are intertwined one way through the security alliance of NATO, a second way through the single-currency region known as the

Eurozone, and a third way through membership in the European Union—which, to top it all off, has governing institutions of its own.

But in addition to the complexity, there is a very specific strangeness about Israel's diplomatic posture in Europe, one that flows from the history that unites the Jewish people and the peoples of Europe—a fraught relationship, filled with hope and sorrow and madness, going back centuries and reaching its nadir in the darkest corners of the twentieth century.

It is to Israel's paradoxical relationship with Europe that we now turn.

CHAPTER 7

THE EUROPEAN PARADOX

In August 2022, I assumed my post in Berlin as Israel's ambassador to Germany. The role is, of course, a sensitive one for any Jewish diplomat—and especially one representing the Jewish state that gained its independence in the tumultuous wake of the Holocaust. It is a role fraught not only with enormous diplomatic challenges, but also with personal ones for any Israeli.

All the more so for a descendant of German Jews who deeply loved the nation that ultimately betrayed them in ways that beggar the imagination.

Again, this has not been my first tour of duty in Germany. For that we need to go back to 1988, when Germany was still divided between the two sides in the Cold War, as it had been for more than forty years. Israel had no relations with Communist East Germany, and I was given my first foreign assignment as second secretary at the Israeli embassy in Bonn, the West German capital.

Bonn would be my first of several deployments in Europe. I would go on to serve as a diplomat twice in London as well—once as the spokesman for the Israeli embassy from 1995 to 1998, and then again as Israel's ambassador to the United Kingdom from 2007 to 2011—both of which took place while Britain was still part of, and a central player in, the European Union.

Over the course of these intensive tours of duty in the capitals of perhaps the two most important European nations, I saw firsthand both the mindboggling challenges and incredible opportunities that Israel's relationship with Europe presents.

Of course, the history of Zionist diplomacy passed through Europe in some of its most crucial moments. From Herzl's meeting with Kaiser Wilhelm II and the King of Italy and his focus on Great Britain as the "Archimedean point" of the fight for a Jewish national home; to the campaign that led to the Balfour Declaration in 1917, which included garnering support not only in the United Kingdom but also France and the Vatican; to Israel's dependence on Czechoslovakia for weapons in its earliest years; to the 1950s when Israel's principal ally was France and the two nations joined with Great Britain to launch the Sinai Campaign—Europe has played a major role in the thinking of every senior diplomat since the inception of modern Zionism.

Today, Europe is Israel's largest trading partner by far. Its cooperation with Europe in business and investment, culture, technology, and security far exceeds that of any other economy, including the United States. Israel's political institutions and economic approach, moreover, closely resemble those of successful European nations. Indeed, relations between the two are so close that the possibility of Israel becoming an EU member has on more than one occasion been floated publicly, by both Israeli and European political leaders.

At the same time, Europe is also the beating heart of global hostility to the Jewish state and apathy to the forces that threaten not only Israel but Europe itself. It is in Europe that one frequently sees the discredited idea of "containment" still guiding policy: Whether with Russia, or North Korea, or Iran—in every case one finds well-intentioned leaders committed to doing nothing that might anger these weaker but more frightening authoritarian nations. Inevitably, containment ends up being a modern form of appeasement: It does nothing to solve the problem, and instead only incentivizes rogue states and terror groups to continue undermining world order. It is in Europe that Israeli leaders are frequently harassed, that former IDF generals are targeted for criminal lawsuits that prevent them from visiting, that the most vicious of international NGOs and media outlets are headquartered, that Hezbollah terrorists have long been allowed to raise money and organize, and that the largest and most vicious demonstrations supporting Hamas's atrocities have taken place. Outside the Middle East, one finds little on Earth that compares with the degree of venom to which Israelis and Jews are subjected in Europe today.

This is the European paradox—which I discovered not long after I first landed on West German soil.

***

Germany and Israel have held a very unusual place in each other's collective minds and histories since both countries effectively came into being after World War II. Soon after the war, Germany began paying reparations for the Holocaust, both to the Israeli government and to individual Israelis, which continues to this day. West Germany, which reinvented itself as a Western democracy and member of NATO, nonetheless did not establish formal relations with Israel until 1965. East Germany, of course, was locked behind the Iron Curtain and, like its patron the Soviet Union, remained a ferocious opponent of Israel, Zionism, and even the practice of Judaism.

I was excited to land in the West German capital of Bonn in 1988. It was my first diplomatic posting, and I had the fortune of serving under Benny Navon, one of Israel's finest ambassadors, who managed this sensitive diplomatic outpost.

It was in Bonn that I got my first real taste of the specific patterns of Zionist diplomacy abroad: a creativity and spontaneity, a willingness to drop everything and act with force and urgency, and above all a belief that we will determinedly further our nation's interests without waiting for the permission of others. Again, it was under Navon's direction that we invested, aggressively and early, in building relations and understanding with the former East Germany as it made its way out of the Cold War and into the waiting arms of the West.

It was also in Bonn that I understood just how far Israel had come since the days of Herzl, Weizmann, and even Abba Eban. All of them were conducting diplomacy for a people fighting for its survival. All of them had lived in a world without a Jewish state, in which the fate of Jews around the world depended on the good graces of others—and all of them were driven by a determination to give the Jewish people an independent, secure, sovereign life in their homeland.

By the time I arrived on the scene, Israel was an established nation, if less powerful and prosperous than it is today. It was still fighting battles that were existential in their essence, but no longer threatened the immediate survival of the country. The Jewish state had successfully taken its place among the nations and was now prepared to dedicate resources to "going on offense": looking at the shifting winds of international life and making timely moves to build itself further, in security and prosperity, into the future.

I also looked at my posting in Bonn as a way to seek closure with my family's past. My grandparents left Germany in the 1920s and 1930s, settling in Haifa on the slopes of Mount Carmel. They carried with them the conflicting emotions of longing and betrayal—emotions I had imbibed since childhood along with the stories of the concert halls, language, and pastries of Germany before the war, as well as the acute awareness of the Holocaust that every Israeli of my generation received.

What I found, however, was anything but closure. It was, rather, the embodiment of the permanent, living paradox that is Europe's attitude towards Israel, and especially towards the Jews, whom it had both emancipated in the eighteenth century and exterminated in the twentieth. Guilt and resentment, supportive engagement and absurd public slander, the loftiest principles and the dirtiest double-dealing, often at the hands of the same governments or even the same individuals—in Europe, the Jews and Israel have found both peril and promise, both the most bitter forms of hostility, which never disperses but instead merely takes on new forms, on the one hand; and also a profound connection, an affinity of spirit, and the promise of an enormously beneficial partnership in culture, trade, and security.

It is in the nature of paradoxes, of course, that one should not try to solve them. The best one can do is to understand their contours and, in the case of diplomacy, utilize them to our small nation's benefit. And so, I set about to build bonds and fight bias, to accept the paradox and make the best of it in any way I could.

***

Few people remember today that the reunification of Germany, completed in 1990, was not at all an obvious outcome of that period. True, the Soviet Empire had begun to run out of steam, and East Germany had torn itself out from under the Iron Curtain. But West German Chancellor Helmut Kohl faced significant international opposition to the idea of merging East and West into a single Federal Republic of Germany. The Soviet leader, Mikhail Gorbachev, was under pressure to send the Red Army to invade East Germany and reestablish Communist dominance. The British, French, and Italians, recalling the horrors wrought by a powerful Germany during two world wars, were firmly opposed to reunification, and they said so, at least behind closed doors.

We, too, worried about reunification. During the decades that had passed since Israel's independence in 1948, West Germany had, largely as part of its reckoning with the Holocaust, become an important ally for the Jewish state on multiple levels of security, trade, and tourism. West Germans were among the most educated, progressive, and enlightened citizens in the world—and overall highly supportive of the Jewish state. Their cousins to the east, however, lived in a parallel universe. Having been cut off from the free media and bombarded with Soviet propaganda for decades, they perceived Israel as an imperialistic, capitalistic, Middle Eastern proxy of the United States. These assumptions were nourished by the ferocious hatred engendered by the Soviet Union, East Germany's patron, towards the United States and its allies, and were bolstered by the Communist bloc's longstanding, unwavering assault on Zionism and support for the Arab world. And if this kind of brainwashing were not enough, we also had to deal with the residual bigotries of Nazism and the old antisemitism.

Quite simply, most East Germans saw Israel as the enemy.

But the Americans, under President George H. W. Bush and especially his Secretary of State James Baker, saw unification as having the potential to strike a major blow against the Soviets in the Cold War, and an expansion of American influence. Played right, a unified Germany would become a full-fledged partner in NATO, a major free economy, and a Western-facing democracy.

A grand negotiation took place from Washington to Paris and London and Moscow among the "two-plus-four" nations—the two German governments along with the four victorious powers of World War II. Kohl, who had announced a ten-point plan for unification, seemed to be encouraging a rapid *de facto* merger of the two countries, allowing in masses of East Germans and extending West German law into the east. Kohl had to overcome staunch objections from the outside, as well as the domestic opposition of economists, banking industry leaders, and other experts who insisted that merging the nations would bring ruin to West Germany.

In May 1989, the border between Soviet-backed Hungary and Western-facing Austria opened, and suddenly tens of thousands of East Germans poured through those two countries to reach West Germany. On November 9 of that year, demonstrators using sledgehammers and pickaxes tore down the Berlin Wall separating the city's Western and Communist halves. The East Germans held their first free election in March 1990 and brought to power the Social Democrats, the same party that led West Germany.

Events moved far more quickly than anyone had anticipated. Germany wanted to unify, it had the support of both Kohl and Bush, and there was little anyone could ultimately do to stop it.

When the Berlin Wall fell, everyone at the embassy immediately sensed that history was taking a major turn, and that we needed to start planning for it, quickly.

"We are at the dawn of a new and unpredictable age," Navon told me soon after, "and we should prepare accordingly." He then directed the staff to focus on the five states of the former German Democratic Republic, which were being united with the eleven states of West Germany to form the sixteen-state Federal Republic of Germany.

I understood that the key to forging an active collaboration between Israel and East Germany was through culture, art, and music, where a nation's stories are told. Step one would be to create an infrastructure of cultural ties, giving both sides an opportunity to become familiar with each other's stories. Only then could we work toward more official diplomatic ties with the new states on multiple levels, including economic, cultural and people-to-people relationships.

I moved with haste, and in a relatively short time, cultural ties between eastern Germany and Israel were launched with considerable success. Israeli musicians and artists performed in eastern Germany, attracting curious audiences who were seeing Israelis for the first time in their lives. The Germans of the east discovered that the dreaded "colonialist" Israelis were more cultured than they had imagined. The media covered the performances enthusiastically, followed by the politicians. The respective leaders of the former East German states opened their doors to me and asked to learn more about Israel.

With the help of German government funding, we started sending delegations of German parliamentarians to Israel, bringing teachers from the former East Germany to the Yad Vashem Holocaust Museum in Jerusalem, and engaging in a direct dialogue with those responsible for educating the next generation. We paired towns in Israel with those in eastern Germany, set up youth exchanges, organized visits by the leaders of the eastern federal states to Israel, and did everything we could to exploit the historic opportunity.

The Germany that emerged proved to be an exceptionally important ally. In the decades that have passed, and despite waves of anti-Israel sentiment, Germany has remained our strongest ally in Western Europe, with investment, tourism, and especially military and security cooperation at a very high level.

At the same time, successive German governments have too often couched their support in a diplomatic profile that follows the European model, joining in on EU decisions or UN resolutions that reflect less than full support, especially on issues concerning the settlements. Bilaterally, Israel could hardly have a better friend than Germany—as was displayed in the wake of the October 7 attacks, as Chancellor Olaf Scholz and other top government officials made repeated visits in support of Israel, and the Bundestag passed unequivocally supportive resolutions. But when it comes to the international diplomatic arena, to the accusations and fantastical calumnies of the so-called human-rights NGOs, the UN, and other such bodies, Germany's record is more, shall we say, paradoxical.

***

The complexity of building Israel's relations with the two halves of Germany would serve, for me, as an important introduction to the bewildering dynamic of our relationship with Europe as a whole. An entire continent suffused with contradictions and the constant motion of tectonic plates: from the horrors of two world wars, to the perpetration of the Holocaust, to the Cold War that divided the continent for half a century, to their attempts to form an "ever closer union" in the form of the European Union, to the recent massive influx of immigrants from the Middle East, the departure of the United Kingdom known as Brexit, the confusion and trauma of the COVID-19 epidemic, and the eruption of war in Ukraine, which has laid bare Europe's dependence on others for both energy and security.

Europe as a whole is in constant motion. It is confused, sometimes to the point of paralysis. It is locked in a series of clashes over values and policies—immigrants versus "old" Europeans, eastern versus western, unification versus the sovereign rights of nations, and more.

Alongside the general paradox of Europe—the cradle of democracy and liberalism, the site of its most horrific acts of totalitarianism—there is also a specific paradox in its historical relationship with the Jews and Israel. This latter paradox goes back much farther than the twentieth century. Europe, from the time of Constantine, was built on its embrace of Christianity, which was itself built on *both* the demonization of Jews and the canonization of our scriptures. In the Middle Ages, Jews were both welcomed for the economic benefits they brought *and* often persecuted and even expelled as an inferior race worthy of divine punishment. In the modern era as well, pogroms and antisemitic persecutions alternated with the emergence of democracy, the freeing of Jews from the shtetl and involvement in ever-widening spheres of public life.

And so it continues today in its relations with Israel. On the one hand, the European Union is Israel's biggest trade partner, a relationship that has deepened in recent decades as Israel's economic profile has risen to the point of being on a par, in per capita GDP, with Europe's. Israel has excellent relations at the economic and cultural levels with most European nations, and with the EU itself.

Israelis, too, feel the pull of Europe in spite of everything. This flows, in part, from the more distant past—not just from the British support of Zionism in its early years, but also from the aftermath of the Holocaust, and the early years after Israel's independence, when relations first with Czechoslovakia and then France provided a military lifeline to the Jewish state. Israel has modeled itself, since its early years, as a European-style democracy, with a parliament and a coalition government, and with a robust welfare state and a sense of collective commitment that expresses itself in countless ways, including national military service.

On the other hand, European states have also been among the most antagonistic to Israel in international forums, such as the UN, and are host to the most vicious of international NGOs, often causing real harm to Israeli interests.

The result of this paradox is that Israeli diplomats are permanently navigating policies, personalities, and rhetoric that oscillate between extremes of support and hostility—and the stakes of these are often higher than they seem.

I saw this for the first time in Bonn, and also when I was spokesman for the embassy in London in the 1990s. But perhaps nothing drove the point home as powerfully as my tenure as Israel's ambassador to the United Kingdom, which began in late 2007 and lasted until 2011.

Representing Israel in the United Kingdom proved a monumental challenge.

***

Even after Brexit, Great Britain is still a major power in the world. It is the home to media with worldwide audiences. It is a center of the global financial system. And unlike Germany, it is a permanent member of the UN Security Council. Anti-Israel sentiment in Britain, therefore, affects Israel's wellbeing. It is also home to more than a quarter million Jews—second only to France among Europe's Jewish communities—and they directly feel the heat of the antiemitism that seems, at times, to flow in the veins of a significant portion of the population.

Israelis love and admire Britain. We adore its cobbled streets, quaint shops, theaters, castles, and royal weddings. We revere British culture and history, and we admire Winston Churchill's bravery in standing up to the Nazi war machine, and the country's acceptance of Jewish refugees during the war. Deep in the Israeli conscience, there is still gratitude to Balfour and Lloyd George—both of whom have streets in Jerusalem named after them.

At the same time, Britain is one of the most hostile countries towards Israel in Europe. This is because of three unique features that combine to create an especially difficult environment for Israeli diplomats. The media, the academia, and the international NGOs headquartered in London have an outsized influence across the English-speaking world. Together, these three create an environment of anti-Israel sentiment that has no real parallel.

One of the key vestiges of the British Empire is its media empire. Britannia no longer rules the waves, but it still rules the airwaves. British media giants like the BBC, Sky News, the *Financial Times*, and *The Economist*, as well as a wide range of newspapers, such as the *Times* of London, *The Guardian* and *The Daily Telegraph*, enjoy a reach far beyond the borders of the British Isles. Words uttered, written, or filmed in London often create ripples and set agendas thousands of miles away from Westminster. Journalists, editors, and producers in New York and Washington wake up each morning to learn what has already been said that day in London.

Britain is also home to some of the leading universities in the world, such as Oxford, Cambridge, the London School of Economics, King's College London, and Imperial College, alongside dozens of other academic institutions up and down the country, from Edinburgh and Glasgow in the north, to Manchester and Leeds in the middle, to Cardiff in Wales. These universities attract thousands of international students who mostly arrive in Britain in their formative years without firm opinions about the Israeli-Palestinian conflict. Thirsty for knowledge, they often study under ultra-progressive scholars who regard Israel as a violent, colonialist human rights abuser. These students eventually return to their countries and, in time, assume leadership roles in industry, politics, and media.

Besides the media and universities, British hostility to Israel is also rooted in the fact that so many NGOs use London as a base for their global anti-Israel crusades. Over the years, Israel has become a kind of totem for these organizations, which use my country as a magnet for raising funds and resources. Amnesty International, Christian Aid, War on Want, Oxfam, and others were established to fight human rights abuses worldwide, but have discovered that there is money to be made by obsessively, disproportionally, and intentionally focusing on Israel, often at the expense the world's most brutal abuses in places like Syria, Iran, and Venezuela, while continually repeating anti-Israel and antisemitic libels that are decades or even centuries old. Like clergy during the Crusades and the Spanish Inquisition, they are masters at projecting absolute conviction in the purity of their intentions and the righteousness of their cause.

The controversy surrounding the February 2022 Amnesty International report offers just one of countless examples. After decades of anti-Israel rhetoric declaring that Israel is like Apartheid-era South Africa—a claim that originated in the Soviet propaganda in the 1950s and spread as part of its decades-long information war against the West—Amnesty, one of the world's most respected human rights NGOs, based in London, declared that Israel was guilty of the "crime of Apartheid." Not just because of its specific policies vis-à-vis the Palestinians in the West Bank, where Israelis and Palestinians effectively live under different regimes in accordance with the Oslo Accords—but from its very founding as a Jewish state in 1948. The report was, simply, an attack on Israel *in its essence.*

As such, it had the advantage of laying bare what had previously only been implicit: that the rabid attacks against Israel—a liberal democracy whose only significant difference from most European states is the simple fact of its being Jewish—undertaken for decades by NGOs like Amnesty, were never just about specific policies or actions undertaken by the Israeli government. They were always about Israel itself. As such, they were acting, at least as far as Israel was concerned, not as independent rights watchdogs in the service of the liberal democratic order, but as an extension of the great anti-Israel machine that had been pumping out hateful nonsense across Europe since the days of the Soviet Union.[43]

In theory, such a report does not have teeth. Amnesty has no government, no army, and controls no major economies. And indeed, it was not just the United States which rejected the report out of hand—U.S. Ambassador to Israel Tom Nides dismissed it as "absurd"—and so did the governments of the United Kingdom, Germany, the Netherlands, and Canada.

At the same time, when human rights organizations of such magnitude single out Israel in this way, and use their tight relationship with the British media and academia to amplify the reports in a vast, self-perpetuating echo chamber, it forces well-meaning people to make an unpalatable choice: Either Israel really is the world's most evil regime, worthy of a preposterous degree of attention from the world's most noble international organizations—or these organizations are somehow not what they say they are.

The truth is the latter, as is evident to anyone who has visited Israel and seen the remarkable degree of freedom, rights, and civil equality all

---

43 The roots of modern anti-Israel rhetoric in both Nazi Germany and the Soviet Union have been catalogued by several leading scholars. For a good summary, see Jeffrey Herf, "Nazi Antisemitism & Islamist Hate," *Tablet*, July 6, 2022, https://www.tabletmag.com/sections/history/articles/the-nazi-roots-of-islamist-hate (accessed October 20, 2024). See also Izabella Tabarovsky, "How to Beat the New Antisemitism," in David Hazony, ed., *Jewish Priorities: Sixty-Five Proposals for the Future of Our People* (New York: Wicked Son, 2023).

its citizens enjoy, regardless of whether they are Jewish, as is befitting any modern democracy. That's a widely unrecognized truth, which requires some investment to uncover. Most people will not bother, and the result is that entire discourses—legal, political, academic, journalistic—remain convinced that Israel should be seen as a pariah state at best.

Like any democracy, Israel makes mistakes, and like any democracy, we open ourselves to criticism and freedom of the press to a degree unthinkable among the many authoritarian regimes that are somehow immune to criticism from these same organizations. But the one-sidedness and the lack of proportion in their treatment of Israel reaches a stratospheric level of absurdity. For such organizations, the defamation of Israel has acquired the dimensions of an epidemic, as they launch their poison arrows with impunity from the banks of the Thames.

Many British officials, of course, have a realistic understanding of Israel's security challenges. There is substantial British-Israeli intergovernmental cooperation, especially in the areas of defense and intelligence. British policymakers generally know how important Israel is to stability in the Middle East, and some admire Israel's strengths and want to keep Israel on their side, sustaining a relationship based on dialogue and cooperation.

Indeed, Israel has many good friends in the British political system who understand the importance of the bilateral relationship and Israel's contributions to the Middle East and the wider world. Among Israel's strongest friends are Prime Minister Keir Starmer, former Prime Minister Rishi Sunak, former Chancellor of the Exchequer Sajid Javid, MPs Louise Ellman, Joan Ryan, and Ian Austin, former Home Secretary Priti Patel, Cabinet Office Minister Michael Gove, and former Prime Ministers Boris Johnson, Theresa May, Gordon Brown, David Cameron, and Tony Blair.

There is a growing gulf between the understanding that successive British governments have had for Israel's strategic challenges and the intensifying hostility from the wider British public. In a democracy, however, political leaders reflect public sentiment, and it would not take much, under the right conditions, for the hostility to express itself in elections and policy.

There was no clearer warning light in recent years than the 2015 election of Jeremy Corbyn, a supporter of Hamas and Hezbollah who laid a wreath at the graves of terrorists behind the massacre of Israeli athletes at the 1972 Munich Olympics, to the leadership of the Labour Party. Corbyn did not invent antisemitism, but he certainly helped to move it from the conspiratorial fringes to the legitimacy of mainstream discourse. His political and economic extremism, in addition to his antisemitism. was a major contribution to Labour's collapse in the 2019 general election, after which he was ousted from the party.

But the dark forces he represented will not be easily uprooted from the political landscape. In the years since Corbyn's dismissal, Labour has continued to be dogged by a sense of pervasive antisemitism and Israel-hatred in its ranks, despite efforts of its new leader Keir Starmer to root them out. In September 2021, the party conference passed a resolution condemning Israel's "ongoing Nakba in Palestine," using the Arabic term for the "catastrophe" of Israeli independence in 1948; and two months later, Israel's ambassador to the United Kingdom, Tzipi Hotovely, was forced to rush out of a speaking engagement at the prestigious London School of Economics as violent protesters of the Left swarmed her car.

Starmer rightly condemned these events, but it's clear that anyone who thought the ferocity of the British Left's anti-Israel sentiment would vanish with the defeat of Corbyn was mistaken. There is much work to do.

During my time as ambassador, the United Kingdom was the vanguard of anti-Israel prejudice in Europe. We at the embassy had to deal with growing calls for academic and economic boycotts, mass protests in the wake of the Gaza conflict known as Operation Cast Lead in 2008 and 2009, the fallout of Israel's legal situation and reputation after the hostilities in Gaza, and the outrageous abuse of the idea of universal jurisdiction as Israeli officials started to be threatened with arrest while traveling overseas.

But for me, personally, it reached its most virulent expression during my visits to university campuses.

***

The ancient hallways of the University of Edinburgh display portraits of its most illustrious alumni, and such figures as the inventor Alexander Graham Bell, former Prime Minister Gordon Brown, and the author J.K. Rowling peer at you as you walk by. Grand staircases climb among the labyrinthine floors that greet visitors at this prestigious academic institution, which has graced the Scottish capital for 400 years. If you stay absolutely silent, you can almost hear the footsteps of historical figures in the hallways. If you really listen hard, you can also hear the echoes of angry voices at the university's entrance, awaiting my arrival.

An hour before my scheduled lecture in the magnificent graduation hall, the Palestine Solidarity Campaign organized a demonstration outside. Some 200 students chanted refrains condemning Israel, calling it "IsraHell." They brandished placards ranging from legitimate expressions of protest to swastikas and racist slogans, such as "Star of David = Swastika." Near the entrance I spotted a few placards with my name in blood-red letters alongside appellations such as "Child-Killer" and "Envoy of the Zionist Devil." What can one say to twenty-year-old students holding signs like these? I wondered what might have led them to this point, and I briefly considered engaging them in dialogue. But inside, in a lecture hall filled to the brim, hundreds of students were already waiting to hear me speak.

In the wake of the 2006 Second Lebanon War and the 2009 Gaza war, the mood in Britain was especially hostile. Every morning, I awoke to newspapers crammed with mostly negative coverage.

One regional council in Scotland decided to boycott books by Israeli authors and remove them from the shelves in public libraries. Another town declared a boycott of Israeli goods. I remember wondering: How many Israeli products were even sold in this small, far-flung town such that the local council saw fit to proclaim a boycott? "Nothing, it's just symbolic," explained Carly Maisel, who organized my public appearances at British universities and later became my chief of staff. Carly, a talented, sharp-tongued British Jew driven by Zionist ideals, threw herself fully into the embassy's public diplomacy.

It was a time of heightened hostilities on the Gaza border, as well. In late December 2008, Israel launched Operation Cast Lead in a bid to suppress the incessant rocket fire from the Gaza Strip, which had intensified after Hamas seized power in the Strip and made the lives of Israelis in the south a living hell. Hamas had bombarded the towns of southern Israel with rockets, and the IDF had justifiably retaliated, but many in Britain reacted to Israel's response with opprobrium and scorn, which sometimes spilled over into violence.

At the embassy, the phone did not stop ringing. We scrambled to respond to reporters seeking clarifications, to field constant requests for challenging media interviews, to meet British MPs demanding urgent answers, and to dart between universities for lectures in front of mostly bellicose crowds. Embassy staff advised me not to travel to Edinburgh. "It's a hostile place," Carly said, "they'll blow up your lecture." Indeed, whenever Israeli representatives came to British campuses, all hell broke loose as students stood up, shouted, and hoisted banners against Israel. They did not want to engage in dialogue, nor did they wish to receive answers. They were driven by a single-minded zeal to send the Israeli speaker packing.

As ambassador, I made a point of accepting almost every invitation to give an interview, deliver a speech, or make a public appearance—especially at the most challenging hotspots. Just showing up and confronting a hostile audience had value in itself. I refused to hide behind a barricade of security guards, and I took no personal offense at insults hurled my way.

Standing in front of hundreds of political science students in Edinburgh, many of them seemed to have come to listen. But it was obvious that others were hiding banners under their seats, and I would receive a frosty reception inside as well as outside. Indeed, five minutes into my speech, one student jumped up, waved an anti-Israel placard, and sealed his mouth with masking tape in an act of protest. Six other students popped up behind him and did the same. I ignored most of them and continued my lecture. When one student asked me, "Why are you attacking Gaza?" I answered:

> Do you think that the citizens of Dover would be eating Dover soles quietly for lunch if missiles were launched against them from Calais in France? Well, you don't have to be a rocket scientist to understand that if rockets fall on your head, you are entitled to defend yourself.

In the world of diplomacy, especially in Britain, the most pressing challenge is to respond calmly and precisely to allegations. Don't dodge tough questions, don't lose your temper, and don't get agitated. Rather, respond with quintessential British equanimity, matter-of-factly but sarcastically. It is not easy to pull off, especially in front of an intelligent, inquisitive, and skeptical crowd of students, and the task is infinitely trickier when someone is waving a banner reading "Murderer" in your face, and you can hear vulgar chants against your country outside.

And so, when I was asked, "Why don't you talk with Hamas?" I answered simply: "A terrorist organization like Hamas does not recognize my country's right to exist. So, what do you want me to negotiate with it about—the flower arrangements at our funeral and the choice of wood for our coffin?"

One student, a fair-haired and blue-eyed British chap, got up and started reciting a litany of Israel's alleged "war crimes" in Gaza. I cut him off and said, "My dear friend, take another look at the page you're holding and read out exactly what you were told to say. You've forgotten at least two critical points against Israel. Be careful, you don't want to get told off." The embarrassed young man unfolded his message sheet to check his mistake and started hesitating. I continued: "Not good enough! Why are you mumbling? Spit it out!"

This was enough for him. Furious at having been caught red-handed, his face contorted with rage, he broke into a sprint towards the stage. I did not flinch. Officers from Scotland Yard pounced, caught him, hoisted him into the air, and carried him out of the room.

"Is there anyone else," I deadpanned, "who would like to recite questions off a page?" People laughed, and the tension dissipated.

***

It was during my time in London that Israel also faced increasing efforts to attack it through the British legal system. This effort, known as "lawfare," has become an important battlefield in the international campaign against the Jewish state.

In 2009, the Jewish National Fund held a gala fundraiser in London and invited Israel's former foreign minister and then-leader of the opposition, Tzipi Livni, as its guest of honor. A few days earlier, we were tipped off that boycott activists had petitioned a local court to issue an arrest warrant for Livni under the principle of universal jurisdiction, accusing her of war crimes. Unlike sitting ministers acting in an official capacity, Livni did not enjoy immunity against such judicial proceedings.

"Universal jurisdiction" has become a hot new progressive idea in legal circles over the past three decades. According to the International Committee of the Red Cross, this concept allows states "to search for suspected perpetrators of...war crimes...regardless of their nationality and the place of commission of the alleged offence, and either to bring them before their own courts or to hand them over to another state...for trial."[44] Since British law recognizes the principle of universal jurisdiction, anyone can file a complaint about an alleged war criminal to the police, which, in turn, might be able to obtain an arrest warrant in order to interrogate that person.

Indeed, it is through lawfare that the specific combination of NGOs, universities, and the media come together to generate actual harm to the State of Israel. Hatred of Israel is expressed through new legal categories, which are widely disseminated and propounded by respected "experts,"

[44] International Committee of the Red Cross, "The Scope and Application of the Principle of Universal Jurisdiction: ICRC Statement to the United Nations, 2017," October 13, 2017, https://www.icrc.org/en/document/scope-and-application-principle-universal-jurisdiction-icrc-statement-united-nations-unga-2017 (accessed October 20, 2024).

and eventually it ends up becoming conventional wisdom among certain classes and winds up hijacking a country's legal system for its nefarious political ends.

In Livni's case, even if the arrest warrant was not going to lead to her being led off in handcuffs, the mere fact that it was issued set a dangerous precedent for Israel, particularly for IDF officers and members of the Knesset visiting Britain. The judge was following standard procedure in issuing the warrant without considering the merit of the complaint itself, which would be brought before another judge in a follow-up hearing. The judge was not an expert in the laws of war and had no means of investigating whether Livni had committed the crimes she was accused of. He was only authorized to consider the request for the arrest warrant, and the narrow focus on procedure at the expense of the merits of the complaint was enough to jeopardize the former minister's visit.

The result of it was that boycott activists successfully weaponized the law to serve their agenda. The idea that a former foreign minister of Israel might be held for interrogation by British authorities about IDF operations was preposterous. Even if the police investigation ultimately led to nothing, the arrest of Tzipi Livni would have given the Boycott, Divestment, Sanctions (BDS) movement a media victory and a boost of morale.

I placed calls to Number 10 Downing Street, the Foreign Office, and the Ministry of Justice, demanding that the arrest warrant be revoked immediately. British officials can be highly creative in finding diplomatic solutions, but they all gave me the same answer: "Sorry Ron, our hands are tied, the law's the law."

Their flaccid response forced us to advise Livni to postpone her visit to London. We could not afford to have television screens and newspaper front pages around the world carrying images of Livni being arrested at Heathrow Airport and carted off for questioning.

To be clear, the problem here went far beyond the harm done to Israel: It was clear that prosecuting the leaders of democratic nations for exercising their right to defend themselves was creating a dangerous precedent, an abuse of the system, and a form of harassment that would potentially hamstring democratic nations, including Great Britain itself, from properly defending themselves in the future. It was serious business. Our British colleagues, however, could not have cared less.

Even after Livni postponed her visit, the story refused to go away. A short while later, we received a request at the embassy to attend a court hearing about the arrest warrant. Pro-Palestinian activists had alleged that we had "hidden" Livni in Britain and thus helped her to evade arrest. Absurdly, we had to prove that Livni had not set foot on British soil. It just shows how ridiculous and annoying these demands are. It would have been very simple for the British authorities to check whether Livni passed the border control and entered the UK. But they preferred to exhaust us and demand "proof." We had to obtain security footage from the gala event to prove to the judge that Livni had not been there. The judge was satisfied. The British Foreign Office was of course aware of the absurdity of the case, but did not lift a finger to correct the distortion.

How curious, I thought, that a former Israeli foreign minister was barred from entering London, while the foreign minister of Iran, a state sponsor of terrorism, was free to pass in and out of Heathrow Airport as he pleased.

The arrest warrant for Tzipi Livni was not a one-off occurrence. Time and again, we found ourselves fighting to keep Israeli politicians and senior military officials from getting arrested. Doron Almog, a former IDF major general who today heads up the Jewish Agency, flew to London in 2008 to raise money for a rehabilitation village for children and adults with serious mental and developmental disabilities, which he had founded with his wife Didi. The lawyer who had gone after Livni quickly petitioned for an arrest warrant for Almog over his alleged involvement in the demolition of the houses of terrorists during his military service.

When Almog landed at Heathrow, the embassy received a tip that police were waiting for him at the terminal with an arrest warrant in hand. It was swiftly agreed that he would stay in his seat on the El Al plane that had brought him over and would fly straight back to Israel.

When Aviv Kochavi, who later served as the IDF chief of staff, concluded his service as commander of the IDF forces in Gaza, he was admitted to a study program at the Royal College of Defence Studies in London.

Eager to arrange for immunity against attempts to get him arrested, we proposed having him accredited as a military attaché at the Israeli embassy. Diplomacy is the art of reaching such collegial solutions, but the British Foreign Office displayed a remarkable degree of disinterest in finding a creative solution. Kochavi, a brilliant officer, went on to complete his studies at Harvard. The British lost a golden opportunity to improve their own military capabilities by learning from one of Israel's most creative military minds.

I informed the British Foreign Office that it was putting me into the unpleasant position of having to advise Israelis, especially from the defense and military establishment, to turn down Britain's invitations for strategic dialogue—which would hurt our bilateral military, intelligence, and defense cooperation. My words fell on deaf ears. Israel had found itself on a *de facto* blacklist that undermined its sovereign equality and freedom of action. But one incident in 2009 made British officials realize that they had to act.

Israeli Defense Minister Ehud Barak was planning on visiting London in September 2009 to deliver a speech to members of the British Labour Party in his capacity as the chairman of the Israeli Labor party. Pro-Palestinian activists petitioned for an arrest warrant, accusing him of having perpetrated war crimes during recent hostilities in Gaza. British law did not allow courts to issue arrest warrants against certain officeholders, including presidents, prime ministers, and foreign ministers on official business. But under the British interpretation of universal jurisdiction, defense ministers had no such blanket immunity.

The presiding judge at a magistrates' court in London (who, again, had no means or mandate to explore the merits of the case) agreed to issue the arrest warrant for Barak. Once it was out, British officials said that their hands were tied since—no surprise—nobody was above the law. Barak landed in London. He was not arrested at the airport, but the warrant hung over him like the sword of Damocles, and any police officer could have arrested him during a meeting or dinner at a London restaurant. Barak was briefed not to accept an envelope from anyone during his stay in Britain, because if it contained an arrest warrant, he would have to turn himself in.

We appealed to the British attorney general, government ministers, and members of the House of Lords. Behind closed doors, none of them concealed their support for Israel, but none wished to say so publicly. Some even advised us to circumvent their own system and set up working meetings for Barak with British officials, so that his visit might be considered official business and the exposure to an arrest warrant thereby minimized.

When the media learned about the warrant, the British political establishment went into a tizzy. The British tried to have their cake and eat it, too, as they so often do: to respect the rule of law but to avoid a grave diplomatic crisis with Israel. I picked up the phone to British Foreign Secretary David Miliband, who showed a similar disinterest in finding a creative solution. Instead, he told me that he was "not against" asking the courts to revoke the arrest warrant for Barak. "I'm not against it," is a British euphemism for "Sorry, chap, you're on your own."

Miliband, who is Jewish, was in no hurry to have the warrant overturned, lest he lose support in the Labour Party by expressing sympathy for Israel.

"Just imagine that Ehud Barak gets arrested," I told a gathering of British MPs. "What would you expect other Israeli defense officials to do? Do you think they'll keep coming to Britain to enhance the security and intelligence cooperation between our nations? You, with your own bare hands, are sabotaging Britain's own security interests."

"But the law's the law," they replied robotically.

"Yes, I got that," I snapped back. "I guess I'll have to talk to the people actually responsible for passing laws in your country."

On the afternoon of the first day of Barak's visit, lawyers from the British Ministry of Justice appeared in court. This time, the presiding judge understood the wider significance and relied on a loophole to invalidate the original arrest warrant. I imagine that a sigh of relief could be heard at Westminster, not just at the Israeli embassy.

After the warrant was overturned, we kept up the pressure on British decision-makers. Our efforts to get Britain to revise its legislation and related procedures on universal jurisdiction produced some surreal moments. We often found ourselves, absurdly, at roundtable discussions with our lawyers in London and officials from the British Ministry of Justice, drawing up lists of Israeli figures who had been invited to the country, calculating the likelihood that they might be arrested, and working out whether they met the legal criteria for immunity. These sessions were as embarrassing as they were draining, but they prompted our counterparts to understand how Kafkaesque their situation was. "Your legal system has been taken hostage by boycott activists," I told them. They nodded in desperation.

Ultimately, our appeals to British interests paid off, and the British recognized the need to change the law on universal jurisdiction and the procedures surrounding it. In 2011, Britain amended the law to require the director of public prosecutions to sign off on arrest warrants requested by private individuals, after being convinced that a case involves genuine war crimes rather than being a political stunt by activists abusing the legal system.

Yet the attempts to use the tools of international criminal law—such as arrest warrants and rulings of the World Court and the ICC—continue as part of the systematic campaign against Israel. Since October 7, abuse of the international legal system for the purpose of harassing Israel and limiting its right to defend itself has roared back to the parlor rooms and dinner parties of Europe's elites.

***

I first came face to face with the uniquely European form of self-righteousness as a junior diplomat in Germany and Britain in the 1990s. From a more elevated vantage point later in my career, I tried to decipher *why* Europe behaved this way, despite its shared values with Israel, an island of democracy in a region that otherwise repudiates all of Europe's political principles. Is this only an issue of Europeans' disapproval of what they define as the "occupation"? I don't think so.

What is striking about European officials generally is their one-sided approach to the Israeli-Palestinian conflict: They tend to disregard or belittle Israel's security needs, marginalize Israel's rights, and challenge its authority, while tolerating and sometimes actively supporting efforts to negate Israel's international legitimacy and its right to defend itself, and its citizens and their property.

This mindset has multiple layers. The foundation is old-fashioned anti-Jewish bigotry that has resonated throughout Europe for centuries. When people express hatred of Israel and believe it should never have been created, and when they criticize Israel for things they don't criticize anyone else for, they are operating in the realm of bigotry, not criticism.

If someone suggested that Spain—despite its long history of imperialism and colonialism—should not exist because of its ongoing suppression of Catalan independence and occupation of various islands in the Atlantic, and that therefore the Spanish are not a people entitled to nationhood, that would be dismissed as absurd. No one would take it as "criticism of Spanish government policy." When someone says that Israel, the one Jewish-majority country in the world, should not exist, or that it has no right to defend itself when it is violently attacked by its enemies, that is simply anti-Jewish bigotry. That such antisemitism is often cultural rather than political among Europeans, and more instinctive than conscious, does not make it any better. It makes it both more potent and harder to deal with.

Another layer is what one may call Europe's "double guilt complex" concerning its own history. On the one hand, European colonialism involved a great deal of atrocities and contemptible behavior, and today many Europeans blame this history for many of the gravest current problems in their former colonies. They feel guilty and, as a result, effectively absolve these countries' current regimes of responsibility for corruption, human rights violations, and oppression of their domestic political opponents.

On the other hand, Western Europeans after the war felt similarly guilty over the fate of the Jews in the Holocaust, and still do today. This produced broad political support for the establishment of Israel at the time. With time, this guilt also manifested itself in waves of Europeans arriving to volunteer on the collectivist kibbutzim, in an almost utopian view of Israel as a model society and egalitarian paradise. In Israel's early years, the constant threat of invasion by its Arab neighbors elicited concern and empathy in a Europe wracked with guilt.

The Israeli-Palestinian conflict is the area where, for many Europeans, consciously or unconsciously, the two guilty feelings come together. Collective guilt is a difficult burden to live with. People need valves to release the pressure. Many Europeans buy into a narrative in which the Palestinians are a peace-loving, non-violent people oppressed by a brutal Israeli occupation, a colonialist enterprise born of Europe's own evils, and they are willing to ignore the Palestinians' consistent refusal to negotiate peace deals or the violence undertaken by Palestinian "liberation" groups against Israeli civilians as being a form of "legitimate resistance." They ignore the fact that terrorists' families are given lifelong stipends through an incentive program often called "pay to slay," and that suicide bombers are martyred by the Palestinian Authority, with posters idolizing them and public squares named after them.

It is this bizarre psychological reality that made it possible for quite a few well-meaning Europeans to disbelieve, at first, many of the accounts of the worst atrocities committed by Hamas on October 7, 2023.

This narrative allows some Europeans to relieve their own guilt regarding the Jews by embracing the neat and symmetrical (though nasty and false) idea that the Palestinians are the new Jews, oppressed and helpless, whereas the Jews have now become the "Nazis," and perhaps were all along. Sometimes it is stated explicitly, but more often it wafts, unspoken yet unmistakable, in the air. Indeed, according to a survey conducted by the Bertelsmann Foundation in 2021, 36 percent of Germans fully or somewhat agree with the statement: "What Israel is doing to the Palestinians today is essentially the same thing as what the Nazis did to the Jews in the third Reich."[45]

This is not especially new. Almost twenty years ago, the French Jewish philosopher Alain Finkielkraut observed that in the post-Holocaust era,

---

[45] Jenny Hestermann, Roby Nathanson, and Stephan Stetter, "Germany and Israel Today: Between Connection and Alienation," Bertelsmann Stiftung, September 2022, https://www.bertelsmann-stiftung.de/en/publications/publication/did/germany-and-israel-today-en (accessed October 20, 2024).

European progressives do not allow the existence of enemies, only Nazis and victims. Victims enjoy the status of "the Other," who must be protected against the reincarnated Nazis, whoever they may be. And in this context, it becomes all too easy to recast Israelis as the new Nazis and Palestinians as the new Jews.

> [Europeans] were so utterly concerned for the Other that the figure of the Other eventually replaced that of the *enemy*. Thus, the Palestinians are no longer the enemies of the Israelis, but their Other. The result is clear: Being at war with one's enemy is a human possibility; waging war on one's Other is a crime against humanity...the relationship is charged with racism, and everything racist must disappear. Thus, the enemy stands squarely in the camp of recognition, while the racist, by virtue of his words and his actions, is excluded from it.... Conclusion: Where morality has made room for the enemy, he re-emerges, recast in a demonic form, as the *enemy of the Other*—that is, as the enemy of humanity. With this enemy, there can be no compromise.[46]

Nazism, of course, is not the only comparison made. In more polite company, Israel is described through the more fashionable slur of "colonialism"—another form of European guilt, this time referring to centuries of conquest and exploitation of foreign lands and peoples by European powers.

Israel, however, is not a colonialist enterprise. It is very much the opposite, signifying the return of the Jewish people to its homeland, the land of its ancestors, as part of the realization of its national aspirations and self-determination. To achieve it, Jews had to overthrow—both diplomatically and through force of arms—the British colonial regime and declare Israel's independence as the sovereign nation of a historically oppressed

---

[46] Alain Finkielkraut, "In the Name of the Other: Reflections on the Coming Anti-Semitism" *Azure* (Autumn 2004), pp. 29 and 30.

people. Zionism is, by definition, an anti-colonial movement. At the same time, the Palestinian leadership has mastered the use of violence, incitement, and terrorism as the means to a political end. But Europe is a land where reality and fashionable narratives scarcely overlap.

The persistence of this European belief in Zionism-as-colonialism demands explanation, and the most fruitful conclusion I've been able to arrive at is that on some level, it is an effort to retroactively mitigate the Europeans' own crimes against their Jews. This manifests itself in manifold ways in European politics, philosophy, and culture. At the extremes of the spectrum are overt Holocaust denial, generally from the Right, and the denial of the Jewish right to self-determination, almost always from the Left. In a more subtle (and thus potentially more dangerous) way, it expresses itself in calls to downgrade bilateral relations with Israel and to treat the country exclusively through the lens of the Palestinian issue. In civil society, it often expresses itself in forums that pretend to foster dialogue between Israel and Palestinians but in practice are structured to appear more like a trial—with the Palestinians as accusers, the Israelis as defendants, and the Europeans in the role of judge and jury.

But perhaps the most fascinating—and intractable—source of friction between Europe and Israel is not about European guilt at all. It concerns, rather, a fundamental disagreement about the meaning of national sovereignty and the nation-state.

Europe, again, has a hard time with nation-states, dating back to the fallout from World War II, when the nations of Europe embarked on a project to gradually limit their sovereignty, and the nationalist sentiment that sustains it, in favor of the creation of a pan-European superstate. This project, which has culminated in the European Union, promotes collective European decision-making in a range of policy areas, with a view to enshrining social and economic equality across an ever closer union, and to systematically excising the dangerous forms of nationalism that, it is said, devoured Europe through war in the first half of the twentieth century.

Some have argued that Israel's existence poses a persistent challenge to this entire project. Its success as a thriving Jewish nation-state, granting civic equality and promoting a vibrant and free public discussion, pulls the rug out from under the European view that such things are impossible, backwards, or just one step away from fascism. It is a matter of consensus across virtually the entire Israeli political spectrum that Israel is the nation-state of the Jewish people. Everyone agrees that Israel must remain "Jewish and democratic," and the only argument is over what exactly this means. Europe, meanwhile, is so allergic now to nationalism, which it equates with bigotry, that the term "nation-state" has become almost unutterable in polite liberal society.

Another attempt to get to the roots of the idea is to point out that the whole idea of national self-determination in the nineteenth and twentieth centuries emerged as a *response* to colonialism and imperialism. It holds that a group of people who feel they are a nation—with a common heritage, culture, land, and language—have the right to free themselves from imperial rule. The nation-state, in other words, is anti-imperialist and anti-colonialist in its essence. This is just as true for the peoples who fought for liberation from the Austro-Hungarian Empire as it is for those who fought for liberation from the Soviet Empire, and it is true of course for the Jews, who were the persecuted among the peoples and also fought for their liberation. But today the fashionable narratives have been switched, and the Jewish state has been relegated, through the force of European bigotry, to the wrong side of history.

Though most European nations supported the 1947 UN Partition plan, which called explicitly for the creation of a "Jewish state" and an "Arab state," they would be uncomfortable with that terminology today. Yet, they say that they favor a two-state solution for Israel and Palestine, which amounts to the same thing. Their peculiar way of looking at things allows them to support Palestinian nationalism as a way of making amends with Arab victims of imperialism—but not to support Jewish nationalism and self-determination, which are seen as somehow retrograde.

Part of the explanation for this apparent paradox goes back, yet again, to the Holocaust. This immense trauma gave rise to two rival postwar identities, one European and one Israeli. Europeans, reeling from two world wars executed mainly on their own territory, were shocked by what they could do when they had too much power, while Jews were shocked by what could happen to them when they had too little. Having the luxury during the Cold War of cultivating a pacifist ideology while the United States provided most of Western Europe's military defense, modern European identity, based on the disavowal of military power in general, believes that all things may be resolved in dialogue. But Israeli identity, based on the disavowal of powerlessness in general, commits the Jewish state to defending itself by itself, safeguarding its might and its ability to exercise force when needed.

For more than half a century, the effort to create an "ever closer union" of European states was, on the face of it, a model of success. Thanks to NATO and the collective defense pact with the United States, which greatly reduced the military threat to Europe, questions of defense and security slipped down the public's agenda. Over the decades of the Cold War, Europeans grew enamored with the signing of treaties, aimed at arms control, troop reductions, and non-proliferation. Captivated by what they saw as the protective power of treaties, they reduced their own investment in security and defense. This dynamic was made abundantly clear during the 2022 Ukraine war, as NATO nations like Lithuania and Poland felt protected by their treaty with the United States, whereas Ukraine found itself fighting for its very existence against invading Russian tanks and artillery. It took only a few months for two non-NATO countries that had taken a position of neutrality for decades, Sweden and Finland, to apply for membership in NATO.

But the Europeans misunderstood something fundamental, even in the face of the Ukraine war: that treaties alone, without the will and wisdom to enforce them, do not provide protection. Without repeated statements by the American president making clear that the U.S. would defend "every inch" of NATO territory by force of arms, it's not at all clear that the war would not have spread across Europe.

In parallel, Europe developed a lively discourse on human rights. But Europe could only afford the luxury of advocating human rights around the world as long as its fundamental security and stability were ensured.

The European approach, however, has been imploding for the past decade, as the EU has been hammered by crisis after crisis, including waves of refugees and migrants, sprees of Islamic terror, political instability, economic collapse, Brexit, social polarization, paralysis flowing from an inability to form consensus, the impotent collective response to the COVID-19 pandemic, and the post-October 7 waves of antisemitism and riots. Compounding all this is the growing threat of Islamic fundamentalism, rooted not only in recent waves of immigration but second- and third-generation migrants from Muslim countries. The latter were born in Europe, but politically correct, fashionable narratives actively hindered their integration into European society. Europe's naiveté left it poorly equipped to deal with these mounting challenges.

Europe's enduring guilt about the Holocaust and colonialism, combined with its romantic instinct to sympathize with the perceived underdog, appears to have thrust it into one the most challenging periods in its modern history, with grave repercussions both for Europe and for the whole international system.

From this perspective, Israel, as both the Jewish state and the ultimate reference point for European guilt, frequently finds itself as collateral damage for Europe's own internal struggles.

***

If you drive past Jerusalem east toward the Dead Sea, you begin to lose radio reception as you speed down a sharp descent among towering amber hills. About halfway to Jericho, you might see some grayish shacks by the side of the road.

The white signs on these flimsy structures proudly display a blue symbol with a wreath of yellow stars, above the text: "Donated by the European Union." Living in these hovels are Palestinians who received material assistance from the European Union to settle in a fiercely disputed piece of territory. If the sign were more accurate, it would add: "This structure was illegally built here by the EU, in violation of the Oslo Accords and international law, with the aim of bypassing direct negotiations between the parties."

The Bedouin village of Khan al-Ahmar is just one example of European funding for programs that aim to establish facts on the ground and force Israel to change its policies in the West Bank. It is located in what the Oslo II Accords call "Area C," the 60 percent of the West Bank in which Israel is granted full security and civilian control, including full authority over planning and zoning. But the EU wants this disputed territory to be part of a future Palestinian state, so it has funded illegal Arab construction there to create facts on the ground. To do so, European states have defied a ruling by the Supreme Court of Israel, issued after a nine-year legal battle, defining the structures as illegal. And by disputing the legitimacy of a Supreme Court judgment, European states are essentially undermining the Israeli judicial system, which is one of the foundations of Israeli democracy. The European Parliament even went as far as to call the impending eviction a "war crime."

A well-oiled European machine stands behind numerous other efforts to undermine Israeli law and international agreements. For example, Britain, the European Union, and EU member states bankroll the Norwegian Refugee Council (NRC) to the tune of millions of dollars a year to conduct a legal war of attrition against Israel. It is a large-scale initiative to exploit Israel's democratic institutions, and specifically its courts, to undermine Israeli authority, challenge Israeli policies, and jam up its legal system. According to the watchdog group NGO Monitor, the NRC files hundreds of lawsuits a year in Israeli courts using private lawyers and Israeli and Palestinian political NGOs, some of which are involved in efforts to boycott Israel. The project's mission, according to official documents from donor states, is to pursue high-profile litigation in order to advance the EU's political interests in the region. The NRC sets itself a target of thousands of lawsuits each year to achieve its goals. By backing this campaign, the Europeans are lending a hand to lawfare against Israel.

The European Union, in other words, is consciously choosing to challenge Israeli democracy. In addition, some European countries are indirectly supporting the fight against Israel, through their own democratic institutions. The French government, for example, actively funds a large number of anti-Israel boycott organizations, such as the Platform of

French NGOs for Palestine—even though the boycotts they promote are illegal *under French law*.

Much of the criticism and delegitimization directed at Israel is not aimed at improvement, but at weakening, undermining, and ultimately destroying Israel's ability to defend itself. What makes the European role here so noteworthy is the enormous gap between its pretended high purposes to serve morality, humanity, and peace, on the one hand, and its actual cynicism in siding with undemocratic, violent, corrupt, and terrorist forces that aim to bring Israel to its knees, on the other.

I have posed this paradox to EU officials on numerous occasions, and they respond mainly with eyerolls and deflection. They insist that funding is allocated for specific projects, subject to certain guidelines and in accordance with basic values, and not to the organizations themselves. According to NGO Monitor, this excuse is an insult to one's intelligence. In many cases, EU funding constitutes 50, 60, or even 75 percent of these organizations' overall budgets, and they even use the EU flag to adorn their anti-Israel activities. When the funding is so extensive, the European Union cannot plead ignorance.

***

One final point about Europe must be made, which perhaps is something of a pet peeve. But for me the most blatant, repetitive, odious habit of European leaders and diplomats—somewhere between a religious mantra and a nervous tic—is their unceasing call for dialogue in response to all situations. *Dialogue über alles!*

This may sound odd coming from a career diplomat. Talking, after all, is what we do. And, indeed, it is true that dialogue is for the most part a good thing in itself, and solutions reached through dialogue are generally preferable to unilateral action or violence. But when dialogue becomes the goal, rather than a means to an end, when its use inevitably excludes the use of power in order to create the illusion of achievement at the international level, it can easily become a burden rather than a blessing.

The fact is that European diplomacy indeed views dialogue as a goal in itself even when dealing with the darkest regimes in the world. The most glaring example of the past decade from Israel's perspective concerns Iran. Although I think the 2015 nuclear deal with Iran, the JCPOA, was a terrible agreement that paved Iran's path to a nuclear capability under a protective international umbrella via its "sunset clause," the agreement would not have happened without the active urging of European countries who have long insisted on maintaining a positive relationship with a country whose leaders openly call for the destruction of another country, use blatant antisemitic messages to justify it, and work tirelessly to fund and promote terrorist activity around the globe.

Due to the addiction to dialogue-for-its-own-sake, and despite the fact that significant parts of the continent's security are still entrusted to the United States even today, some European governments nonetheless adopt a position of moral superiority over American "militarism." The price of this approach is often far too high. And in the case of Iran, the result is a *de facto* tolerance for a regionally destabilizing, extremist Islamist regime that seeks to acquire nuclear weapons. At the end of the day, this has the capacity to undermine global stability and certainly to endanger Europe and the security of its citizens.

The European tendency to ignore Hezbollah's spread across Europe is another example of the pathology of dialogue. Hezbollah is a recognized international terror organization, backed by Iran, with tentacles spanning the globe. In 2013, the British government leaned into its fantasy and created a legal fiction. It split its idea of Hezbollah in two, declaring that the terror group had a military wing and a political wing—though the organization itself, including its leader at the time, Hassan Nasrallah, denied that such a division exists and openly mocked it. The rest of Europe jumped on this fabrication. The idea was to placate the Iranians, their main sponsors, by only designating part of Hezbollah as a terrorist organization. Hezbollah, like all opportunistic terrorist groups, responded by turning Europe into one of its main financial and logistical lifelines, second only to Iran, which is responsible for 70 percent of Hezbollah's $1.1 billion annual budget, according to the U.S. Treasury.[47]

Hezbollah has used Europe to build a network of terror cells, crime families, and front organizations that funnel donations earmarked for orphans towards military purposes, illegal drug distribution networks, and money laundering syndicates across Europe.[48] This network has two purposes: to bolster Hezbollah's bottom line, and to create a European organizational infrastructure for Hezbollah and Iran, waiting for instructions to pounce.

This network has a state-like structure, with the requisite adjustments. The basis of Hezbollah's cobweb-like operations in Germany, for example, is Lebanese Shi'ite crime families who immigrated to Europe in the 1970s, settled down, became fully equal German citizens, and built criminal empires to exploit Germany through drug-trafficking establishments, money-laundering schemes and fake charities, such as orphanages. It is not unusual to see parades with Hezbollah flags on the streets of Germany or in luxury cars owned by wealthy Lebanese émigrés near the Brandenburg Gate. They are responsible for widespread organized crime, and the German authorities stand by helpless, clueless about how to respond to the crime syndicate funding an international terrorist infrastructure right under their noses. Grafted onto this criminal enterprise is a pro-Hezbollah Lebanese Shi'ite ideology, and the ringleaders donate some 20 to 25 percent of the proceeds of their crimes to the Hezbollah war machine in Lebanon.

---

[47] Liz Sly and Suzan and Suzan Haidamous, "Trump's Sanctions on Iran Are Hitting Hezbollah, and it Hurts," *The Washington Post*, May 18, 2019, https://www.washingtonpost.com/world/middle_east/trumps-sanctions-on-iran-are-hitting-hezbollah-hard/2019/05/18/970bc656-5d48-11e9-98d4-844088d135f2_story.html (accessed October 21, 2024).

[48] The Abba Eban Institute for Diplomacy and Foreign Relations, "Main Projects: The Janus Initiative," https://www.abbaeban.runi.ac.il/policy-and-technology-program (accessed October 21, 2024) Daniel Cohen and Liron Shilo, "Ending Hezbollah's Stronghold Over Lebanon," *The National Interest*, January 5, 2020, https://nationalinterest.org/feature/ending-hezbollahs-stranglehold-over-lebanon-110586 (accessed October 20, 2024).

European law enforcement agencies did practically nothing about this abomination. For years, Europe failed to establish special task forces, neglected to build effective systems of cooperation with international enforcement agencies, and gave little consideration to the burgeoning menace to its citizens—one that unites drugs, organized crime, and terrorism.

In recent years, as U.S. sanctions have weakened Iran, Europe has emerged as Hezbollah's biggest cash cow—all of it thanks to the Europeans' invented distinction between the organization's military and political wings. Before 2019, European countries (with the exception of the Netherlands) preferred not to touch this situation with a ten-foot pole, either unaware of the extent of the Shi'ite terror threat or fearful of provoking a Hezbollah retaliation on European soil or damaging their bilateral relations with Lebanon.

Finally, after an international diplomatic campaign to which I was proud to make a modest contribution in late 2019, Germany took a significant step in the right direction when its parliament, the Bundestag, called for the whole of Hezbollah to be designated a terror organization. The German government responded by issuing a full executive ban against Hezbollah in April 2020, accompanied by a few very significant operational measures. Germany was not alone. It was joining parallel changes in Great Britain and several Latin American countries—the fruits of an international diplomatic effort, which I hope are the harbingers of spring. Until such time, European leaders' sanctimonious deafness will continue to endanger their own citizens.

Nowadays, the global terror risk and the migration crisis are making one thing clear: If the nations of Europe continue to allow their legal system to be hijacked by nefarious operators sponsored by hostile regimes, they may find themselves powerless to protect their citizens when terror organizations like Hezbollah—which, again, is largely controlled by Russia's ally Iran—are able to act freely on European soil. The addiction to "dialogue" at all costs, without assertive action, risks engulfing the continent in bloodshed.

***

The tumultuous developments of the past few years, especially in the wake of the Ukraine and Gaza wars, have laid bare the perils of subordinating one's core national interests to the dream of an interdependent world—a dream promulgated by Europeans more than anyone else. For decades, Europeans saw themselves as the vanguard of a new world order, in which technology, global supply chains, the internet, and political unification would create a new world that left behind the old irrationalities of national pride, sovereignty, and the wars they inevitably brought.

Russia's invasion of Ukraine in February 2022 blew a hole through the middle of that dream. Europeans suddenly discovered they had become overly dependent on Russia for oil and gas, on Ukraine for wheat, and on the United States for defense. This came soon after the COVID-19 pandemic in which the EU's ability to make decisions collectively was also severely hampered to the point of paralysis. As I write these words, governments are still reeling in the face of staggering inflation, supply-chain disruptions, worker shortages, protests, and a war to the east that shows no signs of slowing down.

Germany, in particular, has recognized the need to undergo a seismic shift in its national security doctrine. Chancellor Scholz uses the phrase *Zeitwende*, or an inflection point in history. The paradigm shift includes two main elements: first, an evolution away from the long-held German position that emerged in the wake of World War II, that war is absolutely evil, unjustifiable under any circumstances. Today, Germany understands that it must arm itself in defense of democratic values. (The fact that the Green Party, long known for its pacifist approach, is among the most vocal supporters of arming Ukraine with advanced weapons, shows the paradigm shift in the German public opinion.) Second, Germany understands that its dependence on Russian gas and oil is not sustainable and has begun investing in alternative energy resources that it hopes will allow it to attain energy independence in a few years.

Given the changes in Europe, Israel cannot afford to be apologetic in the face of harsh and one-sided European criticism and invasive activity. For decision-makers, this means connecting the dots among various European initiatives and understanding that they form part of a deliberate, coordinated policy—an active assault against a sovereign state.

The inescapable conclusion is that Israel must create a diplomatic balance of power towards Europe by adapting itself to the Europeans' own two-pronged approach. It must be uncompromising in the defense of its national security interests, while pursuing a policy of social, economic, and technological cooperation as if there were no political controversy. At the diplomatic level, Israel must dismiss Europe's political diktats and remain steadfast about exercising its authority in the face of international interference. At the social and economic levels, Israel must focus its best efforts not only on foreign governments but directly on civil society and industry.

At the same time, Israel should work to strengthen its ties with the nations of Central and Eastern Europe—the countries that lay beyond the Iron Curtain until the fall of the Soviet Union and joined the European Union at the turn of the millennium. They are motivated by different values than their Western European neighbors and do not blindly worship the cult of human rights at the expense of self-defense. Like Israel, they understand the significance of the nation-state and the urgency of protecting it. This makes them better placed to understand and empathize with Israel's challenges. Stronger Israeli ties with Central and Eastern Europe may nudge the European Union to temper its criticism of Israel, bolstering Israel's international stature.

I am fully aware that there are negative aspects to Israel's alliance with right-wing, conservative, populist governments, such as in Hungary. There is a risk that they will use their warm relations with Israel to whitewash antisemitism and xenophobia and undermine human rights. But Israel must pursue a two-track approach. It can build collaborative relationships with populist governments while clearly and uncompromisingly denouncing any antisemitism tendencies. For years, foreign countries have taken a similarly bifurcated approach towards Israel, warmly embracing it on matters of consensus and ferociously criticizing it on matters of dispute.

Why should Israel not take the same approach towards its own international partners?

Tectonic shifts have roiled the European continent in the past decade, raising major questions about the future of the European Union, and a rethinking of the role that individual European nations may play on the international stage. This has been brought into sharp relief by the war with Ukraine, in which European nations issued the most ardent denunciations of Russia but, when push came to shove, struggled to act with unity when it came down to sanctions or supply of desperately needed arms to Ukraine. Europe revealed itself to have fundamental vulnerabilities—not least of which are its reliance on Russia for the supply of oil and natural gas—and its individual nations were hard pressed to act on their own while the EU as a whole looked mostly paralyzed.

There is an old saying that within every crisis lies an opportunity. Israel must identify the opportunities for change in Europe and leverage them to its advantage.

Europe is the cradle of Western civilization. It laid the foundations for democracy and liberalism. It defined and shaped the values of human rights, liberty, and equality. But Europe was also the central arena of the deadliest wars in history, as more than a hundred million people lost their lives in two world wars that were started in Europe in the first half of the twentieth century. And Europe was, of course, also the slaughterhouse of six million Jews in the Holocaust.

The violence in Europe triggered the most ambitious peacemaking project of the twentieth century, when states agreed at postwar conferences and conventions to abjure violence and rebuild a new international order.

Today, Israel enjoys a productive and wide-ranging relationship with Europe. Israel conducts full diplomatic relations with European governments and shares ample intelligence with European armies and agencies. There is extensive scientific and academic cooperation in research and development, and the skies of the Mediterranean are full of planes carrying tourists in both directions.

But Europe is also an intoxicating, mendacious fantasy. When it comes to the Jewish state, Europe provides a master class in how to disentangle proclaimed values from actions on the ground. The unfortunate fact is that most European nations, by commission and omission, have subjected Israel to hostility at international forums for years and even decades.

CHAPTER 8

THE UN—ADVENTURES IN DIPLOMACY-LAND

Nearly a decade passed between my departure in 2002 from Washington, where I served as political counselor at the Israeli embassy, and my arrival in New York as Israel's ambassador to the United Nations in June 2011. In between these two postings on American soil, I served as director-general of the Foreign Ministry, where I learned much more about the machinery involved in coordinating Israel's diplomatic efforts around the world, the training of new diplomats, the relationship between the prime and foreign ministries in setting foreign policy, and the process of securing budgets for the Foreign Ministry, which always seemed like a losing battle; and then as ambassador to the United Kingdom, where I cut my teeth on the endless battle against anti-Israel propaganda, and the anti-Semitic venom it thinly veils, across Britain and much of Europe.

Both of these roles added crucial experience that helped to prepare me for the twists and trials of Turtle Bay. Indeed, more than twenty years' experience in Israel's foreign service had all led to this moment—and I would need to take advantage of it all. Though I had spent much of my career battling efforts to delegitimize Israel, whether in Bonn or London or Washington, I was still surprised by the intensity of the antagonism at the United Nations.

Representing Israel at the United Nations was, in a crucial way, different from my earlier posts, or the one I occupy today in Berlin. When dealing with national governments in foreign capitals, you can often feel immediate results—for better or worse. You can grapple with real-world cooperation in defense, technology, business, and culture. You can speak with your counterparts in the language of interests rather than ideology. Part of your job may include dealing with propaganda and harassment—especially, as I saw, in London. But in general, you can see with your own eyes how state-to-state relations translate into actions of real consequence. The outcomes can be measured in eight- or nine-figure deals, in joint military operations, in shared intelligence, in a whole range of decisions that affect the lives of every Israeli.

The United Nations is different. It is one or two steps removed from the bilateral relations among nations. It focuses almost entirely on the dynamics of a kind of diplomatic fantasy world—in which very few of the people you meet have the authority to make decisions, and they never really seem to mean what they say. Hostility and support never feel quite real, but more like the antagonism of lawyers in a courtroom—who later may go out for coffee or drinks together as if nothing happened.

The UN is kind of like an amusement park for diplomats. Yes, they are there in principle to advance the interests of the nations they represent. Sometimes they do so quite effectively. But they are also there to play on a field that is detached from those interests, enjoying budgets and perks that are largely disconnected from the impact of their words or actions. They also claim to be there to advance the central values on which the United Nations was founded—quality, human rights, a better world—but frequently act in ways that are little more than lip service to these vaunted principles.

Somehow, the aggregate of all the representatives of the nations of the world are supposed to come together and create institutions that do not solely reflect power interests, but also lofty ideals. This is, of course, an impossible goal. And no one has paid the price of this dissonance as much as Israel. All too frequently I have seen nations with which we have good relations in the "real world" suddenly speaking and voting in ways that clearly betray not just our interests, but basic democratic values or any sense of justice.

This does not mean, however, that such votes and decisions are devoid of consequence. On the contrary: Whether it be through the development of new concepts of international law geared to limit my country's ability to function, especially in military conflict; or the consequences of global embarrassment by being pilloried, day in day out, in a forum that carries a great degree of prestige; or the funneling of hundreds of millions of dollars into hostile NGOs that undermine our own sovereign rights—the UN is actually a high-stakes poker game masquerading as a circus, which in turn is masquerading as the most important forum in the world.

Nor is the problem just a matter of specific hostile resolutions in the General Assembly or the Security Council, or the overall climate of hostility that demands immense resources to contend with. It runs much deeper. The entire institutional structure of the United Nations, I quickly discovered, embodied a systemic and institutional bias against the only Jewish state in the world.

***

The most obvious example of this institutional bias dates back to the early years of the UN. Outrageously, embarrassingly, over a period of many decades, Israel was the only nation excluded from UN regional groups.

In the UN system, the world is divided into five geographic groups: Africa, the Asia-Pacific, Latin America and the Caribbean, Eastern Europe, and the "Western Europe and Others Group" (WEOG). In addition to key Western European states, WEOG includes the United States, Canada, Australia, and New Zealand.

By belonging to a group, states are able to get elected to posts and positions, attend committees, and participate in UN agencies and bodies. If a state fails to fall into any group, its envoys cannot apply for posts. It cannot easily form alliances or cooperate with other states, and it is denied the basic rights to which every other UN member state is entitled.

Until the year 2000, Israel was the only country in the world that was not a member of any regional group. And not because it didn't want to be. Israel was denied membership in the Asia-Pacific group, even though—or, rather, because—the Palestinians had been members since 1986, despite not actually having a state. The African, Eastern European, and Western European groups had used a series of polite excuses to turn Israel away when it asked to join their clubs.

And so, despite the United Nations having helped to bring Israel into being in 1947, and admitted it as a member in 1949, this global monument to the equality of nations subjected the Jewish state to clear structural discrimination for more than half a century.

In 2000, in the twilight of Bill Clinton's presidency, U.S. Ambassador Richard Holbrooke invited Israel to join WEOG. The group had just one condition. It used a three-year rotation cycle to nominate members for UN posts, and no state was willing to forgo its turn. Israel would have to wait three additional years before competing for UN posts on the group's behalf. There was a fierce argument at the Israeli Foreign Ministry over whether to accept the offer. Personally, I saw the stipulation as an insult. Foreign Minister David Levy listened attentively to me and the other senior diplomats, and reasoned that the offer might not come again, so Israel should accept it. He should be credited for thinking strategically, with an eye on the long run. Israel joined WEOG and, after a three-year wait, its diplomats started assuming official roles at the United Nations and getting elected to important committees.

Israel's membership card, however, turned out to have some additional fine print. The invitation only extended to joining WEOG at the UN headquarters in New York—not to its other sites in Geneva, Vienna, and Nairobi. Why? No reason was given. To be clear, the group's members had absolute discretion over admitting states, so their conduct cannot be blamed on a need to reconcile any pressure by Arab member states.

Many years later, on November 29, 2013, Israel finally won a golden ticket to WEOG in Geneva after Foreign Minister Avigdor Liberman and his deputy Ze'ev Elkin threatened to withhold Israel's cooperation with UN human rights reports. Following that, Israel also gained admission to the Western group in Vienna—in 2018. The United Nations has another main office, in Nairobi, Kenya. As of this writing, seventy-five years after

Israel joined the United Nations, the Jewish state is still excluded from its own regional group at the UN Office in Nairobi. Why? Just because.

Having joined a regional group, Israel gained the power to navigate various UN institutions, yet there, too, it found little solace. As a matter of principle, the United Nations is permanently preoccupied with Israel, exerting a completely disproportionate focus on the Jewish state.

To justify this, the UN must diverge from its traditional double standards, according to which there is one standard for dictatorships and another for democracies. In the case of Israel, there is a special and unattainable standard, a *triple* standard, which exceeds anything that is expected of democracies and sets a bar so high as to be, presumably by design, unreachable.

This triple standard expresses itself through any number of bodies, which may have once been aimed at doing some good in the world, but have instead concerned themselves mainly with the task of bashing Israel.

Of all such bodies, the most obvious is the General Assembly.

***

The UN General Assembly is, of course, the central body of the United Nations. There, the nations of the world discuss every issue under the sun, and then craft resolutions. Each country gets one vote, regardless of its respect for human rights, democratic values, or international obligations. The result is much as you would predict: Global power politics thinly disguised as democratic decision-making.

The General Assembly aspires to be seen as the world's parliament. Its 193 member states convene to argue, negotiate, make plans, pass resolutions, and make deals. No resolution is free from ulterior motives, and every vote gives something to one member at the expense of another. The politics is dishonest rather than straightforward. It pretends to be high minded and fair when it is really low and crooked. Nothing can be taken at face value, and it is always important to question the politics behind the airs and graces.

Moreover, too many of the actions taken in the General Assembly have one thing in common; they focus, to a comically disproportionate degree, on a single member state: Israel. It is there that the triple standard is felt most acutely. Unlike Security Council resolutions, which are binding and can be followed up with enforcement measures, the General Assembly's resolutions are purely declaratory. This has the unfortunate result of making it easier even for so-called friends of Israel to adopt them. But they can still inflict damage.

And so, we find that the same body that in 1947 passed the Partition plan that gave the Jewish people the international license to create a sovereign homeland of their own, an equal among the family of nations, has spent decades trying to betray it. In 1975, the General Assembly passed a resolution declaring Zionism—the belief that the Jewish people should have a sovereign state of their own—to be a form of racism, and didn't rescind it until 1991.

Each year, even today, the General Assembly passes no fewer than twenty-one anti-Israel resolutions. Every year, its members just copy and paste the same texts, change the date on them, and vote to condemn Israel for its actions in Judea and Samaria and the Golan Heights. While this in itself is ridiculous, the content of these resolutions is even more so. For example, every year the UN calls on Israel to hand over control of the Golan to Syria and the Assad regime. Even in the middle of the Syrian civil war, when Assad was massacring his own people, the UN wanted to give him control of this piece of land and the people living there.

Since 2015, the General Assembly has passed no fewer than 125 condemnatory resolutions against Israel—compared with 6 against Iran, 7 against North Korea, 18 against Russia, and 9 against Syria.[49]

This insane imbalance was brought home, somewhat comically, during a meeting of the Fourth Committee of the United Nations General Assembly in November 2013. The committee members had just finished voting on a series of resolutions condemning Israel in relation to West Bank, Golan Heights, Palestinian refugees, and more when they suddenly

---

49 UN Watch Database, "Is the UN living up to its founding principles?" https://unwatch.org/database/ (accessed October 21, 2024).

heard the voice of an interpreter who had forgotten that her microphone was still on:

> I think when you have...like a total of ten resolutions on Israel and Palestine, there's gotta be something, *c'est un peu trop, non?* [It's a bit much, no?] I mean I know... There's other really bad shit happening there [in the region], but no one says anything about the other stuff.

The chairwoman swiftly interjected to say that there was a technical glitch, the startled interpreter apologized—and the hall burst into laughter. When everyone laughs at a joke, it's usually a sign that nobody needs an explanation.

When the United Nations admitted Israel as a member state in 1949, it had 58 members, most of which were democracies. Today, only 87 of its 193 member states are democratic, per the UN's own definition. The UN operates "democratically," in the sense that each state gets an equal vote, but most of the hands raised are attached to the long arms of dictators. The result, of course, is the opposite of the promotion of democracy in the world. Because every member state has an equal voice at the General Assembly, democracies are always outnumbered. And a vote cast by the United States—the United Nations' biggest financial contributor—carries the same weight as small states like Kiribati and tyrannies like North Korea.

Natural coalitions form to take advantage of this game of numbers. The Arab states (the 22 members of the Arab League, including the Palestinians), have coalesced with other Muslim countries (the 56 nations of the Organization of Islamic Cooperation) and the rest of the Non-Aligned Movement (a broad alliance of 120 nations, mostly from the developing world), to form an anti-Israel diplomatic bloc at the United Nations. Together, they constitute more than two-thirds of the UN states, and they cause the United Nations to pass more than twenty anti-Israel resolutions a year.

Given this numerical superiority, Israel has virtually no chance of winning meaningful votes. The Non-Aligned Movement also severely punishes states, both inside and outside the bloc, that do not fall in line. It can limit their access to oil reserves, withdraw collective support at critical votes, and thwart appointments to UN posts.

If that were not enough, sometimes the bloc is joined by the 27 nations of the European Union, driven by their ostensibly acute sense of justice, but also their desire to exercise greater global influence, or their eagerness to win coveted positions in the UN, including in the Security Council—a prize that, due to the numbers, cannot be achieved without the Arab states' support. The Palestinians and their supporters are therefore able to promote their initiatives quietly, knowing they can win a majority without much effort.

I saw this with my own eyes as ambassador. In 2013, the Sixty-Eighth Session of the UN General Assembly adopted no fewer than 21 resolutions against Israel, compared to just *one* each against Syria, Iran, North Korea, and Myanmar. From 2012 to 2015, the General Assembly adopted 83 resolutions against Israel and only 15 against *all the other member states combined*. Reasonable observers should ask themselves: Is Israel really responsible for nearly 85 percent of the world's problems?

One resolution, in 2014, called on Israel to compensate the Lebanese government for an oil spill that happened during the 2006 Second Lebanon War. The General Assembly passed the resolution with a majority of 170 states (including European ones), eight years after the war had ended. It, of course, made no mention of the war itself, which erupted after Hezbollah—the Iran-backed terrorist group, and the most powerful political, social, and military organization in Lebanon—killed three Israeli soldiers and abducted two more. Nor did it allude to Hezbollah's deliberate targeting of Israeli civilians, cities, and critical infrastructure during the hostilities. Needless to say, the United Nations never lifted a finger to investigate the Second Lebanon War's major economic and environmental consequences for Israel.

The anti-Israel conduct of Arab states and their supporters at the United Nations did not surprise me. I expected little from the envoys of Saudi Arabia, Libya, Syria, and Venezuela when it came to human rights and other issues. These are among the darkest regimes on Earth, countries where people are silenced, jailed, or disappeared for expressing opinions.

Rather, the true challenge for Israel lies with the countries with which it shares values, nations that should be joining it on the same side of the barricades—the supposedly "like-minded" nations of Europe. I used to have high expectations of the Western democratic bloc to be the world's moral backbone. Yet it was at the United Nations that I experienced my most bitter disappointments in my many years as a diplomat, when I discovered the extent of the duplicity of many European countries as they single out Israel without a modicum of decency or even self-awareness.

Oui. C'est un peu trop.

***

But despite its high profile, the General Assembly is not necessarily the most harmful body with respect to Israel. The UN body associated perhaps more than any other with the anti-Israel agenda is the UN Human Rights Council (UNHRC), headquartered in Geneva. Under Item 4 of its permanent agenda, the Human Rights Council deliberates on human rights violations in every country around the world—except for one, the State of Israel.[50] Israel is the only state to merit its own clause, Item 7, which is limited to alleged violations by Israel and thus singles it out for opprobrium.[51]

Consequently, in its first decade after its founding in 2006, UNHRC passed 68 resolutions condemning Israel, compared with 67 for the

---

50 UN General Assembly, Sixtieth session, "Resolution adopted by the General Assembly: 60/251. Human Rights Council," April 3, 2006, https://www2.ohchr.org/english/bodies/hrcouncil/docs/a.res.60.251_en.pdf (accessed October 21, 2024), The UNHRC's 2006 original mandate was to "address situations of violations of human rights, including gross and systematic violations, and make recommendations thereon." Agenda Item 4, further to A/HRC/RES/5/1, August 7, 2007, focuses on "human rights situations that require the Council's attention."

51 Agenda Item 7 demands a specific focus on Israel in terms of the "human rights situation in Palestine and other occupied Arab territories," "human rights violations and implications of the Israeli occupation of Palestine and other occupied Arab territories," and the "right to self-determination of the Palestinian people."

entire rest of the world combined. In 2016, for example, it passed two resolutions on Syria (at the height of its civil war, which included a genocide and large-scale, violent dislocations), one on North Korea, and five on Israel. In other words, the UN's premier human rights body chose to condemn Israel more often than Syria, North Korea, Iran, and Sudan combined—the last two not even being condemned at all. After the council published the infamous Goldstone Report in 2009—its pseudo-investigation of the 2008–2009 Israel-Gaza war that was so grotesque that even Richard Goldstone, the South African judge after whom it was named, later regretted his involvement—I wrote in the *Times* of London, as the Israeli ambassador to the United Kingdom, that the report was like asking Jack the Ripper to lead a murder investigation at Scotland Yard.

The Jack the Ripper parallels go beyond the Human Rights Council. The obsessive focus on Israel does a disservice not only to Israel but to other nations. For example, the United Nations has a special agency (UNRWA) to deal exclusively with Palestinian refugees. It was created on December 8, 1949—just a few months after Israel became a member. Six days later, the UN created another body, aimed at taking care of *all other refugees in the world*, called the UN High Commission for Refugees (UNHCR).

This is no blip in the system. The Arab states represented at the United Nations, who at the time were uniformly and openly dedicated to Israel's eradication, decided that their cause could be best served by giving the Palestinian refugees special treatment. So, they brought about the creation, and continue to maintain today, a tailor-made agency just for them and above all others. As explained by Adi Schwartz and Einat Wilf in their 2020 book, *The War of Return*, the establishment of a Palestinians-only refugee agency was specifically designed for the purpose of permanently foreclosing a humane solution to the plight of Palestinian refugees, so that they could instead be leveraged against Israel in the future.[52]

As of 2021, prior to the Ukraine war, the UNHCR estimated that the world contained 74.5 million (non-Palestinian) refugees and internally

---

[52] Adi Schwartz and Einat Wilf, *The War of Return: How Western Indulgence of the Palestinian Dream Has Obstructed the Path to Peace* (New York: All Points Books, 2020).

displaced persons in 137 countries, in need of urgent assistance—these are the UNHCR refugees. Yet over the years, the United Nations has invested through UNRWA far more money and resources per capita for Palestinian refugees than any other refugee population. In 2020, UNRWA enjoyed an annual budget of $1.13 billion and 28,756 staff members: one employee for every 198 refugees and a budget of $198 per refugee. The UNHCR, by contrast, employed in 2019 just 18,879 staff members (one for every 3,946 refugees) and spent an average of $115 per person.[53]

How is it conceivable that the United Nations budgets so much more for Palestinian refugees—70 percent more per refugee—than for refugees from Afghanistan, Syria, anywhere in Africa, or any other place on Earth?

The comparison grows more bizarre when one looks at the results of the agency's efforts. Despite being the world's most generously funded refugee agency, UNRWA has failed to rehabilitate the Palestinian refugees. In fact, it has worked to *increase* their number and perpetuate their plight.

The reason for this is that UNRWA operates in flagrant violation of the basic humanitarian logic behind refugee relief. Instead of working to resettle the refugees and integrate them into host countries—to alleviate their plight—UNRWA actively impedes their resettlement, accustoms them to permanent refugee status, and does nothing to integrate them into wider society. This is not only the case in host countries like Syria and Lebanon, but even within the Palestinian Authority—which, despite being created as the vehicle for Palestinian self-government, nonetheless maintains UNRWA refugee camps.

This is not a result of ineptitude or mismanagement. It is by design.

Unlike the UNHCR, UNRWA treats refugee status as *hereditary*. The result is that not only are these refugees permanently stuck in camps, their children are as well. With each generation, more refugees are created.

---

[53] United Nations Relief and Works Agency for Palestine Refugees in the Near East, "Annual Operations Report 2020," August 10, 2021, https://www.unrwa.org/resources/about-unrwa/annual-operational-report-2020 (accessed October 21, 2024); UN High Commission for Refugees, "Figures at a glance," https://www.unhcr.org/en-us/figures-at-a-glance.html (accessed October 21, 2024); and UN High Commission for Refugees, "History of UNHCR," https://www.unhcr.org/en-us/history-of-unhcr.html (accessed October 21, 2024).

The results are as predictable as they are startling. Over time, the number of registered "refugees" entitled to UNRWA funding and assistance has risen substantially. In the 1950s, the highest estimate put the number at 860,000 souls; as of 2020, that figure is 5.7 million. In fact, according to UNRWA, their number is significantly higher than all the Palestinians who lived in Palestine in 1948. Indeed, the number of people alive today who were considered refugees when UNRWA was founded is actually rather miniscule.

The consequences are absurd. Many of the UNRWA-defined "Palestine refugees" are in their twenties and thirties, lead normal lives in Arab or Western countries, have academic degrees, and enjoy decent incomes. Neither they nor their parents were forced to flee their homes, but according to UNRWA they are still refugees and entitled to international aid. But most important—on top of their demand for an independent state—the Palestinians continue to demand a "right of return" for millions of refugees to homes inside Israel, to cities like Safed, Jaffa, Lod, and Haifa. This demand, supported by the framework and heavy funding of the United Nations, is obviously one of the biggest obstacles to peace.

UNRWA is not a passive player in all of this. Its offices and spokespeople are, in effect, an arm of the pro-Palestinian movement. Take, for example, UNRWA's approach to education. Palestinian schoolchildren, studying in UNRWA schools, are given textbooks filled with hatred of Israel, with antisemitism and pure racism, as well as with terror-supporting messages. In addition, some UNRWA schools in Gaza have served as storage facilities for Hamas weapons—rockets whose entire purpose is to target Israeli civilians. During Operation Protective Edge in 2014, Hamas used schools as rocket launchpads, UN health clinics as ammunition depots, and UNRWA offices as terror command posts. There was, of course, no acknowledgment or protest from UNRWA. When the IDF struck an UNRWA school that had been converted into a rocket warehouse, the United Nations reacted angrily and set up a commission of inquiry, despite Israel's unambiguous evidence about the site.

In the Gaza war that began in October 2023, UNRWA's complicity in Hamas's atrocities was revealed for the whole world to see. In addition to allowing Hamas to use its schools and other facilities for terror operations and weapons storage, evidence emerged that dozens of UNRWA employees took part in the atrocities themselves or were directly involved in keeping Israeli hostages. A lawsuit filed in Manhattan in early 2024 revealed, moreover, that UNRWA chiefs in Gaza were fully aware, and failed to report, that Hamas had siphoned off more than $1 billion in humanitarian aid for military purposes.

Unfortunately, the Human Rights Council and UNRWA are only the most glaring examples. Though some UN bodies have been hijacked primarily for the anti-Israel cause, other bodies, which are normally dedicated to good causes, nonetheless find the time and resources to take up the fight.

Take, for example, the United Nations Children's Fund (UNICEF), which is entrusted with the sacred mission of protecting children. In 2013, UNICEF published a report called "Children in Israeli Military Detention," which accused Israel of the "widespread, systematic, and institutionalized" abuse of Palestinian minors in detention. This choice of words was no coincidence. The idea was to describe Israel's actions using the language of international law, for the purpose of assembling a legal case against the Jewish state. These words were addressed directly to the chief prosecutor of the International Criminal Court (ICC) in The Hague, with the aim of turning the report into an indictment against Israel, since the phrase "systematic and widespread" alludes to the burden of proof for the crime of Apartheid.[54] The report was written by local UN staff: Palestinians on the organization's payroll with no pretense of objectivity. But typically for the United Nations, far too often and especially in the case of Israel, the information was never double checked, as is common procedure with other countries and in different types of reports. Nor did Israel get the opportunity to respond to the manufactured allegations. The report became an official, ostensibly objective, UN document.

Or consider a resolution from May 2016 by an organization considered to be entirely professional in its essence—the World Health Organization

[54] Pursuant to Article 7 of the Rome Statute (2002), the charter of the International Criminal Court at the Hague.

(WHO). The WHO, which is a UN agency, adopted a resolution titled "Health conditions in the occupied Palestinian territory, including east Jerusalem, and in the occupied Syrian Golan." It accused Israel alone of "human rights violations" affecting "mental, physical and environmental health" in these areas. The resolution was sponsored by the Arab states in collaboration with the Palestinian UN delegation; and among those voting in favor were not just Iran, Venezuela, and Syria, but also many Europeans nations, including Britain, France, and Germany.

Like many anti-Israel resolutions, this resolution has also been brought up for a vote every year since it was first introduced in 2008. Another example concerns Israel's truly heroic efforts to help victims of the brutality inflicted by the Assad regime during the Syrian civil war. At the same time that Israel opened a special hospital on its border with Syria to treat the same people that Assad's forces tried to kill, as Israel was welcoming into its land Syrian women and children against whom Assad had used chemical weapons, the WHO saw fit to condemn Israel for the medical conditions on the Golan. Yes, it went after the country that saved Syrian people and gave a free pass to the country that killed Syrian people.

The WHO knows perfectly well that the Israeli healthcare system is among the best in the world by global standards—the Bloomberg Global Health Index, for example, ranked it tenth in the world in 2020.[55] It is also fully aware that as a result of their cooperation with Israel, the health conditions of the Palestinians has been dramatically improved.[56] But at the United Nations, professionalism and politics are two parallel universes, and the organization's bodies do not shy from abusing their professional standing, structures, and mechanisms for political purposes—and no political purpose is more widely embraced than attacking Israel.

But all of these are merely the most visible aspects of the UN's systemic institutional bias against the Jewish state. Less known is that the

---

[55] WorldHealth.net, "Bloomberg's Global Health Index for 2020," June 18, 2020, https://worldhealth.net/news/bloombergs-global-health-index-2020/ (accessed October 21, 2024).

[56] Ben-Dror Yemini, *Industry of Lies: Media, Academia, and the Israeli-Arab Conflict* (The Institute for the Study of Global Antisemitism & Policy, 2017).

UN has a special committee dedicated to what it calls "The Exercise of the Inalienable Rights of the Palestinian People." Not that the UN ever thought that the Jewish people had inalienable rights. Among the great activities of this committee is the annual International Day of Solidarity with the Palestinian People. Just so you know how cynical the UN is, that day is held on November 29—the day in 1947 when the UN voted to establish a Palestinian State next to a Jewish State—a resolution that the Palestinians rejected.

Nor is this committee alone. A special division of the UN Department for Political and Peacebuilding Affairs (DPA) is dedicated to Palestinian rights, and there's even a dedicated United Nations Information System on the Question of Palestine. I challenge anyone to find the basic information in that system that indicates that the Palestinians could have had a state back in 1948, had they wanted it.

Last, but definitely not least: the UN special rapporteurs and envoys. Time after time it seems that the UN goes out of its way to find people who are already severely biased against Israel to investigate the Jewish state. I won't even go into the fact that the UN always feels the need to investigate Israel and not Hamas, Fatah, and the other terror organizations that instigate the violence. For years, the UN special rapporteur on human rights in Palestinian territories was Richard Falk, a man who, among his other merits, argued repeatedly that the Bush administration was secretly behind the 9/11 attacks. In 2021, after Operation Guardian of the Walls, the UN chose a South African lawyer named Navi Pillay to head the probe. Pillay used to head the UN Human Rights Council, where she blithely ignored human rights violations around the world and focused most of her energy condemning Israel claiming that Israel exercised "apartheid" and "egregious violations of human rights" against the Palestinians and war crimes in Gaza. In 2012, a bipartisan letter of the US House Committee on Foreign Affairs condemned her for her "repeated inaction with respect to human rights abuses, while engaging in biased efforts against Israel and other Western democracies."[57]

[57] UN Watch, letter to Ambassador Susan E. Rice, from Representatives Ileana Ros-Lehtinen (R-FL) and Eliot L. Engel (D-NY), May 24, 2012, https://unwatch.org/

When it comes to Israel, the UN tends to drop all pretense of impartiality. In many cases, it doesn't even bother pretending otherwise.

***

It is against this backdrop of the permanent, severe structural and institutional bias against Israel that our enemies find the ideal conditions for conducting what can only be called diplomatic warfare.

For decades, dating back to the Cold War alliance between the Soviet Union and the Arab states and continuing to this day, UN institutions have been allocating money and providing jobs for the purpose of writing anti-Israel reports, holding seminars promoting anti-Israel agendas, and adopting reams of biased resolutions—all with the aim of constricting Israel, undermining its legitimacy, defeating its spirit, weakening it position, and ultimately undoing the achievements of 1948. As we have seen, this extends to fully hijacking certain bodies—like the UNHRC and UNRWA—or compelling otherwise well-meaning bodies to pay lip-service to the hatred of Israel demanded by the anti-Israel bloc—as is the case with UNICEF, the WHO, UNESCO and many others. These organizations' reports on developments in Gaza and the West Bank are written by UN employees from around the world, but mainly by local Palestinians, including some who are affiliated with organizations that support or even conduct terror. Everybody knows exactly what the reports will say before even a single word has been written.

Carl von Clausewitz, the legendary early-nineteenth-century Prussian general, once described war as "the continuation of politics by other means." In my various positions, especially at the United Nations, I discovered that the converse is true as well—that the politics of diplomacy can be a continuation of war through other means. And in this war, we at Israel's UN mission were at the front lines.

The events I experienced at the United Nations were neither one-offs nor accidental, but part of a comprehensive and sustained campaign

wp-content/uploads/2022/03/Bipartisan-Letter-on-Navi-PillayS-anti-Israel-bias-May-24-2012-1.pdf (accessed October 21, 2024).

of diplomatic warfare, rooted in a calculated strategy on the part of the Palestinians and their cheerleaders.

Although diplomatic warfare has always been an important tool in the fight against Israel, in recent years it has taken a conspicuously central role. This is mainly because of the historical failure of other methods.

The war against Israel has been fought in stages. From the UN Partition plan in 1947 until the Yom Kippur War of 1973, it was led by the Arab states, mostly with Soviet backing, which sought to bring Israel down by military force, and included dozens of operations, hundreds of terror attacks, and five wars. It met its symbolic demise with the 1979 peace treaty with Egypt.

In the second stage of this struggle, beginning in the early 1970s, the Arabs focused their war on two main tactics: terrorism and economic warfare. Major assaults, such as the murder of Israeli athletes at the Munich Olympics or the hijacking of airplanes in the 1970s, were met with stern worldwide opposition and failed to achieve significant political gains. More effective, if briefly, were economic boycotts and an oil embargo against the West, triggering the global energy crisis of the 1970s. OPEC became a player on the geopolitical stage, cutting production and raising prices. Greatly enriched, the Arab bloc directed pressure against many African states, which had enjoyed flourishing diplomatic and economic relations with Israel. The pressure forced them to completely sever ties with Israel, following the near-compulsory recommendation of the Organization of African Unity (now called the African Union).

But at the end of the day, this, too, fell short. The world reduced its dependence on Arab oil, the United States flexed its own economic muscle when it illegalized participation in boycotts against Israel, and the Arab states lost much of their power to bully others. By the end of the 1980s, the Soviet Union was collapsing, and the Arabs lost their superpower patron. Israel continued to develop economically, technologically, and commercially.

The third stage of the offensive unfolded during the second half of the 1990s and the first decade of the new millennium, when the Palestinians intensified their fight against Israel by means of terror—including the new tactic of suicide bombings. Although Palestinians signed the Oslo Accords with Israel in 1993, this didn't prevent them from building their terror arsenal. If anything, it gave them far more resources and freedom to do so. From late 1995 until May 1996, Palestinian groups like Fatah, Hamas, and Islamic Jihad launched a series of gruesome terror attacks, including suicide bombings in public buses and coffee shops. The same strategy returned with a vengeance in the early 2000s, with the second intifada: a far more vicious round of suicide bombings and other attacks which killed more than 1,000 Israelis.

Following the Israeli withdrawal from the Gaza Strip in 2005 and the Hamas takeover the following year, the strip turned into a major base of terror operations that included the launching of rockets into Israeli population centers and the digging of underground "terror tunnels" for crossing the border to kidnap or murder civilians—both of which were met with rounds of military retaliations, as well as Israeli technological solutions including the Iron Dome anti-rocket system and, most recently, a sophisticated anti-tunnel system that includes an underground barrier and sensors along the entire Gaza border.

In 2023, Hamas's terror kingdom launched what may (we may hope) be its final assault on Israel, an unprecedented invasion involving thousands of terrorists, killing more than 1,200 Israelis and triggering the most destructive retaliation in Gaza ever undertaken by Israel. It is too early to fully assess the results, but it seems clear that, at a minimum, it has brought extreme hardship to Gazans, no serious strategic or political achievements for the Palestinians, and a radical diminishment of Hamas's fighting capability.

In recent years, terrorism has failed to achieve strategic benefits for the Palestinians, but the diplomatic war has raged on. The ends are the same, but the means have become more sophisticated and therefore—in the long run—more dangerous. With the signing of the Abraham Accords in 2020, the failure of the old strategies has become overwhelmingly evident. The creation of a warm peace with the UAE, Bahrain, and Morocco has dealt a blow to the rejectionist strategy at least as great as the peace with Egypt.

What the Abraham Accords revealed is that the Palestinians today no longer have the unified backing of the Arab world. Sure, there is still plenty of lip service paid to the Palestinian cause. But the days when the Palestinians could count on militarily powerful Arab states for significant material support for violence against Israelis are, more or less, over. Yes, Hamas received funding from Qatar, acting it seems at Iran's behest. But 10/7 ultimately has proven to be just another, if spectacular and belated, failure to destroy Israel through violence. All the Palestinians have left now are the diplomatic, economic, and legal approaches in their fight against the Jewish state—and they have pursued them with everything they've got.

The purpose of Palestinian diplomatic warfare, it should be clear, is not to achieve peace. It is not about mounting pressure as a negotiating tactic towards getting the best deal possible. It is, rather, to wage a permanent war, whether through delegitimization, boycotts, or the creation of a Palestinian state without accepting the Jewish state of Israel or its basic security needs. Such a state would not only include internationally dictated borders and a capital in Jerusalem, but also the influx of millions of UNRWA-defined Palestinian "refugees," spelling the end of Israel as the nation-state of the Jewish people and its *de facto* destruction. This diplomatic warfare offensive has included filing war crimes complaints against Israel at the International Criminal Court at The Hague, trying to get it on commercial blacklists and travel bans, and lobbying states to impose sanctions.

Over the years, Israel has expended vast resources in fighting terror and conventional warfare, developing world-leading expertise in cutting-edge military methods from counterterrorism to drones to cyberwarfare, but it has invested precious little in the diplomatic war. Consequently, it is lagging far behind its foes in both budgetary allocations and strategic planning. The Palestinians raised and spent hundreds of millions of dollars in adapting to the ever-changing vocabulary of Western civil rights discourse, and branding themselves as victims while Israel gazed helplessly at the international institutions dragging it into diplomatic rearguard battles.

Reports like the Goldstone Report, commissions of inquiry, attempts to arrest Israeli officials abroad, boycotts of Israeli goods, and the deplatforming of Israeli lecturers at universities around the world represent just a few of the successes of the Palestinians' diplomatic warfare. Time and again Israel finds itself getting kicked around, forced to deploy its finest lawyers and produce evidence of its own right to live. It is floundering in quicksand.

I do not use the term "diplomatic warfare" lightly. Terror and conventional warfare against Israel have an immediate objective: to kill as many Israelis as possible. Israel is all too familiar with buses exploding in city centers and with other murderous acts that have created thousands of bereaved families. But conventional warfare, and especially terror, also have other, longer-term objectives: to sow a feeling of helplessness among the Israeli population, and to force political change by sparking a global and internal Israeli debate about the justice of Israel's very existence. Terrorists aim to upend public opinion in Israel and divide it over questions of morality, justice, and Israel's place in the world. Diplomatic warfare has the exact same long-term ends, only through different means.

Diplomatic warfare is less spectacular, and therefore more insidious. While conventional warfare leaves a trail of blood and burnt metal in its wake, diplomatic warfare leaves a trail of resolutions, legal precedents, and international documents, which continue to preoccupy Israel and its institutions years later. As every law school freshman learns, precedent is the best means of setting norms. What begins as a Palestinian anti-Israel initiative morphs into a set of international norms, which are henceforth cited in international statements and quoted in academia and the media. International conventions concerning human rights and war crimes have clauses inserted into them, under pressure from the anti-Israel bloc, deliberately aimed at targeting Israel and then serving as proof of Israel's alleged criminality. Israel thus risks being defined as a rogue state and serial violator of international law—not just because of its actions, but because of its very existence.

Whatever the Palestinians and their supporters claim, the goal of diplomatic warfare is not to promote a peace settlement between Israel and its neighbors. It is a call to frame all forms of terror as legitimate "resistance" against Israel, which is the "root cause" of all violence, and to paint it in the international mindset as *inherently* responsible for war crimes and crimes against humanity.

In other words, their goal is not to make propaganda. They make propaganda to achieve their ultimate goal of "liberating" all of Palestine by undermining international support for Israel and undermining Israel's domestic morale.

It is all entrenched in layer upon layer of legal, cultural, and political narratives, built and maintained over more than seven decades, hiding behind every imaginable form of virtue signaling, and headquartered in the vast moral catacombs of the United Nations.

***

There is an accusation, repeated *ad nauseum* despite being entirely wrong, according to which every legitimate criticism against Israel is tagged immediately as diplomatic warfare. This is nonsense, but it requires elaboration.

How can you tell the difference between legitimate criticism and diplomatic warfare? I would suggest there are three simple tests.

The first is how it compares to criticism of other states. Does the United Nations pass similar resolutions and voice similar criticism in relation to comparable or worse conduct by other states, democracies and non-democracies alike? If the answer is no, then we are talking about diplomatic warfare.

The second is the systematic, coordinated *pattern* of falsehoods. Anti-Israel activities are generally part of a recurring set of organized operations—a flood of joined-up similar initiatives creating a kind of echo chamber of mutual validation. Consider, for example, the passage of three consecutive resolutions by the WHO (May 2016), the UN Security Council (December 2016), and UNESCO (May 2017), which all either denied Israel's connections to the Temple Mount and Jerusalem or accused it of violating Palestinians' rights there. This was not "legitimate criticism" around a temporary issue. It was, rather, a coordinated campaign around a specific falsehood. The dots clearly connected. In parallel, the campaign spreads the falsehood throughout the international arena, academia, and the media. It is not a battle *for* the rights of the Palestinian people, but *against* the right of the Jewish people to live in their homeland, by denying fundamental truths about the Jewish past.

The third respect is its effort to effect long-term structural change in the perception of Israel or the criteria through which it is judged. This includes not only the development of new narratives but also new norms. Most of these activities are part of a protracted campaign, with repercussions that will be felt for years. Their purpose is to build a criminal file against Israel at international institutions, including the International Criminal Court.

The diplomatic war on Israel—like the conventional and terror wars that came before—will ultimately fail. It is not an imminent existential threat to Israel, the way an Iranian nuclear weapon would be, but it is a real threat with existential goals and strategic-level effects. The success of the Palestinians' war must be judged at different levels of Israel's functioning: its economy, society, international ties, relations with Diaspora Jewry, tourism, higher education, culture, science, and technology. These are all suffering already and may yet suffer further if Israel fails to invest in the fight.

***

When I became Israel's ambassador to the United Nations, it was clear that my first priority was to alter the course of the diplomatic war by returning fire and foiling anti-Israel campaigns. My doctrine rested on constant initiative, prevention and deterrence by going on offense, and national dignity. Taking the initiative meant using the UN stage to emphasize Israel's strengths and contributions to the world; going on the offensive meant taking proactive measures against those who wished us harm; and national dignity meant no more apologies—we would represent Israel out of a conviction in the truth and justice of its cause.

All of Israel's UN ambassadors over the years had encountered structural and institutional bias against Israel and had fought against it, day and night. I respected them deeply and learned a great deal from many of them. During my tenure, I tried to build on their work by introducing a more assertive and explicit operational doctrine—one that brought us into more frequent confrontation with UN officials and ambassadors who were acting against Israel's national interests.

Together with members of Israel's UN delegation, I formulated a simple, comprehensive strategy that was inspired by the examples of Israel's greatest diplomats of the past: If we wished to be perceived as a legitimate state in the family of nations, we would have to behave like one. If in the past it meant insisting on the symbols and signs of an independent state that the world would need to get used to, today it meant playing up and down the length of the UN field, not just defending the goalposts.

I took lessons from other forms of Israeli warfare. Like traditional counterterrorism, for example, the effort would require coordinated operations guided by strategic thinking. This included, first and foremost, planning intelligence-based diplomatic offensives to thwart and deter diplomatic attacks. It would require leveraging personal contacts for reconnaissance, cross-referencing intelligence with other information from the international arena and the Israeli intelligence community, and building an offensive diplomatic strategy incorporating an array of tactics and techniques, such as the careful use of traditional and social media.

We applied the doctrine of countering diplomatic warfare, for example, in 2015, when UN officials tried to surreptitiously add Israel to a blacklist of violators of children's rights in conflict zones alongside ISIS and al- Qaeda. The report with the blacklist is an annual publication from the Office of the Special Representative of the UN Secretary-General for Children and Armed Conflict. The 2015 report was written by special envoy Leila Zerrougui, an Algerian, who had set herself the objective of blacklisting Israel for its alleged conduct during Operation Protective Edge in 2014. She and her staff worked behind the scenes, without informing Israel or any of the professional actors in the field, and without requesting an official response to her allegations.

Personal connections are among the most important and basic tools in any diplomat's toolbox. In this case, the Israeli mission's legal advisor, Amit Hoyman, received a crucial heads-up about Zerrougui's plan. We realized that we were facing a diplomatic assault that would drag our government into an international legal battle. To prevent it, we would need to mount a complex, multi-arena, cross-organizational, international response. My team and I did so on two main fronts, initiating both preventative and offensive action. We put out a "diplomatic warfare alert" to notify all the relevant actors in Israel and to rally them to action. We also reached out to diplomatic missions of friendly states to corroborate the intelligence.

On the preventative front, we aimed to delay the report's publication and thwart Israel's inclusion on the blacklist. We did so by getting UN Secretary-General Ban Ki-moon, who had appointed Zerrougui as his special envoy, to dispute her improper working methods and the integrity of her report. I appealed personally to Samantha Power, the U.S. ambassador to the United Nations, and to US National Security Advisor Susan Rice, who had been my counterpart for two years as Power's predecessor. I sent them both a terse and forceful message: "Zerrougui is exploiting the UN stage to pull off a major anti-Israel heist, which will cause long-term damage. It is your responsibility to stop her." President Obama was in the middle of his second term, and his administration was still trying to placate Israel in the international arena in the hope of resuscitating Israeli-Palestinian peace talks. The Americans listened attentively and were furious that Zerrougui's office had kept them out of the loop. At the same time, to guarantee that the message reached President Obama himself, I conveyed an urgent request to Prime Minister Benjamin Netanyahu: *Please discuss this directly with Obama.* Netanyahu obliged.

I also appealed to Ban Ki-moon and demanded that he put an end to the anti-Israel incitement and biased reports. I reminded him that as his special representative, Zerrougui was his subordinate, and that his failure to prevent the report's publication would be a personal shortcoming. Zerrougui's secretive working methods, I insinuated, confirmed that her motives were far from professional and that she was trying to deliberately circumvent him. The message got through.

The offensive front was more public. Despite the challenging media environment for Israel after Operation Protective Edge, I launched a media campaign against Zerrougui and criticized her ferociously in the international press. It is natural to retaliate against anyone who attacks you, but this is practically taboo at the United Nations, where the convention is not to publicly criticize UN officials for doing their jobs. I rejected that convention. Public officials all over the world, whether appointed or elected, should be subject to public scrutiny and accountability, and there is no reason to make UN officials an exception to this rule.

Zerrougui retaliated by leaking to the media that the Israeli ambassador was pressuring the UN secretary-general to scrap a "professional" UN report. On my end, I kept reminding everyone who asked that despite her nationality, as a UN official, Zerrougui was supposed to represent the United Nations, not just the government of Algeria. At the same time, by a remarkable coincidence, reporters started publicly questioning Zerrougui's professional integrity as a senior UN official in light of her undeniable anti-Israel bias.

Our efforts bore fruit: Zerrougui's report was published, but Israel was kept off the blacklist. Had we not mounted our campaign, we would have surely woken up one morning to the news of a diplomatic attack, and the United Nations would have made the anti-Israel report into an annual ritual, using it to justify other anti-Israel resolutions and actions, including possible sanctions.

The Zerrougui report and many other episodes at the United Nations underscored to me that just as conventional battles require intensive ground operations, so do diplomatic battles. The goal is to foil anti-Israel plots by remaining both vigilant and active, launching focused preemptive strikes, gathering valuable intelligence in real time, and always safeguarding your nation's honor.

Ultimately the doctrine I initiated at the UN focused on five key elements, which I share both for the benefit of future diplomats and also to give a deeper understanding of the kind of work that has become a central component of Zionist diplomacy and will likely remain so for the foreseeable future.

First: Go on offense.

Like the Polish cavalry facing the German war machine at the onset of World War II, Israel often has shown up to diplomatic tank battles on horseback. As a result, it spends most of the time playing defense, failing to define its criteria for victory and not always fully understanding its mission.

My first priority as Israel's UN ambassador was to overhaul everyone's thinking and habits within the Israeli mission. For years, Israel's default mode during UN debates had been—in the diplomatic tradition—to listen, absorb, dutifully write everything down, and send long-winded cables back to Jerusalem. Our diplomats also suffered from a long-ingrained professional reticence. Reacting immediately to every attack creates unpleasant situations. It exposes the speaker to criticism and increases the likelihood of mistakes. To react immediately requires diplomats to shoot from the hip self-confidently and with a total mastery of the facts, to be unhesitating and unapologetic.

This is no trifling matter. As most people know from their work and social lives, it is never easy to be a lone voice in the wilderness against conventional wisdom. It is even harder at the United Nations, where diplomats who express positions outside the consensus may find themselves sidelined in debates, while those who embrace the groupthink are embraced.

My fellow UN ambassadors from other countries often told me, "Ron, drop it—you're one of us, a like-minded democrat with the same values and moral standards as us. It's the Arabs we have no expectations from." The offer on the table was clear: Make this small concession on the text we're negotiating, and we'll keep seeing you as one of our own.

Time and again, I urged my fellow diplomats at the Israeli mission to keep fighting, even if it meant being excluded from polite society at the United Nations. We did not need to win anyone's affection, but their respect. Experience had taught me that even those who disagreed with us respected us more when we adhered to our principles than when we folded in the hope of fitting in.

When I entered the role of ambassador, I announced that from now on, our default mode would be to respond in real time to every attack on Israel. Any decision to hold back because of professional or political sensitivities would require my express prior approval, and such permission would be granted sparingly. I promised my colleagues that I would personally lead this new approach in my appearances at the main UN organs—the General Assembly and the Security Council—and I would give my full backing to anyone who made mistakes in that context. The idea was to encourage action and discourage inertia, writing off the cost of the inevitable mistakes along the way.

We put this idea into practice by maximizing our "right of response," the UN procedural rule governing the right to a final say in public sessions, which serves to guarantee that every voice gets heard. In every forum where Israel had a seat, we immediately signed up for a right of response before a single word was uttered. Sometimes anti-Israel allegations cropped up in debates on such unrelated issues as global warming. Our goal was to stay alert and ensure that no anti-Israel statement went unchallenged.

In order to optimize our response in each of the hundreds of domains in which Israel is assailed at the United Nations, we divided our team members by fields of expertise and created printed talking points that encompassed all the main topics under debate. Is Israel violating women's rights? Is Israel polluting the oceans? Is Israel abusing children? Please, come and hear the truth about Israel and its neighbors. When the distortions are cast aside, Israel comes out on top. Sometimes telling the truth is the best option, even at the United Nations.

We compiled a separate list of the languages spoken by members of the Israeli mission. Pride of place was given to diplomats who spoke Arabic, an official language of the United Nations—a fact that we leveraged to our advantage. I instructed my people to respond to envoys in their own language. The envoys from Arab and European states, and audiences watching the livestream of UN debates from home, were astonished to hear pro-Israel remarks and criticism of the Arab world's corruption, violence, and incitement *in Arabic* from Israeli diplomats.

Soon enough, we noticed a change for the better. The feeling of success boosted morale in the delegation. We also observed a discernible numerical drop in attacks by Arab ambassadors against Israel. The moment we started grabbing the microphone at every forum, Israel's detractors understood that we were going to hold them to account. The fiery glare of the spotlight quickly turned on them, and no envoy wished to receive a stern phone call from his capital asking why his country had suddenly become the focus of UN debates.

Humor proved especially useful. Fresh in the role, I approached the Palestinian envoy, Riyad Mansour, as he left a debate about Israel at the Security Council and headed towards the microphones outside. "Mansour, Mansour," I said, looming behind him, "every time you approach the microphone, take a look over your shoulder. I'll be there to refute your lies."

Creativity was one of our sharpest tools in our battle for attention. In a world awash in information, we had to reinvent ourselves every day to stand out against other headlines and eye-catching pictures. One European ambassador at the Security Council even told me that his political counsellor had said he would be late for a delegation meeting because he wanted to hear some of "Ambassador Prosor's dark humor." Jeffrey Feltman, the UN undersecretary-general for political affairs and a former US State Department official who was often critical of Israel, wrote that he often found himself "reading draft UN statements, thinking about how proposed words would sound in Ron's sharply focused ears, and anticipating his probable reaction to the various formulas under consideration."

Second: Work both traditional and social media.

During Operation Protective Edge in 2014, when Hamas launched hundreds of rockets from the Gaza Strip and Israel came under an onslaught of diplomatic attacks, we coordinated our media efforts and made a point of using both traditional and social media—the latter of which, at the time, was still a new discipline in diplomatic circles. Hamas was systematically violating the intermittent ceasefires negotiated throughout the war as it tried to drag Israel into deeper entanglements. Ban Ki-moon, the UN secretary-general, did what the United Nations does best and called on both sides to exercise restraint, even though Israel had respected the ceasefire. By the umpteenth call for restraint since hostilities broke out, I could no longer bring myself to respond with the same tedious rigamarole of sending his office a letter. The outrageous injustice of the UN approach, and the mounting casualties on the Israeli side, called for a different kind of response.

One Friday afternoon, the secretary-general issued another of his routine calls for restraint. This time, the Israeli mission's talented and energetic spokesperson, Savion Medaleion, together with the equally creative Tal Dror, decided to wage a public diplomacy guerrilla campaign on the United Nations' Facebook page, which had more than one million followers. We replied to the secretary-general's statement with a post directly on the Facebook wall, skipping the formal diplomatic jargon:

> Dear UN,
>
> This morning you released a statement.
>
> Your statement said that you were disappointed that the parties were unable to agree to an extension of the ceasefire.
>
> I couldn't help but notice that you didn't mention one of the parties, which happens to be the party that violated the ceasefire.
>
> This party has a name—they are called Hamas.
>
> Hamas is our enemy.
>
> Let me introduce you to them.
>
> Many countries around the world designate Hamas as a terror organization.
>
> Hamas' charter calls for the destruction of the State of Israel.
>
> Hamas has fired over 3,000 rockets at Israel over the past month.
>
> They kidnap and kill children.
>
> They dig terror tunnels in order to carry out mass terrorist attacks.
>
> They breached all the ceasefires that Israel accepted.

> If I wasn't familiar with the UN, I would think this is a parody.
>
> But because I am familiar with the UN, I know this is a tragedy.

When we hit "post," it was late at night Israel time. The next morning, we woke up to discover thousands of likes and comments, mostly from ordinary Israelis who had effectively joined our public diplomacy campaign. Many had also made posts of their own, telling the UN secretary-general exactly what they thought about the organization's approach. The campaign quickly went viral, and we discovered the importance of using social media—creatively and with humor—to powerful effect. Today it may seem old hat, but at the time it was quite innovative, especially in the stodgy realms of international diplomacy. The point is not just what we did at the time, but to point out the need for constant innovation, constant learning of new means and methods.

Savion and Tal are important to this story for another reason, as well. I would be remiss if I did not make mention of the many extraordinary women who have played decisive, if not quite as famous, roles in the history of Zionist diplomacy. Best known, of course, is Golda Meir, who grew up in Milwaukee and Denver and served as one of the central leaders of the Yishuv before statehood, as foreign minister for a decade from 1956 to1966, before becoming prime minister in 1969. Ora Namir, a former government minister who served in the late 1990s as ambassador to China, contributed greatly to the expansion of relations with the world's most populous nation, including the first-ever visit of a Chinese president to Israel. And so many others, like Collette Avital, who served as ambassador to Portugal and then as consul general in New York before turning to politics, have made crucial contributions to Israel's diplomatic efforts. But despite the many hundreds of women who have served in our diplomatic corps, few have reached the top levels. This is a mistake that has undoubtedly harmed our national interest in countless ways, and which must be rectified.

But while the new media are crucial to the future of diplomacy, old-timers may rest assured—the traditional media are not dead. Nobody who has ever served as an ambassador in New York or London, which are both global media capitals, would rush to eulogize them. *New York Times* editorials are still read by millions, including world leaders. Interviews in the *Times* of London can be shared online hundreds of thousands of times and be cited by countless other outlets. *Financial Times* and *Wall Street Journal* articles attract attention from across the world of business and politics.

Let's take another example from the 2014 Gaza conflict. I realized that talking about Hamas's terror was not enough—people were growing tired of it. We decided to try a different angle, focusing on the financial infrastructure behind it. I called out Qatar, Hamas's biggest financial backer at the time, in an op-ed in *The New York Times*, published on August 24 with the headline: "Club Med for Terrorists."[58]

The idea came to us during the media frenzy of the war. I was giving several interviews a day to Israeli and international media, as part of a public diplomacy campaign conducted with the IDF spokesman, Israel's National Information Directorate, government ministers, and ambassadors. We all put ourselves forward to speak in every available broadcasting slot, at every hour of the day, lest a single TV studio be left without an Israeli presence. During one brief pause during an interview blitz, waiting in the lobby of the CNN studios at Columbus Circle in Manhattan, we decided that our role was to expose to the world not just the activities of terrorist organizations, as we had been doing on television, but also their supporters—chief among them Qatar. The idea became a wide-reaching diplomatic event. The op-ed resonated globally, with even Arabic media covering it, and journalists and diplomats at the United Nations started referring to Qatar as the "Club Med for terrorists."

A few weeks later, the Qatari ambassador to the United Nations met her Egyptian counterpart, Maged Abdelaziz, and told him that she

---

[58] Ron Prosor, "Club Med for Terrorists," *The New York Times*, August 25, 2014, Sec. A, p. 19, https://www.nytimes.com/2014/08/25/opinion/qatar-club-med-for-terrorists.html (accessed October 22, 2024).

preferred not to deliver another speech against Israel unless she absolutely had to. "Let others denounce Israel," she explained. "One speech isn't worth all the explanations I'm having to give the Foreign Ministry in Doha after the Israeli ambassador attacks us in *The New York Times*."

Third: Build personal relationships.

When I entered the United Nations, I was surprised at the camaraderie with which I was received by the other countries' envoys, including those with which Israel had no formal relations. We would have friendly conversations, and they would tell me of their profound admiration for Israel. Imagine how dumbstruck I was to then hear the same ambassadors vigorously denouncing my country in public just a few hours later. I decided to play the same game and separate my friendly personal relations with the other ambassadors from my searing responses to their public attacks against Israel. This often created absurd situations, in which I attacked a particular ambassador one morning and met him for coffee that same evening. That's the United Nations: *House of Cards*, international edition.

Personal relationships, however, are an investment that often pays off long after one has left a given post. Italy's ambassador to the United Nations at the time, Cesare Ragaglini, had been Italian Foreign Minister Franco Frattini's chief of staff when I held a parallel position for Israeli Foreign Minister Silvan Shalom. Sir Mark Justin Lyall Grant, the British ambassador to the UN, had previously served as director-general for political affairs of the UK Foreign Office when I was ambassador to London. The German ambassador to the UN, Harald Braun, had been my counterpart as his country's political counselor in Washington.

I had also forged personal ties with ambassadors from Arab states. The Egyptian ambassador, Maged Abdelaziz, had been President Hosni Mubarak's chief of staff for seven years, partly overlapping with my period as director-general of the Israeli Foreign Ministry. Mubarak was fond of Israel's foreign minister at the time, Silvan Shalom, and my collaboration with Abdelaziz was based on mutual respect. Years later, when we met again at the United Nations, we kept in close touch and often had lunch together. Obviously, I never deluded myself into thinking that warm personal ties with Abdelaziz and other Arab ambassadors hinted at their secret fondness for Israel, but they gave me a better understanding of trends in the Arab world. Such ties also matter for the purposes of diplomatic reconnaissance—receiving timely tips about diplomatic plots against Israel and understanding the prevailing mood in other countries and regional groups.

The United Nations had 193 member states when I reported for duty in 2011, and I asked to meet every ambassador who would oblige, including those of countries with which Israel had no diplomatic relations. Before every meeting, I reviewed the brief my team had prepared about them and their country. Every word that came out of my mouth was tailored specifically for a particular nation's interests. The German ambassador, for example, was interested in sanctions on Iran. The envoy of the Ivory Coast was interested in agricultural technology. I came to each meeting knowing that it could have an important impact on relations between our countries.

Two ambassadors were conspicuously absent from my calendar—those of Iran and Syria.

In my first weeks in New York, I understood that one of my central tasks was to leverage the organizational structure of the United Nations, and specifically the fact that every state has exactly one vote, to our advantage. Since Italy counted as much as the Ivory Coast, we did not neglect the smaller nations, applying an inverse function to our diplomatic algorithm. In business terms: Investing in smaller enterprises would yield greater returns. This was what we had in mind when we organized an event to salute the presidents of Micronesia, Palau, and the Marshall Islands during the General Assembly annual debate in September 2014. Israel had been the first country to recognize their independence from the United States thirty years earlier and to understand their significance at UN votes.

Israel's troubles in the Middle East are rarely the top priority for smaller, resource-scarce states. Their votes on Israel-related resolutions are often up to the personal discretion of the ambassador, who is not always acquainted with the issues. I discovered that in such cases, often an important element in an ambassador's considerations on how to vote was our personal relationship, not the content of the vote itself.

Sometimes these personal relationships gave me moments of relief at an organization that mostly gave me grief. Before one important vote, I approached one Latin American ambassador with whom I had developed a cordial friendship. "Are you with us?" I asked him.

"Of course!" he replied.

"So will you vote for us?"

"Of course not."

I asked him why and was astonished to hear how much pressure the Arab states were exerting to sway his vote. I looked at him. He looked at me.

"You look unwell," I said. "Perhaps you might have to end up skipping the vote, on account of your illness?"

The ambassador took a long look at me, then started laughing. "You're right, Ron, I think I'm feeling a bit under the weather," he said, coughing. "Maybe it's the flu." He was absent from the show of hands the following day, and a single vote moved from the "ayes" to the abstentions.

During my round of introductory meetings, I headed out to meet the Ivory Coast ambassador and was told there was no need to drive—the Ivorian mission was just a few floors below Israel's in the same building. I stepped into the ambassador's office. "Nice to meet you," I said. "I'm Ron Prosor."

"I'm Ambassador Youssoufou Bamba," he said, extending his hand warmly.

A huge grin spread across my face. "Ambassador Bamba, you might not know it," I said, "but every child in Israel knows your name." The ambassador was surprised and smiled politely.

The next day, I returned to his office with a crate full of packets of Bamba—the peanut-butter puffs beloved by Israeli children. Bamba burst into laughter. We became close friends. He briefed me, helped me with key votes, and opened doors for me with other African ambassadors. In one special meeting, I surprised the Tanzanian ambassador by revealing that I had lived in his nation's capital, Dar es-Salaam, when I was eight years old, the son of a diplomat posted there. I have magical childhood memories from Tanzania, which I eagerly shared.

But my first and most important meeting in New York was, naturally, with Susan Rice. Meeting the ambassador of Israel's greatest strategic ally, the United States, demanded meticulous preparation covering issues of vital importance to Israel's national security, and a good working relationship was key. Rice is a tough, straight-talking, unimpeachably honest individual. She had been a member of President Obama's original team long before he was elected—she was his confidante, a member of his cabinet, and a friend of First Lady Michelle Obama. She was also a consistent critic of Israeli policy, and especially of Prime Minister Benjamin Netanyahu and Foreign Minister Avigdor Liberman, and my uncompromising defense of the Israeli side often pushed our conversations up the decibel range.

The first meeting with Rice went well, although she was on the more critical flank of the Obama administration when it came to the US-Israel relationship. When the White House demanded that Israel apologize to Turkey for the *Mavi Marmara* incident, for example, Rice made it abundantly clear to me that an apology was not only essential for Israel, in her view, but an American interest vis-à-vis Turkey. "Every now and then, you could do something to help U.S. interests," she lectured me once. "We do so much for you and pay a heavy price for doing so."

Rice also accepted the Palestinian narrative of the weak against the strong, with the implication that we would have to make major concessions. To my view, her approach did not always take into account the bigger picture, which included the Palestinians' incitement, violence, and avoidance of negotiations. Yet despite our differences, our first meeting was successful and started a fruitful and positive professional relationship, based on mutual respect, honesty, and admiration for each other's insistence on our country's national interests.

Fourth: Aggressively seek UN posts of influence.

When I arrived at the United Nations, I stumbled across Yuri Fedotov, the former Russian ambassador to Britain, with whom I overlapped during my service in London. Fedotov, it turned out, had been picked to head the UN Office on Drugs and Crime in Vienna, and came to New York on a professional visit. Fedotov and I had been friendly, and I was happy to see him again. Next to him was Dmitry, his political counsellor from London. "What's Dmitry doing here?" I asked.

Fedotov smiled. "There was rigorous competition for the role of my chief of staff in the UN Office on Drugs and Crime in Vienna," he said sarcastically. "And by complete coincidence, Dmitry got the job." But this was no coincidence. Diplomats tend to move between posts with their trusted advisors. The former Egyptian envoy Maged Abdelaziz, in his new job as the secretary-general's special advisor on Africa, was also surrounded by Egyptian officials who just "happened" to pass the interview committee. This is the United Nations' *modus operandi*, a productive arrangement for states to safeguard their interests.

Appointments at the UN Secretariat and the various committees are made on a quota basis, and all member states are entitled to representation in the United Nations' professional organs. But as always, there is one rule for regular member states and another for Israel. I quickly discovered that we would have to fight for our legitimate place at the table even at the "neutral" Secretariat.

I told my team that we would start lobbying for Israelis to be appointed to various positions in the UN Secretariat. We would bid for every role, committee, and sub-committee that we could, even if we were rarely going to win.

We fought for every position that opened up—including for myself. I was elected vice president of the General Assembly and had the honor of calling up Israel's prime minister to speak when, in September 2012, Netanyahu delivered his famous speech about the Iranian nuclear program, in which he held up a cartoon bomb to illustrate Iran's progress.

This strategy was put to the test in February 2014, when it was the turn of Israel's regional group to nominate a deputy chairperson for the Fourth Committee, which deals with special political affairs and decolonization. The Fourth Committee is a particular source of angst for Israel, responsible for almost half of the anti-Israel resolutions produced by the General Assembly. It goes without saying that the Fourth Committee, like the General Assembly itself, is controlled by a majority formed around the Arab bloc. The moment I was told about the election for the deputy chairmanship, we decided to go for it, against the advice of the Foreign Ministry, which was worried about the optics of losing the vote. This may make sense in domestic politics, but, at the UN, if you don't try, you will never succeed.

After an intensive diplomatic campaign, WEOG chose Motti Amichai, an experienced diplomat and Israel's former consul in Istanbul, as its candidate for the role of deputy chairman of the Fourth Committee. The Arabs declared war on his nomination and used every weapon in their arsenal to torpedo his appointment. They applied pressure on WEOG and made threats against UN institutions, including threats to cut funding. The Israeli mission fought on every front for the Israeli candidacy, even against members of the Western group itself, who nearly succumbed to the Arab pressure campaign and backtracked on the nomination. Eventually Amichai was elected to the post.

We also resolved that Israel should have a foothold in the Fifth Committee, the United Nations' budget committee and *de facto* treasury. Few states invest much effort in this committee, because its business sometimes sounds grey and dreary compared to more "sexy" institutions like the Security Council. Israel had also not always noticed its latent potential; only in recent years has the penny dropped that the Fifth Committee can be used to influence the entire organization. In 2015, we nominated Yotam Goren, a young and energetic Israeli diplomat, for the role of deputy chairman. He was duly elected as the first Israeli to hold the post. With time, the Israeli representative on the committee became one of the most diligent gatekeepers of the United Nations' administration, able to ensure the probity of the organization's budget while representing Israeli interests in the UN budget, positions, and other resources. Another successful appointment was that of a high-ranking IDF intelligence officer, Major Jonathan Conricus, to a key role in the UN Office of Military Affairs which runs the UN's global peacekeeping operations. It was the first time an Israeli had filled such a role.

Not all our efforts met with success, of course. An intensive campaign to nominate Shimon Peres to serve as the first Israeli undersecretary-general of the UN, in the post of special envoy for peace and innovation, ran aground. We felt our chances were actually quite good—Peres, after all, had been instrumental in getting Ban Ki-moon elected as secretary-general, and the United States supported Peres's candidacy. These were not enough, however, to overcome Arab opposition in the mind of the secretary-general—a weakness of resolve he had displayed on several occasions with regard to Israel.

At the same time, our efforts proved how unfounded the Foreign Ministry's fears of the "optics of failure" were. We lost nothing, and in fact made it clear that Israel would insist on putting forward candidates for every position at the UN, no matter how lofty.

These efforts continued to bear fruit after I left. In 2017, Danny Danon was appointed ambassador, as I had been, to serve as one of the twenty-one vice presidents of the General Assembly—a one-year post that allows the ambassador to chair meetings and set agendas. His successor was Gilad Erdan, who was appointed to the same post in 2022.

Fifth: Be creative, swift, and entrepreneurial.

In the international arena, and especially at the United Nations, there is a vast gap between the warm relations that various states maintain with Israel in fields such as economics, culture, and agriculture, and their hostile voting patterns. Israel is a powerful player in the fields of security, cyber-technology, high technology, agriculture, water desalination, sustainable development, social and gender equality, culture, and art. The United Nations is a suitable stage to showcase Israel's strengths, and Israel should be on the constant lookout for opportunities to add value to the global conversation.

This was what we had in mind by inviting Rita Yahan-Farouz, the famous Iranian-born Israeli singer who performs under her first name as "Rita," to give a concert at the UN General Assembly hall. The idea struck me when I watched her sing in Farsi in New York in 2012. Her voice is astonishingly beautiful, and I savored every note even without understanding the lyrics. I thought: If Iranians could hear her sing, she would surely sweep the Iranian record charts, politics and ayatollahs be damned. But then again, why shouldn't Iranians hear her? I happened to know a few top dogs at the United Nations, and they would surely love the message of an artist who could bring people—and sworn rivals—together.

Rita loved the idea. The challenge now was to get the UN to love it, too. This was, to put it mildly, tricky. The next morning, I asked members of the Israeli mission to explore how to stage a performance by Rita at the General Assembly.

"Impossible," they said, without skipping a beat.

"Don't tell me what we can't do," I snapped back. "I can work that out by myself. Tell me *how* we can do it anyway."

Their initial reaction, frankly, was entirely reasonable. Other than during the annual observance of United Nations Day, only three artists in history had ever performed in the General Assembly hall: Beyoncé, Bono, and Stevie Wonder. The idea of bringing an Israeli artist, at the invitation of the Israeli mission, to perform on a stage that has hosted only a handful of the world's biggest superstars—and to have her perform in Hebrew and Farsi, just to add some tension in the building—seemed outlandish even to me.

But these are exactly the challenges I relish.

As anyone who has served a day of military service can tell you, the most important people at any base are the quartermaster and the chef. We cultivated close ties with the UN management, including the heads of security and logistics.

At the same time, I scheduled a meeting with the secretary-general and explained to him that Israel had no dispute with the Iranian people, only with the ayatollahs who held them hostage. The United Nations was exactly the right place to send a message of peace and dialogue. Our message was simple: Israelis wished to forge a sincere dialogue with the Iranian people.

The secretary-general took the bait. I had made sufficient use of jargon from the United Nations' international development goals to speak to his heart. Before leaving, I invited him to open the event. He spotted the potential complications and promised to think about it. I persisted and asked him to give me two openings in his calendar, and he obliged.

Off we went. We spent a whole year planning the performance. The UN staff did not miss an opportunity to heap further logistical and security difficulties on the event, and we had to raise a substantial sum of money. Funding from the empty coffers of the Israeli Foreign Ministry was obviously not an option, but the Iranian Jewish community in the United States generously covered much of the cost.

As Rita's concert drew near, we sent invitations to the envoys of every UN member state, including the Iranian ambassador, who repaid us with a letter of complaint to the president of the General Assembly, insisting that the show be cancelled. He was acutely aware of the urgency of his demand: Many media outlets in New York had already shown interest, and the Iranians found themselves powerless to drive back the waves of curiosity, which had reached Tehran. But the General Assembly president and UN secretary-general honored their commitments to me and dismissed the Iranians' querulous concerns. Most Arab states responded by simply boycotting the event.

On the night of the performance, on March 5, 2013, the General Assembly hall was ready to party. The media crammed into the press gallery. The ambassadors of 128 nations thronged into the hall, and ushers added extra chairs for audience members invited from outside. Unsurprisingly, the Iranians sent nobody. In his opening remarks, Ban Ki-moon said that the concert was a symbol of peace and coexistence.

The performance was a huge success. Everyone was enthralled by Rita, and global media outlets reported on the event with gushing praise. CNN invited Rita for a special interview. Several weeks later, we were still receiving emails from Iranians around the world thanking us for the gesture and expressing hope that one day, Rita might perform in Tehran. For that one night, Israel was no longer discussed in terms of conflict and war, but as the multicultural, creative, and peace-loving nation it is.

Following the dictum that "if you can't measure it, you can't manage it," we started systematically measuring our operations, successes and failures alike, and used our insights to learn lessons and take further action. The Israeli mission submitted draft resolutions and hosted events with Israelis making groundbreaking contributions in technology, medicine, and humanitarian assistance. We requested and received a stage to show off every field in which Israel had an influence. The mission's agenda covered issues ranging from coping with disabilities, to agricultural technologies, to solar energy and water purification, to gender equality, and more, and everyone in the team worked in synchrony.

My concept of entrepreneurial diplomacy looked at the UN as a huge global marketplace, which produces a solid supply of anti-Israel delegitimization but also contains a growing demand, even a thirst, for Israeli innovation. One way we fought delegitimization was by boosting Israel's supply in sectors in which it enjoyed a comparative advantage, trading on its reputation as the "start-up nation." The effect was to offer at least some measure of balance against the constant flow of delegitimization. When we mapped out the different countries and their particular needs, we noticed that Israel could also help by providing solutions to many of the world's challenges. We decided that Israel should sponsor a UN resolution on entrepreneurship for development.

The Foreign Ministry in Jerusalem heard about our initiative and expressed concern: The General Assembly had only ever passed two Israeli-sponsored resolutions since Israel's admission in 1949. Whatever entrepreneurial spirit the Foreign Ministry had was crushed by its fear of defeat. They said that I was overestimating my team's abilities at the United Nations, but we pressed ahead, and in 2012 started promoting a draft resolution on "entrepreneurship for development."

We had no illusions about how Syria, Yemen, and Pakistan would vote. Even the weakest Arab states, those most dependent on UN resources, indicated that they would vote against the resolution simply because it was ours. Nevertheless, I knew that our Western allies would take our side, as would many countries in Asia, which were hungry for innovation.

African states traditionally vote with the Arabs on Israel-related resolutions. On a good day, after lobbying, some of them might abstain. But this time I was determined to pitch this resolution to the African ambassadors and explain its benefit for their countries. Thanks to sheer grit and personal ties, the African ambassadors—including the ambassador of Togo and my good friend, Ambassador Bamba of the Ivory Coast—became the biggest advocates of the Israeli resolution. They sent me reports from the African regional group's meetings, filling in the tally chart of who was still against us, who was on the fence, and which arguments we had to tighten. We fought for every vote till the last minute. For every phone call an ambassador received from me, he received four from the Arabs.

Despite the Palestinian rearguard offensive, 102 UN member states representing all parts of the globe co-sponsored the Israeli resolution. The feeling of fighting a war of attrition gave way to cautious optimism. Ultimately, 129 states supported the resolution, which was reaffirmed in later years. Israel sponsored another resolution about agricultural technology soon thereafter, and it, too, succeeded in gaining a majority at the General Assembly.

Some of our diplomatic initiatives were more reactive, and one of the issues we had to react to was a spike in antisemitic incidents around the globe. In my last year in New York, in January 2015, we held the first high-level UN forum on the fight against antisemitism, in an auditorium that normally pulsated with anti-Israel and antisemitic pronouncements every day of the week. It took place two weeks after a string of horrific terror attacks in Paris. We lobbied for the publication of a joint statement, and forty states committed to fight antisemitism.

The event was attended by government ministers from Germany and Canada, the French-Jewish philosopher Bernard-Henri Lévy, and Rabbi Yaacov Monsonego, whose eight-year-old daughter Miriam was murdered in a terror attack at the Ozar Hatorah school in Toulouse in 2012. U.S. Ambassador Samantha Power delivered a particularly moving speech about the victims of the Hypercacher attack in Paris, whose only crime was to buy challah and wine for Shabbat dinner. "Rising anti-Semitism is rarely the lone or the last manifestation of intolerance," she said. "When the human rights of Jews are repressed, the rights of other religious and ethnic groups are often not far behind.... If we fail to expand dramatically the ranks of those fighting anti-Semitism, not only will we fail in our obligations to the Jewish people, but we will see the weakening in our own societies of the rights and bonds that tie us all together."

***

This kind of multifaceted approach to diplomatic warfare is necessary for Israel at all times. But it is often difficult to gauge its impact on the lives and security of Israeli citizens. It's not so hard to measure in times of war, however. As seen throughout our history, when military crisis erupts, Israel's battles at the UN can make the difference between success and failure on the battlefield.

On June 12, 2014, Hamas terrorists kidnapped three Israeli teenagers hitchhiking home from school: Eyal Yifrach, Gilad Shaar, and Naftali Fraenkel. For over two weeks, Israel moved heaven and earth to track them down in Operation My Brother's Keeper. On June 30, their bodies were discovered near Hebron in the West Bank. They had been murdered on the night of their abduction. Events snowballed, and a nonstop volley of rocket fire at Israeli towns from the Gaza Strip forced Israel to launch, on July 8, a broad military operation in Gaza, which lasted fifty days. It was called Operation Protective Edge.

The moment that news reached New York about the kidnappings, we at the Israeli mission contacted the UN secretary-general and demanded a formal condemnation on behalf of the United Nations. Ban Ki-moon denounced the abduction in limp and reserved terms, as we had come to expect, and most UN organs remained indifferent. The UN spokesman made a point of emphasizing in his daily press briefing that the United Nations had no unequivocal proof that the young Israelis had been kidnapped by Hamas at all, a fact that was quite clear to the whole world by this point, except for the United Nations.

The moment an incident like the kidnapping of the three boys takes place, Israel's whole foreign policy apparatus moves to a war footing, putting into motion what I call the "complementary diplomatic operation": a set of actions in the international arena to provide legitimacy and room for maneuver for an Israeli military response. Obtaining a condemnation by the UN secretary-general is the first step towards building the legitimacy for an Israeli retaliation, giving it a window of opportunity to act forcefully, and equipping it with the necessary tools to achieve the political goals that ultimately underpin any military campaign.

For example, the Second Lebanon War erupted in 2006 when Hezbollah killed and abducted Israeli soldiers in a cross-border ambush from Lebanon and started raining rockets on northern Israel. The international legitimacy that Prime Minister Ehud Olmert's government was able to obtain for action in Lebanon, including by delaying the passage of a Security Council resolution, enabled it to embark on a military campaign against Hezbollah unprecedented in its scope. The response was so fierce that even Hassan Nasrallah, the leader of the Iran-backed guerrilla group, said that if he had known how Israel would react, he would have thought twice before provoking it.

By contrast, in 1996, Israel had launched Operation Grapes of Wrath to retaliate against a volley of Hezbollah rockets fired at Israeli towns. But then disaster struck: More than a hundred Lebanese civilians were accidentally killed when Israel shelled a UN compound in the village of Qana in southern Lebanon. On this occasion, the harsh international response and a Security Council resolution forced Israel to suspend the operation almost immediately. The international fallout sabotaged Israel's pursuit of meaningful political and security achievements.

In recent years, as TV audiences have gained front-row seats to the hostilities and awful images from conflict zones pop up on every smartphone, it has become more urgent for Israel to respond quickly through coordinated, complex diplomatic efforts. Every day that Israel is at war, the legitimacy of its defensive actions comes under further assault.

Israeli decision-makers, both political and military, now understand that their combat objectives must be tightly defined and time-bound. Military generals always prefer to stretch out the process of building up forces in and preparing for combat before unleashing the full extent of their firepower. They believe that this creates deterrence and has important operational value—the bigger the force on the field, the less likely they'll need to use it. But this is a luxury that Israeli generals rarely have, because a protracted buildup of international pressure can end up indirectly costing lives, because time constraints force Israel to intensify its use of force, thus producing the *opposite* of what was planned.

Sooner or later, international pressure is always brought to bear—whether the UN Security Council passes a resolution, or the U.S. president picks up the phone and demands that Israel stop the operation—and such interventions usually do the trick. Israel is forced to halt its offensive, and the result is that the fundamental conditions that caused the war in the first place remain largely unchanged, setting the stage for further conflict. Israel's decision-makers must therefore seriously consider speeding up the timetable and landing a painful blow on the enemy right at the start of an operation—a decisive strike to hasten the end of the war.

During the hostilities in 2014, we launched a major diplomatic campaign with the aim of providing as strong as possible a diplomatic umbrella to allow the IDF to do its job. We initiated a series of intelligence-operational update sessions, in which we flew senior Israeli Air Force and intelligence officers to New York to brief selected members of the Security Council as well as the secretary-general, armed with maps and high-resolution satellite images of the battlefields. Ambassador Power, a member of President Obama's cabinet, received real-time updates about developments on the battlefield and reported straight back to the president.

On top of all this was the campaign to present the truth of events to the general public. In a world of instantly available information, this front is often no less important than the others. International public opinion is critical, and addressing it is part of any operation's core objectives. *Hasbara* is not about being liked, but a substantial lever for the fortification of Israeli power, giving it the legitimacy to act. Israel does not need the whole world to be *happy* about its actions, just to acquiesce.

In many cases, explaining Israel's case to the world is a virtually impossible task. It takes far less time to publish a blatant lie than to paint a fact-based, accurate reality. These challenges become infinitely more complicated during wartime because in an official state-led effort, every dot and comma must be approved by several different actors, such as legal counsels, the IDF, the national security advisor, and more. The other side, by contrast, relies on fabrications and distortions and can make decisions more quickly and efficiently. This challenge requires Israel to think and operate flexibly and to react more rapidly than other states are used to, all while under fire.

The solution to this complexity lies in understanding that every incident can potentially inflict international diplomatic damage and must therefore be addressed, preferably in advance, by gaming out possible scenarios. Doing so requires tight coordination between worlds that are often at odds: intelligence and diplomacy. One is used to the shadows, the other to the spotlights.

My very smart friend Douglas Feith, a member of the Bush administration and a true friend of Israel, analyzed this point in depth in an article he wrote with Shaul Chorev, discussing the future of war.[59] Feith and Chorev show how in recent years, conventional warfare goals are also rooted in the media and public perception, rather than on the traditional battlefield alone. Therefore, they argue, diplomats and others concerned should be integrated into war games and training. Their contributions can be as decisive in a war as bombs and bullets.

***

Two days after the launch of the operation, on July 10, the Security Council convened an emergency debate at the behest of the Arab states, which hoped—to no avail at this stage, due to U.S. pressure—to pass a resolution condemning the Israeli operation. The challenge facing us was to expose evidence from the field of Hamas's brazen war crimes, and to engender solidarity with Israelis, who were coming under non-stop rocket fire. While we worked on my speech, our cell phones kept buzzing with incessant alerts of fresh rocket sirens in Israel, and we decided to sound the "red alert" siren—a shrill, undulating screech—during my speech, in front of the world's media:

---

[59] Douglas Feith and Shaul Chorev, "Lessons from Israel and the U.S. about the New Way of War," *Mosaic*, May 7, 2020.

> As I speak, there is a storm of rockets being fired by the Hamas terrorist organization in Gaza. Hamas is intentionally and indiscriminately threatening the lives of three-and-a-half million innocent men, women, and children in Israel from north to south—from Beersheba to Tel Aviv to Haifa. In the last three days, 442 rockets have been fired into Israel—that's one every ten minutes....
>
> Fifteen seconds [play sound of siren]. That's how much time you have to run for your life. Imagine having only fifteen seconds to find a bomb shelter. Now imagine doing it with small children or elderly parents or an ailing friend...
>
> A generation of Israeli children is growing up under the shadow of this threat. This abnormal way of life has become the "normal" way of life for many Israelis—and it is absolutely unacceptable. No nation, no people, and no government could tolerate this.

Sounding the siren achieved its goals. First, we grabbed the attention of the envoys, most of whom had never heard the "red alert" siren that warns Israelis of incoming rocket fire. The siren from my phone was heard well beyond the walls of the Security Council hall and reached news outlets around the world. What does it mean for children to have fifteen seconds to run for shelter under a hail of missiles? We hit our immediate target just by getting the news agencies and UN committees to raise the question.

This stunt also had a less obvious consequence. Political counsellors from various UN member states installed the Red Alert app on their phones to keep abreast of the situation. In so doing, they brought a taste of the threat facing Israel into the meeting rooms of their national delegations and received minute-to-minute reminders of what had become the daily reality for tens of thousands of Israelis.

The Palestinians pushed the Security Council to convene non-stop sessions during this period, dragging its members back to work on the weekends and even at midnight. They tried to grind us down. For the first twenty days after the operation began, we managed to block their attempts to promote a resolution condemning Israel. It was essential to prevent them from submitting such a draft resolution, and all the more so to prevent a debate on possible resolutions and having to rely on the U.S. veto, which would leave Israel and the United States looking isolated. In practice, we pursued two complementary paths: Thwart resolutions that would jeopardize Israel's abilities to achieve its goals, and present the truth of the situation in Israel on the international stage.

We made sure to flood the United Nations with accurate information. We invited the IDF military attachés in Washington to the Security Council to brief the ambassadors, and we briefed the envoys of the Council's permanent members one by one to make sure they understood the full picture and were not relying on incomplete reports and mendacious propaganda. When a U.S. ambassador pores over photographs of terror tunnel openings and aerial shots of rocket launchpads in the heart of residential areas, you can be sure she will stand with Israel and will be more confident in her work and the justice of her cause.

Late at night on July 28, the Security Council convened to ratify a declaration by the president of the General Assembly calling for a ceasefire and urging respect for international law. It was an unsubtle signal to Israel that it no longer enjoyed legitimacy for the continuation of its military campaign and that its window of opportunity for such action was swiftly closing.

But we had done our part. Israel was able to continue its campaign against the rocket-launchers and terrorists well into August.

We at the UN mission had given our armed forces and decision-makers back home weeks of cover to carry out their mission and protect our citizens, and laid the groundwork for dealing with the inevitable next phase, the commissions of inquiry and accusations that always come in the aftermath of a war that we knew had been justly and honorably fought.

***

After one grueling day of diplomatic warfare at the United Nations, coming on the tail of a long night, my team and I left the UN building and passed the iconic row of flags outside, representing 193 nations. Twenty-five flags featured a cross; fifteen displayed a crescent. Only one flag proudly bore a Star of David—the blue and white flag of the world's only Jewish state.

During my service at the United Nations, I felt that it was my duty to protect this one flag on First Avenue in Manhattan from the tempest inside the building that threatened to tear it down.

The triple standards, the hypocrisy, the diplomatic warfare, and the institutional and structural discrimination against Israel at the United Nations undoubtedly made it difficult for us to do our jobs. But they also made it easier for us to maintain our conviction in the justice of our cause. From the ambassador to the interns, we all worked tirelessly to make sure that this one flag could flutter with pride among those of the world's nations, where it rightfully belongs.

CHAPTER 9

A NEW MIDDLE EAST FOR THE CHILDREN OF ABRAHAM

Meanwhile, back on planet Earth, a series of events over the course of a decade and a half began to alter the fundamental realities of the Middle East, and of Israel in particular. The implications for Zionist diplomacy were profound.

Most obvious was the remarkable improvement of Israel's basic strategic and economic posture. The end of the Lebanon war in 2006, it turned out, marked the beginning of an extended period of quiet on Israel's northern border with Lebanon and Syria. Although there were a series of armed conflicts against Hamas in Gaza, these were smaller in scale—and became even less worrisome for Israeli civilians with the development and, in 2011, deployment of the Iron Dome missile intercept system.

Certain economic developments were significant enough to rise to the level of strategic shifts, as well. Israel had spent decades, like many countries, dependent on others for energy sources and in a constant state of water scarcity. In the 2000s, however, discoveries of massive natural gas fields in the Mediterranean, combined with the development and large-scale deployment of seawater desalination plants along the Mediterranean coast, transformed Israel, quite suddenly in historical terms, into a country that not only could fulfill its own needs but also *export* both natural gas and fresh water.

And the Israeli economy grew and grew. The "start-up nation" became a magnet for direct foreign investment and a dynamic economic engine. To choose just one of many indicators: From 2005 to 2020, Israel's real per capita GDP went from $28,809 to $37,489—a rise of more than 30 percent—compared with about 10 percent for both the United States and the European Union. In September 2010, Israel joined the OECD, marking it as one of the world's thirty-plus leading economies. Israelis had always looked to Europe as a land of relative prosperity; but by 2021, Israel's per capita GDP was comparable with that of Germany and ahead of both the United Kingdom and France.[60]

But there were other changes as well—changes that pushed in the direction of an inexorable rapprochement between Israel and the Arab world. The controversy surrounding the 2003 Iraq war made America's relationship with the Middle East into a more politically delicate subject in the United States, especially regarding the use of its own military muscle there—despite the presence of large military bases across the Persian Gulf. In the mid-2010s, the Obama administration threw all its weight behind a campaign to cut a nuclear deal with Iran that would, in his words, transform the Islamic Republic into a "very successful regional power." The effect was to drive many Arab states, terrified of an expansive, empowered, destabilizing regime in Tehran, to the conclusion that they should reconsider their cold ties with Israel.

For generations, the conventional wisdom held that all roads to peace went through Ramallah, that there could be no Arab-Israeli peace without first resolving the Palestinian-Israeli conflict. This was the entire rationale behind the Oslo Accords—that solving the central conflict would open doors across the region. The peace treaties with Egypt and Jordan could have presented evidence to the contrary, but the coldness of that peace (and

---

60 World Bank Group, "GDP per capita (constant 2015 US$)–Israel, United States, European Union," https://data.worldbank.org/indicator/NY.GDP.PCAP.KD?end=2020&locations=IL-US-EU&start=2005&view=chart (accessed October 23, 2024), and World Bank Group, "GDP per capita (current US$)–Israel, Germany, United Kingdom, France," 2021, https://data.worldbank.org/indicator/NY.GDP.PCAP.CD?end=2021&locations=IL-DE-GB-FR&start=2016 (accessed October 23, 2024).

the 1981 assassination of Egyptian President Sadat) seemed, if anything, to instead prove the point. Non-belligerence? Perhaps. But real peace—the kind with tourism and trade and investment and friendship—would remain but a dream so long as the Palestinian problem continued to burn.

And then the Abraham Accords happened. In the summer and fall of 2020, four nations—the UAE, Bahrain, Morocco, and Sudan—entered into full normalization agreements with the Jewish state. Quickly it became clear that these were no mere non-belligerence deals. They would include everything that Israel had longed for: trade, tourism, cultural exchange, investment, and close cooperation on security.

These accords have already brought billions of dollars of annual economic activity and close security cooperation, and have thus far weathered the storm of the 2023 and 2024 Gaza war, especially with the Gulf states that are much closer to Iran geographically, and much more threatened by it, than we are.

It also helps to bring down walls of hatred and false perceptions of each other, while promoting the most important and sustainable element for long-lasting peace: people-to-people relationships.

But the Abraham Accords didn't emerge out of thin air. On the contrary, they were the culmination of decades of efforts, mostly behind the scenes, to build real bridges with the business-savvy nations of the Gulf and beyond.

My own involvement began in the mid-2000s, when I served as director-general of Israel's Foreign Ministry. Looking back, I can see it as a case study in the kind of innovative, entrepreneurial bootstrapping diplomacy in which Israel has become quite proficient.

***

A few minutes after I crossed the Israel-Jordan border in 2004, the Israeli deputy ambassador in Amman, Danny Nevo, received a phone call. An officer on the Israeli side of the crossing tipped him off that the director-general of the Foreign Ministry had crossed the border. The deputy ambassador was unnerved. What was I doing, visiting Jordan without his knowledge? He began to suspect that I was on my way to meet King Abdullah or the Jordanian foreign minister—without him.

As the hours went by, Nevo's suspicions grew. There was nothing in the media or in the Foreign Ministry's diplomatic cables about a meeting between me and any senior Jordanian officials. Perplexed, Nevo called the border crossing. "Did he come back?" he berated the border control officer. "Are you *sure* the director-general of the Foreign Ministry crossed the border?"

"Yes, it was Prosor," he confirmed. "He crossed the border into Jordan, but he hasn't come back."

Nevo persisted. "*Where is he?*"

The source of his bafflement was, at that moment, drinking a fine cup of coffee hundreds of miles away in Dubai, one of the seven emirates of the UAE in the Persian Gulf. An hour earlier, I had arrived, together with an aide, aboard an Emirates flight out of Amman for a series of clandestine meetings. There began the long process of tightening Israel's relations with the Gulf states.

Outwardly, the Arab states had been uncompromising in their hostility to Israel since before the Jewish state was founded. Their rejectionism was expressed in their refusal to take part in the 1947 UNSCOP process that ultimately led to Partition; in their refusal to recognize the new Jewish state; in their participation, directly or indirectly, in the attempt to destroy it through force of arms in 1948 and beyond; in their launching of a broad international boycott against corporations that did business in Israel, in international sports and culture, and more.

But beneath the surface, there were always contrary forces at play. Some states, like Morocco, maintained historically positive relations with their Jewish communities, as well as large expat communities in Israel that remembered fondly the land of their birth. Some had no real sympathy for the Palestinians and could not understand why their own national development needed to be held back by faraway politics. This was especially the case for large Muslim states outside the Arab world, like Indonesia and Turkey. Still another contrary current came from the Kingdom of Jordan: After the Six Day War in 1967, Jordan, which had lost the West Bank and eastern Jerusalem to Israeli forces, licked its wounds and would be in no hurry to join the attack of the 1973 Yom Kippur War. In September 1970, in the midst of the Jordanian civil war known as Black September, Syrian forces amassed on Jordan's northern border and began to invade. Israel called up its reserves and mobilized forces on the Golan Heights, sending a clear signal that it would not allow a Syrian invasion of Jordan—and the Syrians withdrew. Jordan suddenly discovered that having Israel as a neighbor had its advantages.

Another complicating factor involved the Arabs' superpower patron, the Soviet Union. Much of the Arab unity against Israel was backed by Soviet support, but that came with a price. Egyptian President Anwar Sadat wasn't willing to pay it and envisioned his nation's future as ridding itself of the Soviet presence in his country—including the presence of thousands of Soviet military "advisers"—and wanted to find a path to the American umbrella in the Cold War. This desire ultimately led to the 1979 peace treaty with Israel, which had long been an American condition for its support of Egypt.

When the Soviet Union collapsed, leaving the United States as the only remaining superpower, new possibilities seemed to arise, and new calculations took hold. In 1993, Israel and the PLO signed the Oslo Accords, followed by the peace treaty with Jordan in 1994. Meanwhile, resentment against the Palestinians began to grow across much of the Arab world. During the 1991 Gulf War, which began with Iraq's invasion of Kuwait, the Palestinians took the side of Iraq—angering most of the Arab world, which had joined in coalition with the United States to liberate the invaded country. The Palestinians did the same after 9/11, dancing for joy on the rooftops of Ramallah, further angering America's Arab allies, especially those who saw al-Qaeda as a threat to their own regimes.

Throughout this period, Israel grew both militarily and economically, and many Arab leaders began privately to ask themselves: Is the Palestinian cause *really* worth all our sacrifice in economic, strategic, and other ties with Israel and, indirectly, with the United States?

Morocco was one of the pioneers of closer ties with Israel. An Israeli-Moroccan rapprochement seemed only natural thanks to the unique persona of King Hassan II, who treated the Moroccan Jewish community with great respect and considered that a benefit to his kingdom; indeed, some of his closest advisors were Jews. The relationship went public after the signing of the Oslo Accords, and in 1995 Israel opened an official mission in Rabat. Tunisia was next in line. In 1996, after decades of ties at various levels, the Israelis and their Tunisian counterparts seized the opportunity of the PLO's departure from Tunis to open "interest offices" on each other's soil. In 1996, Israel opened interest offices in the Qatari capital, Doha, and the Omani capital, Muscat.

The initiative to open interest offices was the result of multilateral working groups formed between Israel and Arab states immediately after the Oslo Accords. The idea was to establish confidence-building measures (CBMs in diplomatic jargon) that would support future bilateral agreements in areas such as water, the environment, refugees, and arms control, and would lay the groundwork for a final Israeli-Palestinian peace accord. Israeli representatives met their Arab counterparts at several international forums in Muscat, Casablanca, and other cities in the Arab world to promote joint economic initiatives and projects, with the aim of upgrading and deepening Israel's relations with the Palestinians and the Arab states.

But, ultimately, these relationships collapsed in late 2000, in the wake of the failure of the Camp David negotiations between Israel and the Palestinian Authority and the latter's decision to launch the second intifada. Several years of diplomatic efforts evaporated into thin air almost overnight when most Arab states announced that they were severing diplomatic ties with Israel immediately due to its alleged "aggression" in the West Bank and Gaza.

Of course, there was no unprovoked Israeli aggression. The intifada was, again, launched by the Palestinian Authority in the wake of the collapse of the Camp David II talks. In hindsight, the loss of regional cooperation and the closing of the Israeli missions turned out to have been orchestrated by the Arab League, which wanted to express support for the Palestinian terror onslaught. The Arab League's decision was particularly problematic for Egypt and Jordan, which had binding peace treaties with Israel. It was one thing to close an interest office and quite another to shutter an embassy anchored in an international treaty. The states that had signed peace treaties with Israel were therefore exempted from the Arab League resolution, but Israel's interest offices all had to close.

In reality, however, cracks began to appear in even this watered-down decision. One interesting story made its way to me from Doha. Qatar's foreign minister (and future premier) Hamad bin Jassim was ordered to comply with the Arab League resolution but found elegant ways to drag his feet.

Once, Arab League officials called him and claimed that the light was on at the Israeli interest office in Doha.

"I don't know what's going on, I'm not their security guard," replied Bin Jassim, quick on his feet. "Maybe they left a light on to keep burglars away?"

***

The model that I had in mind for building relations with the Arab world back in 2004 was similar to the one I had used successfully as first secretary at the Israeli embassy in Germany a decade and a half before, at a time when Israel forged ties with the Communist east. At the time, we imported Israeli culture, bringing dance troupes over to the former Communist bloc to reach people's hearts. Only after laying these cultural foundations did we embark on a new chapter of diplomatic relations.

I intended to roll out this model again to revive relations with Arab states, with one key difference: Instead of building on cultural ties, we would leverage trade. I knew that if we managed to lay the foundations for commercial and development projects between Israel and pragmatic Arab states, we could bridge the suspicions and distrust that divided us. Only then could we start forging durable diplomatic ties with these nations' leaders.

Like East Germany during the Cold War, the Arab world, too, does not have a Western conception of diplomacy. This observation might sound trivial, but the difference of approach is a significant barrier to establishing ties. It is hard to overstate the importance, for example, of being personally and intimately acquainted with Arab rulers and their families. Unless they meet an untimely death, Arab leaders and their advisors tend to hold lifetime positions, and their ministers can remain in office for decades. If one maintains personal and working ties with them, their door will always be open for you.

There is one particular person in the Israeli Foreign Ministry who has spent years nurturing extensive personal relations with key figures in the Arab world. I cannot reveal his name, but since I nicknamed him "the modern Lawrence of Arabia," I will call him "Lawrence."

Lawrence was far from a typical diplomat. He was more of a field operative, a lone wolf who prowled in diplomatic twilight zones and advanced professionally thanks to his ability to build personal connections. For many years, Lawrence has acted on Israel's behalf forging ties with countries in which no Israeli has ever set foot unarmed. He built extensive contacts in pragmatic Arab countries, and the word at the ministry was that he practically had their leaders on speed dial.

When I assumed the role of director-general, Lawrence was described to me as an expert on the Persian Gulf. Skeptical, I asked to meet him. During our meeting, Lawrence regaled me with stories as well as his plans for relations with the Gulf states. At first, it sounded outlandish. "Your stories sound like a magnificent work of fiction," I told him once. "But as long as I'm in charge, you're grounded, and I don't want you flying anywhere till I work out what you really do."

Over time, however, Lawrence's stories and contacts slowly came into focus, forming a clearer picture. We started to plan our first blitz of meetings in the Arab world.

The first stage was to initiate dialogue about upgrading our bilateral relationship. The method would be to open an interest office in Dubai, as we had done in Doha in 1996. "Our envoys in Doha still work with the most senior figures in Qatar," I emphasized to our hosts in Dubai as we sipped our coffee. We hoped that the knowledge that another country in the region had economic relations with Israel would reassure them.

Of course, I had years of experience in international negotiations and dialogue. But talking to Gulf Arabs was a completely different professional challenge. The diplomatic culture of the Gulf is an undefined fusion of the West and the Middle East. As it happens, the Palestinian issue, ostensibly the biggest obstacle to Israeli-Gulf cooperation, was not the main focus of our conversations and scarcely interested our interlocutors. I got the feeling that they felt obligated to bring it up as lip service, given internal public pressure to do *something* about it.

Before flying out to the UAE, we had done our due diligence. It was essential to gather advance intelligence about the Arab decision-makers we were about to meet. We studied how to address them in conversation, what might offend them, and what might spur them to make certain decisions. We pored over the Gulf officials' family trees—because in the Gulf, as in most Arab countries, "family first" is not just a slogan but a bedrock principle. Entire families controlled this country's resources, made its decisions, and directed its policy in a range of fields, from economics to security and internal affairs. We had to work out, therefore, who held influence over whom and how much. We were surprised to discover, therefore, that one particular decision-maker was most influenced by his cousin, not by his son who ostensibly held an official senior role. In time, our familiarity with the labyrinthine family trees of the Persian Gulf proved to be one of our most important tools for promoting our policies and initiatives in the region.

Israel's vision of regional cooperation was ambitious. We proposed to begin enhancing a network of commercial ties, permitting Israeli companies to operate in the UAE in areas of importance to both sides, such as desalination, agriculture, infrastructure, technology, diamonds, and pearls (this country is a world capital of the pearl trade). We discussed a range of topics, from basic questions such as what level of relations to establish; through to logistical matters, such as whether Israelis could obtain work visas; and finally to seemingly esoteric but hugely important matters, such as how officially to describe our relationship. Slowly but surely, our interlocutors' stern expressions began to relax. By the end, they even grinned with satisfaction.

Shimon Peres, Israel's former prime minister and future president, was for us the godfather of the concept of economic peace. He believed that the rift between Israel and the Arab world could be bridged through cooperation to realize the universal human aspiration for a better future. As prime minister, Peres laid the first practical foundations of his vision in 1996, with the opening of the Israeli economic interest office in Qatar. A decade later, his basic assumptions continued to underpin our discussions. In hindsight, however, I discovered that in the Middle East, even economic interests ultimately take a back seat to geopolitics and pan-Arab interests, which remain a perennial bugbear.

The first pitfall in our talks in the Gulf was mutual suspicion. Just a short time after the terror campaign of the second intifada, distrust and fear were high. If we wished to find a prince, we realized we would have to kiss a frog. We swallowed numerous indignities, and did so without complaint, knowing we had to keep our eyes on the bigger picture. Some of our meetings were scheduled, for example, not in official conference rooms but in less ceremonious venues, including a hotel swimming pool deck. Gulf officials did not want to admit to conducting an open relationship with Israel in broad daylight. We arrived for meetings through the service entrance, to avoid our encounters leaking and provoking a public backlash. Israel, for a long period, was going to have to be the mistress in this relationship.

More than once, it looked like our intensive work deepening our bilateral relationship might be washed away on the shores of this Gulf state's artificial islands. One such near-miss happened after an arduous year of meetings with Mohammed Bin Zayed, the crown prince of the Emirate of Abu Dhabi and deputy supreme commander of the United Arab Emirates Armed Forces.

In the final stages of negotiations over establishing ties, in a friendly and unpretentious meeting, Bin Zayed turned to me and stressed that if our negotiations leaked to the public, he would pull the emergency brake.

There are times when the way you answer a single question can determine the fate of relations between countries.

I looked at him and said, "Let me be honest with you, Your Royal Highness. The State of Israel wishes to deepen ties with you, and I believe this is important for you too. If this relationship takes off as we envisage, its success will be measured in the two-way movement of people between our respective states. So I hope that these relations will become the talk of the town among citizens and businesspeople in both countries—and that's exactly as it should be. Sir, I cannot promise you that our countries' relations will remain a secret."

Time froze. A whole year of negotiations was hanging by a thread. Lawrence went pale and looked like he might have to be airlifted to an intensive care unit if his life's work imploded, as now looked certain. I was feverishly thinking how I could ever explain the collapse of these negotiations to Prime Minister Ariel Sharon and Foreign Minister Silvan Shalom back in Israel.

Bin Zayed stared at me for five long seconds. "I appreciate your honesty," he said, his lips curling into a small smile. The color returned to Lawrence's face and I think I saw a flicker of relief in his eyes. "Let's move on," he continued. "Tell me, what do you need from me?"

I needed no further invitation. I whipped out of my folder a list we had prepared, detailing the various stages of deepening our relations, including an account of differences we might have along the way. Our esteemed host listened attentively and then instructed his people to give us more than we expected.

Sometimes honesty and grit pay off.

***

Following our blitz of meetings in Dubai, Israel began to operate officially in the UAE, but still largely under the radar. Lawrence was put in charge of managing business on the ground, with access to a brilliant team of professionals. I personally handpicked each of the diplomats needed to take this relationship forward.

After months of grueling flights via Europe, marathon meetings, and unexplained absences from the ministry in Jerusalem, I was ready to announce to Foreign Minister Shalom and Prime Minister Sharon: *mission accomplished*. Shalom was proud of our achievement, but the prime minister responded with his characteristic sarcasm. "Oh, Prosor, I see you understand a thing or two about the secrets of diplomacy," he muttered.

Back in Dubai, we were careful to preserve the fabric of this relationship. It was no longer a secret, but we kept it low-key, suiting the interests of both sides. Bit by bit, we expanded our relations with other Gulf states, and trade began to accelerate. Lawrence sent reports back home about the volume of trade, and although his math seemed fuzzy, I resisted my natural instincts and let things continue uninterrupted. I thought it was important for the brand-new team dealing with the Gulf to feel successful and assumed that Lawrence's fertile imagination would sooner or later connect with reality.

We encouraged Israeli companies to start operating in Qatar, Oman, the UAE, and other Gulf states, mediating between them and the authorities. Even before the establishment of formal ties, some Israeli companies already did business in the Gulf under the radar, mostly offering commercial services and goods. After we upgraded ties, they were also able to send goods through third parties in Europe—albeit with nothing marking the containers as Israeli. Later, an Israeli minister even visited Dubai to attend an economic conference, not in the capacity of an official visit. The establishment of official ties made it possible to expand and deepen commercial cooperation, and official visits started being conducted out in the open: Senior figures in the Israeli Diamond Exchange, for example, began flying out to do business with their counterparts.

Gradually, the Gulf authorities' attitudes to Israel changed. Israelis were permitted to visit trade fairs in the Gulf and signed deals with local companies. As matchmakers between Gulf officials and Israeli companies, we took a laissez-faire approach. After making the initial introduction, we took a back seat and let the sides get to business, without the direct involvement of the Israeli government. Only rarely did we need to help Israeli citizens with consular matters, such as visas and permits, and Gulf officials were always glad to oblige.

Our activity in the Gulf spread its wings and took flight. Israeli medical experts were flown over to treat Gulf patients and advise local doctors. Sometimes we even received special requests from government officials to fly out critically ill relatives for medical treatment in Israel's more advanced hospitals. The scope of our activity expanded, and our cooperation deepened, but we kept our ties under the radar because the Gulf states were apprehensive about how the wider Arab world might react to our growing cooperation.

The Palestinians were not indifferent to these burgeoning ties. They gazed dolefully at Gulf countries taking advantage of Israel's knowledge, innovation, and entrepreneurial spirit. They weren't alone. The Iranians were also aware of the blossoming Israeli-Arab romance. "Keep your heads down," Gulf officials warned us. "The Iranians are asking questions." The security arrangements for our visits were tightened in the wake of various warnings, threats, and concerns.

Israel's relations with the pragmatic Arab states reached one of their apogees with a meeting between Foreign Minister Tzipi Livni and Qatar's Emir Khalid bin Khalifa on the sidelines of the UN General Assembly in 2007. The emir invited Livni to join him for an unscheduled meeting outside the UN building. This was after he had already met President Shimon Peres and expressed enthusiastic support for his vision of a "New Middle East" and economic peace. Nobody could doubt that the public embrace by Qatar's supreme leader was the fruit of years of work to foster these ties, and mostly of a confluence of interests between Jerusalem and Gulf capitals.

Qatar is a special player, which plays a double game in order to navigate between conflicting interests in the Middle East. On the one hand, Qatar is a Sunni country, aligned with the Muslim Brotherhood. On the other hand, it shares major economic interests with Iran and is commonly viewed as relatively pro-Iran, supports the Hamas terror organization, and uses its state-owned Al Jazeera media empire to incite and criticize the Saudi regime, the Egyptian regime, and other Arab countries as well as Israel. This is why Qatar was for years subjected to sanctions from the Saudis and others Sunni countries in the region. After all that, Qatar usually manages to survive this dance, due to its strategic importance to the US, which has a very sizable air force base in its territory.

As we worked to forge relations with Arab states, the Qatari leaders maintained somewhat contradictory attitudes to Israel. On the one hand, they were happy to engage with Israel. On the other, they were afraid to outwardly normalize this relationship. Qatari Foreign Minister Hamad Bin Jassim, whom I had met in Doha, personified this tension. Bin Jassim, a highly accomplished man, seemed positively enthusiastic in the run up to the 2005 Gaza Disengagement. Qatar wished to play a more active role in the Middle Eastern arena and saw the Israeli withdrawal from the Gaza Strip as an opportunity to expand its regional influence.

Bin Jassim promised us during our meeting that after Disengagement, Qatar would be the main engine of peace. His promise proved to be empty. The Qataris continued trading with us, and the Israeli interest office in Doha kept working at full speed, but Bin Jassim's promise to upgrade relations with Israel got stuck in the congested pipeline of Doha's other promises. Our complaints about the hostile and biased anti-Israel coverage on Al Jazeera—advocacy that often bordered on incitement—fell on deaf ears. Bin Jassim claimed he was powerless to act.

I am a natural optimist and would normally tell myself that Rome was not built in a day—but as we have seen during the Gaza war, Doha plays a dangerous double game. On the one hand, Qatar provides critical financial and material aid to the people of Gaza and cooperates with Israel in some crucial fields. On the other, owing to upheavals in the Arab world and economic interests it shares with Iran, Qatar has also chosen to take an extremist turn in recent years. It has supported Israel's enemies, including through financial and diplomatic support for Hamas and the Muslim Brotherhood; it continues to host Hamas's top leaders even after the horrors of October 7; it granted asylum to the disgraced Arab-Israeli parliamentarian Azmi Bishara, who was under investigation for spying for Hezbollah; and it has expressed international support for Iran.

This support mostly derived from Qatar's need to survive in the region, but it has created a deep rift between Qatar and many Arab states, led by Saudi Arabia, Egypt, and Bahrain, that severed ties with it altogether for years, and only recently began reconciling. They regard Al Jazeera as a propaganda outlet openly striving to destabilize Arab regimes from within while conveniently ignoring the Qatari regime's own malignant deeds.

We also initiated ties with Bahrain, a small but wealthy kingdom in the Persian Gulf. Manama, the capital, was less impressive than the glitz and glamor of Dubai and Abu Dhabi. The rhythm of daily life was also calmer than the frenetic pace I had experienced elsewhere in the region. In fact, time was much more Middle Eastern—as flexible as a circus acrobat. The scheduled times for meetings with Bahraini Foreign Ministry officials were mere recommendations.

When our hosts saw that my patience for their never-ending delays was wearing thin, they offered to take us sightseeing. After downing a few more cups of coffee, we decided to accept their invitation and headed out to explore the country. They asked whether we wished to see the bridge connecting Bahrain and Saudi Arabia, and I leapt at the opportunity. Back then, in 2005, I was mesmerized by the prospect of catching a glimpse of other countries in the region, long before the romance that has since blossomed with some of them, especially after the Saudi crown prince, Mohammed Bin Salman, came to power.

A secured convoy of Bahraini Foreign Ministry vehicles whisked us away to the Saudi border crossing. The seemingly mundane bridge concealed an almost intergalactic story. Over the years, the crossing had provided an escape route for many Saudis. They crossed it every weekend, fleeing the watchful gaze of their own regime to enjoy the secular, Western delights of Bahrain. There, women could experience the world free from their suffocating traditional dress, and men summoned the courage to take a break from hardline Sharia law and engage in activities for which they might have had their hands chopped off at home: going out, dressing freely, and drinking alcohol. This was not just a border crossing between countries, but a gateway between worlds, shining a spotlight on the innermost cravings of the people who crossed it and on their long-repressed desire to connect to the modern world.

I asked our hosts whether we could cross the border. To my astonishment, they obliged. We crossed the bridge and drove over a mile into Saudi Arabia, and then looped back toward the border. Upon our return, we drove straight back to the Foreign Ministry for a meeting with the Bahraini foreign minister. When colleagues at the Israeli Foreign Ministry asked me where we had been in the Gulf, I replied cryptically: "More than just one country." My answer was geographically accurate in more than one way: These were two Sunni countries, bound together in a tight alliance founded on their common fear of Shi'ite Iran, their hostility towards it, and their anxieties about its perilous imperial ambitions. The agreements signed in 2020, when Bahrain and Israel signed a memorandum of normalization, also signals an indirect Saudi approach that legitimizes Israel. In 2022, Saudi Arabia opened its skies to flights to and from Tel Aviv, cutting by several hours the time it takes to fly between Israel and nations to the east. And the Saudis joined the American-led coalition to help Israel to intercept Iranian missiles and UAVs targeting Israel on April 14, 2024.

Our visit to Bahrain came as its authorities decided to pursue warmer relations with Israel. The timing was no coincidence: They felt liberated to act on their desire to forge ties in the wake of Disengagement, which gave them a veneer of legitimacy to take baby steps out in the open towards the only democracy in the Middle East.

The Bahraini foreign minister, Khalid Bin Ahmed Al Khalifa, a heavy-set, charming man, could not have greeted us more warmly. "Ho, Mr. Director-General, welcome, welcome," he said, patting me on the shoulder with a grin. "You look like someone who likes to eat, so let's eat!" He did not ask about Israeli public opinion the way other Arab foreign ministers did—he already knew much about the Israeli street, he said, from the internet. When I inquired about the exact source of his information—did the honorable minister scour Israel's streets on Google Maps?—he gave a hearty laugh. "I play backgammon online and like to compete against Israelis!" he boomed. "You people are good at backgammon." No doubt, the Bahraini minister was not only a fine backgammon player, but skilled at diplomatic chess.

After a relatively short blitz of meetings, Bahrain joined its siblings in the Gulf and entered bilateral relations with Israel, which it desired for several reasons. Its leaders wanted to strengthen their ties with the United States and knew that good relations with Jerusalem could help them in Washington. They also wanted to create a common front against the Iranians, a kind of pan-Middle Eastern alliance, hoping that Israel would back them against the ayatollahs' regime. Bahrain knew that Israel, unlike other states that had made all sorts of promises, had the means to take firm action against Iran—just as it had fought Iran's Lebanese proxy, Hezbollah. Our Bahraini counterparts took pains to emphasize to us that *they* were the most successful Arab nation, certainly in the Persian Gulf. They spoke with condescension about their neighbors, but all with a view to currying favor with us.

In 2011, the whistleblower site WikiLeaks published documents claiming that Bahrain enjoyed clandestine but tight security cooperation with Israel. The Bahraini authorities denied these reports, but every country in the region, including Iran, suspected it of having a secret fling with the Jewish state. In 2013, Bahrain was the first Arab country to classify Hezbollah as a terrorist organization, and a year later it condemned a particularly gruesome terror attack on a synagogue in Jerusalem.

In 2017, Bahrain's King Hamad Bin Isa Al Khalifa took the unprecedented step of publicly denouncing the Arab boycott of Israel and lifting restrictions on citizens wishing to travel there. Bahrain even supported the United States moving its embassy to Jerusalem and praised Israel for its airstrikes against Iranian targets in Syria. In 2020, Bahrain joined the UAE in signing the Abraham Accords, normalizing relations with Israel.

***

If I had a dinar for every time someone told me, "Nothing will come out of these contacts with the Arabs," I would be as comfortable as an Emirati sheikh. Over the years, many people around me have been skeptical about the prospects for achieving closer ties between Israel and its Arab neighbors.

People naturally want to see tangible results. I am no exception, but I also believe that some of the foundations we laid in the Arab world are still in place today and provide a solid basis for future dialogue. Over the years, I lobbied to translate this relationship into practical terms and endeavored to prevent it from being treated as an illicit liaison. Publicity is not everything, but it *does* matter, especially in diplomacy and particularly in the case of the Arab world. Unfortunately, the State of Israel has resigned itself—to its own detriment—to the traditional Arab view that this is a no-strings-attached relationship.

Israel has consented to two-tiered relations with these states. Under the radar, Israel and the pragmatic Arab states have extensive, far-reaching relations based on covert cooperation and, to a lesser extent, commercial and economic ties. Above the radar, Arab leaders project unceasing hostility towards Israel, both on the international stage and in the ample doses of Israel-hatred that they feed their citizens.

The Israeli government takes the view that these clandestine relations are critical to its strategic interests, even at the cost of neglecting other interests. These relations are undoubtedly of strategic importance to Israel's national security, but by turning a blind eye to this farce, Israel is sacrificing vital dimensions of the potential relationship in a way that jeopardizes its wider long-term interests. It is neglecting people-to-people relations, international support, academic cooperation, and economic development, which should be the cornerstone of bilateral relations. At the end of the day, this oversight risks backfiring on Israel because it leaves the whole enterprise on shaky ground. As far as non-Abraham Accords countries are concerned, the status quo almost exclusively serves the Arab leaders' interests while damaging Israel's broader national security interests, its national dignity, and its portrayal in the international arena.

National dignity is a concept that Western society tends to snootily dismiss as a nationalist or "Oriental" obsession. But as a seasoned diplomat, I believe that states that forgo their national dignity are fated to find their allies joining the widespread mockery of them and their vital interests.

Without an acute commitment to national dignity, skewed international narratives become entrenched with respect to historical events, such as the May 2010 affair of the *Mavi Marmara* ship mentioned earlier, or the canard that Israel perpetrated the 1982 Sabra and Shatila massacre of Palestinian refugees—an allegation unmoored from reality. In the latter case, the killing was the foul work of Lebanese Christian militias, in the midst of that country's brutal civil war. The Kahan Commission that Israel appointed to investigate the killings held Defense Minister Ariel Sharon and the Israeli government partially responsible. The international media wrongly transformed the Commission's verdict into a full-fledged accusation that Israel perpetrated the killings, which was absolutely not true. Many other tales of the same ilk have ended up becoming part of the conventional historical narrative.

Another affront to Israel's national dignity is the fact that no Egyptian president has ever visited the Jewish state since Anwar Sadat came to Jerusalem in 1977, with the sole exception of Hosni Mubarak's attendance at Yitzhak Rabin's funeral in 1995. Israel's acceptance of this fact prejudices its interests and international standing. The message it sends is that normalized relations with Israel are somehow illegitimate. *We may have a peace treaty*, Arab leaders think, *but we can keep relations as obscure as is domestically convenient, and the Israelis won't insist on anything more.*

I've discussed the problematic "cold peace" that has prevailed for decades with both Egypt and Jordan, covering only security but very little in the way of tourism, economic cooperation or people-to-people ties. From my professional experience, states respect strategic thinking and admire countries that fight for their interests and remain true to a vision. If Israel respects itself, other countries will do the same and they will cease to belittle its national interests—or, they will think twice before doing so.

It is often thought that for Arab states, acknowledging ties with Israel is like coming out of the closet and can only be done when conditions are ripe: when Israelis and Palestinians sign a peace treaty. I beg to differ. I believe that in the coming years, especially in the wake of the war between Iran-backed Hamas and Israel, the shared interests of Israel and pragmatic Arab nations will become stronger than ever.

These states are slowly internalizing that, in order to promote their own national, economic, and security interests, they can benefit more by cooperating with Israel than by being constant adversaries. If Israel puts its foot down, this change will usher in an era of overt diplomatic relations with the wider region.

The most obvious example of the wisdom of such an approach is in the signing of the 2020 Abraham Accords, and the fundamental disruption it has meant in the century-long history of Israel-Arab acrimony.

***

The Abraham Accords seemed to appear out of nowhere, but in fact they were the product of more than two decades of investment below the surface.

It has been quite a few years now that the Gulf states—the UAE, Bahrain, Qatar, Kuwait, Oman, and Saudi Arabia—have had their eyes on the threat emerging from across the Persian Gulf. The Islamic Republic of Iran has used its connections with Shi'ite populations in Lebanon, Iraq, and Yemen to flood the region with weapons, build militias, and destabilize regimes. In Syria, too, Iran has recruited Shi'ite mercenaries to fight ostensibly for the Assad regime but in practice to establish a permanent presence and yet another destabilizing foothold. Other nations with significant Shi'ite minorities—especially Bahrain and Saudi Arabia—have been deeply worried about their future. Iran has launched attacks across the region, including at Saudi oil fields. It has developed a sophisticated and powerful military, including advanced drones and cyberwarfare capabilities.

Therefore no one was as alarmed as the Gulf states were with the emergence of the JCPOA in 2015. The concern about an empowered Iranian regime, legitimized and potentially even nuclearized with no restrictions on its destabilizing activities, made it very clear to them how much they would need Israeli support.

At the same time, the Gulf states began to see another looming threat over the horizon: For a variety of reasons, they began to believe that their seemingly endless wealth coming from the extraction of oil and natural gas would not last forever. Much had happened since OPEC wielded enormous power over the West in the 1970s. Technological developments, such as fracking, had allowed countries like the United States, which had once been dependent on Middle Eastern crude, to produce vast amounts of oil by themselves. As climate change became a global concern, enormous sums were invested in the development of renewable sources of energy that would replace fossil fuels. The core of the Gulf states' business model was being threatened, and they started looking for ways to diversify.

Israel offered an incredible target for investment. As the newly crowned "start-up nation," Israel offered a fountain of business ideas backed by a tremendous incubator of human capital. The municipality of Tel Aviv-Jaffa signed more new patents every year than most whole countries. Israel was closer geographically than any European country, and had both the American and European markets wide open to its products and services. It was an investor's playground—and these oil states were looking for highly profitable places to put their money.

All they needed, it seems, was a moment of opportunity, when they could find a way to shake hands with Israel without appearing to completely betray the Palestinian cause.

That moment came in the summer of 2020—in the thick of the worst period of the COVID-19 pandemic. For more than three years, the Trump administration had been signaling a fundamental change in the dynamics of the Middle East peace process—one that would lead to an American-sponsored "Vision for Peace" between Israel and the Palestinians. In January 2020, the administration finally published it at a press conference with Netanyahu. The Palestinians, who had rejected it without seeing it, were not even invited.

The Palestinians may not have realized how quickly the price for their rejectionism would become clear. Barely seven months later, in August, the first of the normalization agreements that would be known as the Abraham Accords was announced, between Israel and the UAE. The Palestinians, yet again, had gotten on the wrong train.

***

Needless to say, the Palestinians were highly displeased by the Abraham Accords and had no qualms about voicing their displeasure—like their unarmed battalions of comrades around the world who automatically respond in accordance with the anti-Israel *bon ton*. While European leaders officially praised the accords, there was clearly a lack of enthusiasm, and even criticism, in influential circles. In part this was because the Abraham Accords went against the long-accepted narratives about peace needing to come first with the Palestinians. Perhaps there was an economic element as well, a fear that a Gulf-Israel alliance could create a bloc that could compete with the EU's interests. The arguments were contorted to the point of breathtaking absurdity. Some argued that by proceeding with a "separate peace" that did not include the Palestinians, the Abraham Accords made real peace harder to achieve. Others suddenly discovered the questionable human rights records of the Arab states in the Gulf and accused the administration of "cozying up to dictators." Still others simply were primed to hate anything this particular U.S. president did, and went on the attack.

All of it was disappointing, to say the least. Anyone who believes in peace should rejoice when there is more peace rather than less.

The fact is that prior to the Abraham Accords, the process of peace between Israel and the Arab world had appeared to have stalled out since the Jordanian accord in 1994. For a quarter century, no additional Arab states made peace with Israel, and those that previously had did not seem to want anything beyond non-belligerence. Any independent-minded observer understood that one could not plausibly cast the Abraham Accords as a negative development. So, other detractors and critics, less willing to say absurd things, chose a different argument—equally disingenuous if more sophisticated: The accords were, if not negative, then essentially "meaningless," because Israel and the Gulf states had already been conducting clandestine relations for decades. This was especially offensive for me, personally: It had taken two decades of hard work to turn the dream into reality, and now it was being dismissed *because* of the efforts of the past two decades!

The absurdity of even the milder claim has, of course, been made clear by subsequent events. Since the memoranda were signed, an entirely new Middle East has been created. First and foremost in the conflict with Iran: Suddenly a regional alliance-in-all-but-name has been formed, with two of Iran's most vulnerable nearby foes—Bahrain and UAE—suddenly under an almost explicit Israeli umbrella, and the Saudis allowing Israel to use its air space and joining in regional missile defense against Iran. Taken together, one could be forgiven for thinking that in a moment of a full-blown conflict, Iran could potentially find itself facing Israeli military assets just across the Persian Gulf.

Some have compared this regional security cooperation to a kind of "mini-NATO" that has come together to contend with an Iran that may well become a nuclear power in the near future. For years, Israelis, Americans, and Europeans have been told that they have to "learn to live with a nuclear Iran." Well, it seems that Iran, whether it gets the bomb or not, is going to have to learn to live with a far more powerful Israeli-Arab alliance that is prepared to confront it.

But the strategic developments since the signing of the accords are matched with economic development. The first three years since the signing has seen a flood of Israelis visiting Dubai and Abu Dhabi, as well as a growing flow of Emiratis coming the other way. Investments and trade have begun ramping up—worth billions of dollars each year. There is every reason to assume that these will only accelerate in the coming years, especially if the Saudis join the accords. (Indeed, it has been widely claimed that Hamas chose its timing of the October 7 invasion in order to thwart an imminent Israel-Saudi rapprochement. If that is the case, then it only delayed the inevitable. The mutual interests, if anything, were brought into sharper relief by the Iran-backed assault.)

The real reason for the Palestinians' opposition to the accords, and the grumbling of their supporters, was quite obvious: The Abraham Accords represent a significant loss of support in the Arab world for the rejectionist cause on which the PLO was first founded and to which the Palestinians remain staunchly committed—perhaps even more significant than when Egypt broke with the Arab world and made peace with Israel in 1979. Egypt was the most powerful country in the Arab League, and the Gulf states are the center of Arab finance. (And while Sudan might not have much money or power, it offered some nice symbolism: The three no's of Khartoum suddenly turned into a big yes.)

The Abraham Accords are, in other words, also a milestone in the history of the Palestinian cause—especially if the Saudis join in. For the first time, the main centers of power in the Arab world have concluded that however much they may sympathize with the Palestinian cause, they can no longer accept rejectionism as the prudent course. Israel, they have concluded, is here to stay and will not only be part of any Palestinian solution, but will play a central role in the future prosperity of the region.

As an Israeli, I can only be happy about this development. Full and fruitful relations between Israel and the Arab world have long been a dream of most Israelis, and the Abraham Accords represent the most tangible, meaningful step in that direction in at least a generation. Israel and the Arab states *should* unite against their common enemy, Iran. Israel and the Arab states *should* come together in business, tourism, and cultural exchange. The Arab-Israeli conflict is truly over in all important ways, having been replaced with a much narrower Palestinian-Israeli conflict—one that will be resolved only through the elimination of Hamas as a significant player and the development of a new order that can offer credible guarantees for the security of every Israeli citizen.

Peace will come only when the Palestinians decide that it's in their interest. The Abraham Accords proved to anyone with two functioning eyes—yet again—that Israel is not interested in conflict. The moment any belligerent nation wants to choose the path of economic development, strategic cooperation, and cultural and tourist exchange, the path of true people-to-people peace—Israel will be waiting with open arms. The Palestinian situation is more complicated because of the enormous distrust emerging from the current war, and the profound issues that will have to be resolved. But as multiple Israeli governments have demonstrated: The moment Israelis are convinced that there is a Palestinian will, we'll know how to find the way.

***

The Abraham Accords were only the beginning of a process. Bilaterally, they've translated into cooperation on multiple levels between Israel and each of the other countries that have signed. They have created both a precedent and a framework for others to join as well.

But they also started something new at the regional level, which has taken the shape of the Negev Forum, which has every indication of becoming a permanent fixture of the new Middle East. And this time, Egypt has decided to join the party.

The Israeli government that took power in 2021, led by Prime Minister Naftali Bennett and Foreign Minister Yair Lapid, made a priority of improving ties with our older peace partners Egypt and Jordan. Bennett's first diplomatic meeting after taking office was with Jordan's King Abdullah II. In September, he met with Egyptian President Abdel Fattah al-Sisi, followed by a visit by Lapid to the presidential palace in Cairo in December.

Their mission: to create a united front across the region in the face of renewed negotiations between the Americans and Iran. In the process, Bennett and Lapid set out to bring the older, "cold" peace partners into the warmth and momentum of the Abraham Accords.

On March 22, 2022, a three-way summit was held in Sharm el-Sheikh, Egypt, with Mohammed Bin Zayed, the crown prince of the UAE, along with Bennett and Sisi. This was almost a month into the Ukraine war—a time when the Emiratis, along with the Saudis, had been refusing to take the Biden administration's calls because of American advances to Iran.

The Americans noticed what was now happening, and the day after the summit, Secretary of State Antony Blinken called Lapid. "I'm coming to Israel on Sunday," Blinken said.

"If so," Lapid responded, "I want to bring everyone here: The Emiratis, the Bahrainis, the Moroccans, and we'll also invite the Egyptians and Jordanians.... Tony, you have to understand: They feel like they've been abandoned by their ally. I'm offering a solution. Come, we'll sit quictly, without interference, without our staffs, and you look them in the eye and tell them that you're not withdrawing from the Middle East."[61]

---

[61] Attila Somfavli, "A New Diplomatic Era: 5 Days. 6 Countries. No Palestinians," *State of Tel Aviv*, June 10, 2022, https://www.stateoftelaviv.com/a-new-diplomatic-era-5-days-6-countries-no-palestinians/ (accessed October 24, 2024).

Blinken agreed, and four days later—a speed almost unheard of in this kind of diplomatic effort—the foreign ministers of six countries met at the luxurious Kedma Hotel in Sde Boker in Israel's northern Negev desert. It was called the Negev Summit, and it began a process that has continued. Six working groups were created to focus on food and water security, energy, health, education and tolerance, tourism, and regional security. Now renamed the Negev Forum, it will—presumably once the war is over—include an annual summit and continued ongoing cooperation.[62]

The Egyptians joined in, as well, which has already translated into warming ties that recently expressed themselves in a joint Egyptian-Israeli deal to supply natural gas to Europe to replace part of what has been lost because of sanctions against Russia stemming from the Ukraine war.

The Jordanians, for now, have chosen to sit this dance out.

Such developments were unthinkable only a few years ago. They represent a sea change in Israel's position in the Middle East. They are also, in many ways, symbolic of what Zionist diplomacy has always been about: Think creatively, move quickly, read the map, and bring people together on the basis of mutual interest.

When it works, it's a wonderful thing to behold.

***

The Abraham Accords mark the most significant Israeli diplomatic success of the past two and a half decades. In many ways, they are also the culmination of more than a century of Zionist diplomatic experience. The efforts that led to them embody the energetic, entrepreneurial, creative, and urgent qualities that have characterized Zionist diplomacy since the days of Herzl and Weizmann. The Abraham Accords and the Negev Forum have reflected the Israeli capacity to correctly analyze power relations and to take advantage of a unique moment in history—in which an American president needed a win, the Gulf states needed Israel, and Israel

---

[62] Ariel Kahana, "Negev Summit to become permanent forum," *Israel Hayom*, June 26, 2022, www.israelhayom.com/2022/06/26/negev-summit-to-become-permanent-forum/ (accessed October 25, 2024).

sought to reap the benefits of its increased economic and strategic power in the region.

In the years since the meetings I conducted in the mid-2000s, the joint Sunni-Israeli interest against Iran has become an open secret. But at the time, these relations were the product of cautious diplomatic legwork, concealed using the most highly classified channels. In most cases, the governments that spoke to us feared that if their cooperation with Israel were to come to light, they would be excoriated and boycotted by their neighbors.

The opening of interest offices in the Gulf, including Qatar and Oman, ranks among the most resounding achievements in the history of Israeli diplomacy. I dare to dream that this model for cooperation—coupled with the increased belligerence of Iran across the region—will encourage more Arab states to join those who have already begun to recognize the benefits that relations with Israel can bring the whole Middle East. The day will come when Israel is no longer the "mistress" in its relationship to any Arab state, but an equal partner. But I have no illusions: The path will be long, arduous, and draining.

Over a period of decades, developments in the Middle East cut in opposite directions and generated powerful political undercurrents and whirlpools. We gave the Arab states with which we had relations everything they wanted: cooperation, defense, trade, technological know-how, and vital services. But whenever we came with a demand of our own, even slightly higher than the basic threshold at which relations began, we were turned down. Arab governments refused to formally recognize Israel or admit the depth of our painstakingly forged relations to their citizens.

In 2010, when Israel was accused of assassinating the Hamas commander Mahmoud al-Mabhouh in Dubai, the Gulf states responded with hostility. Mabhouh had been the architect of countless terror attacks and the chief liaison between Hamas and Iran's Revolutionary Guards. The truth is that nobody in the Emirati government shed a tear for him, but in the Arab world, the pretense is often the official policy. In Mabhouh's case, domestic reasons compelled Arab leaders to publicly denounce Israel, but they chose to go further than public opinion demanded.

My experience in building relations between Israel and its neighbors has left me optimistic, but cautious. Israel must keep its eyes wide open—carefully navigating the ever-present sensitivities, mistrust, and misconceptions while identifying the opportunities that these relationships offer, and making sure that it pursues its own interests, insisting not only on cooperation but also on the mutual respect, recognition, and honor that our nation deserves.

Shimon Peres used to say: "For me, dreaming is simply being pragmatic." As the world continues to be transformed by successive revolutions in computing, communications, artificial intelligence, cyber technology, energy, and more, it has never been more pragmatic than now to dream big. Technology offers an unprecedented opportunity to bring people from different religions, cultures, and socioeconomic backgrounds together. It can be the ultimate equalizer.

Technology allows information to flow beyond borders and barbed wire, shining light in places governed by darkness. Governments used to be able to control the flow of information to their citizens and with it, their citizens' perceptions of other countries. There was a time when the Arab street's perceptions of Israelis were shaped exclusively through the prism of government propaganda. Such perceptions are now harder to control.

Governments can either run scared from this decentralization of information, knowledge, and power, and engage in a game of technological whack-a-mole against their tech-savvy citizens, or they can seek to harness it for the good. If they choose the latter, then the sky is the limit, even, and perhaps especially, in the Middle East.

***

Perhaps the most powerful speech given at the closing ceremony of the Negev Summit in March 2022 was that of Abdullah Bin Zayed, the Emirati foreign minister. On the first day of the summit, a horrible terror attack took place in the Israeli city of Hadera. Two cousins, affiliated with the Islamic State, went on a shooting spree, murdering two people and injuring twelve others. As the six foreign ministers stood together the following morning in an unprecedented gathering, each in turn condemned the attacks. Bin Zayed did as well, and then spoke of the opportunities that had been missed in the decades since the original Camp David accords.

"Forty-three years ago… Egypt and Israel made peace," he began wistfully, and then continued,

> Unfortunately, we've lost those 43 years of knowing each other better, of working together, and of changing the narrative that many generations of Israelis and Arabs have been living. I think what we are trying to achieve here today is changing the narrative, creating a different future, and building on better hope for us and our kids and grandkids.
>
> It's new for [several of us] to be in Israel. This is our first time. So if we are curious sometimes and we want to know things and learn, it's because although Israel has been part of this region for a very long time, we have not known each other. So it's time to catch up, to build a stronger relationship. When I see 300,000 Israelis visiting the UAE in the last year and a half, but at the same time I see 2 million visitors visiting the Israeli pavilion in Expo in only the last six months, it says how curious [we are], and how much we want to know each other.
>
> And this is what I think goes against what happened yesterday [in Hadera]. It's by our standing together, it's by our people-to-people relationship, by creating a better environment for our businesses to work with each other—that's the way we can go after the narrative of hate, of incitement, of terror. We will prevail, no doubt. It's going to cost us, but it matters.

He was followed by the Moroccan foreign minister, Nasser Bourita, who spoke similarly of the difference between the older, cold peace and the new, warmer peace emerging from the Abraham Accords:

> I think we are here today because we genuinely, sincerely, and deeply believe in peace—not that kind of passive peace where we turn our backs to each other and peacefully ignore each other, but rather we believe in a thorough, fruitful, paradigm-shaping, and value-creating peace, the only kind of peace that is a battle worth waging. And I think our presence is a message to that, a message to our people and a message to the people of the region.
>
> We are here to create and to strengthen a positive dynamic.... This dynamic is not just diplomatic; it should be tangible. It should be felt by people, and it should go into concrete positive action which improves the lives of the people and open new horizons for the youth in our region....
>
> I think there should be a spirit of the Negev, which is coexistence, which is tangible results, and which is building for peace and challenging positively those who are enemies of this peace.[63]

Words are only good as far as they go. They must of course be followed by actions. Time will tell if the Negev Forum becomes a permanent and effective fixture of regional cooperation, or just another set of well-intentioned yet ultimately empty speeches. But the message could not be clearer: The future of the Middle East will not look like its past, which

[63] U.S. Department of State, Secretary Antony J. Blinken Joint Press Statements at the Conclusion of the Negev Summit, March 28, 2022: https://www.state.gov/secretary-antony-j-blinken-joint-press-statements-at-the-conclusion-of-the-negev-summit/ (accessed November 25, 2024).

ranged from all-out war to passive-aggressive non-recognition to cold peace, but never went beyond than that.

The region has seen a tectonic shift that is in the process of upending everything, from strategic alliances to economic cooperation, from tourism to culture to trade. Shimon Peres's utopian dream of a "New Middle East" is indeed coming to pass, but through a path he never dreamed of—not beginning with a Palestinian illusion like that of the Oslo Accords, but through real bilateral and regional agreements based on interest; agreements that have the capacity to pull the rug out from under the entire stale and blood-soaked narrative of rejectionism that has characterized the war against the Jews of my country for more than a century and continues in the vicious terrorism, the policies of Syria and Lebanon and Hamas and the Palestinian Authority, and the genocidal rhetoric and aspirations of Iran.

These policies continue today, not just in the terrorist infrastructures that have prospered in both the West Bank and especially Gaza and are backed by Iranian funding, weapons, and training, but also in the diplomatic arena, through diplomatic warfare, lawfare, the protests and speeches seen in elite places around the world. All of it is built on a false reality—one that reframes brutality as "resistance" and antisemitism as "anti-Zionism."

This grotesque world draws its strength from more than a century of hatred. Hatred that expressed itself in European antisemitism, in Arab rejectionism, in Soviet anti-Zionism—and today continues through a large number of anti-Israel NGOs, campus protest organizations, and structures within the United Nations. And it will continue, and it must be fought, and will not be defeated until the Jewish people in general, and the organs of the Jewish state in particular, dedicate much greater resources to the problem.

What became clear in 2020 is that there is an enormous force—not just economic and strategic, but also spiritual and popular—behind the new world that is being created on the ground in the Middle East, largely the result of decades of investment of Israeli diplomacy. A new chapter in the history of Israel, and of Zionist diplomacy, has begun. And because it is grounded first of all in interests, nothing—not even October 7 and the Gaza war—will get in its way.

Every day, the Israel haters detach themselves further and further from reality. Every day, the spirit of Herzl and Weizmann and Abba Eban and all the leaders and diplomats through generations and ages who contributed to the founding and building of the Jewish state, continues to flow through our efforts to create a life for our people that is free of the oppression and persecution of all those centuries past, in which the deepest spiritual resources of our people may be refined and unleashed.

We will continue to build our lives here, in Israel, the only homeland of the Jewish people—and will welcome all those who join us in this remarkable, beautiful endeavor.

EPILOGUE

EISENZAHNSTRASSE 3

Israeli diplomats, you may have gathered, are busy people. Representing an embattled nation, permanently called upon to justify its existence, with limited staff and resources, does not allow much down time. This has been especially true in the diplomatic positions I have held—in Bonn when the Berlin Wall fell; in Washington during the Wye River and Camp David talks, the transition from Clinton to Bush, and 9/11; twice in London under two different British governments; in New York at the UN during an especially challenging period for Israel on that stage; and in Jerusalem as director-general of the Foreign Ministry shuttling to Abu Dhabi, Manama, Tunis, and Rabat.

While all these roles have been excruciatingly intense, none has been as personally moving as Berlin.

For it is here that my own grandparents, Berthold and Elfriede Proskauer, lived when Hitler came to power. This is the place where my father, Ulrich Proskauer, was born in 1927. In 1933, my grandmother, sensing the calamitous danger facing even the most patriotic, secular Jews in Germany, took her family and the few possessions she managed to smuggle past the hawkish eyes of the Nazi regime and emigrated to British-ruled Palestine. The family began a new life from scratch in the Land of Israel. As did so many other families escaping the past and looking to a new future, they changed the family name to something in Hebrew—Prosor, which means "spread the light."

And so, from time to time, I feel the need to walk the streets of Berlin. Inevitably I am drawn to the modest four-story apartment building where my grandparents lived, at Eisenzahnstrasse 3, in the heart of the city. It looks clean and modern, one among many well-kept, pastel-painted buildings, with an unadorned arch over the entrance echoing the rounded tops of the wooden front door and windows. The immaculate sidewalks are shaded by leafy trees taller than the buildings themselves. Across the street is a Chinese restaurant with a bright red awning, incongruously called "Hot Spot," which serves excellent spring rolls.

What is this place? How did Nazi flags once wave here? How were Jews on this lovely, quiet, *ordinary* street suddenly stripped of centuries of proud, flourishing life, stripped of the fantasy of an age of reason and rights and equality, forced instead to cower and flee torture and deportation and death? Walking here today, I cannot fathom it. It sincerely feels like all of it was just a nightmare. But it was quite real.

Germany is a land of dreams and nightmares.

I know the nightmare was real, not just because I have seen the movies and read the books, but because I grew up in Jerusalem, Israel, with parents and grandparents who fled this very place. I grew up in a city where alongside Hebrew and Arabic, I heard German and Yiddish spoken by adults who, like my parents, escaped, and who spoke with broken hearts about those who did not, and of the wonders of German culture that they could not let go of even as it had betrayed them.

I stroll down Eisenzahnstrasse, past a playground where children clamber up a wooden castle and pretend to fight an ancient war, and I take a right onto Paulsborner Strasse. It is a beautiful spring day, as in so many European cities. The sky is clear. I am wearing a light-grey suit and light-blue tie, carrying the same air of discordant finesse as every other Israeli who puts on a suit and tie.

This place is both mine and the opposite of mine. The world has changed and continues to change—and it has stayed the same. Germany today is the opposite of what it was, as is the reality of Jewish life. But it is still Germany, and we are still Jews.

I have come to Berlin as the representative of a sovereign Jewish state, the first of its kind in thousands of years, established for the purpose of making sure my grandparents would never have to flee again. I am the symbol of Germany's ultimate depravity, but also of the failure of that depravity, the eternal life of the Jews, and of the hope that tomorrow may be completely different.

Germany is not what it was, but Germans know exactly why I am here and what I symbolize. The scales have shifted. We all know it.

After three-quarters of a century, who would have believed that the nation-state of the Jewish people would actively contribute to the security of Germany and Europe? Israel today sells advanced air-defense and other military systems to Germany—some of it through deals I have personally helped to broker in my official capacity. The Israeli navy, meanwhile, boasts sophisticated German-made submarines. Back home, the last living survivors of the Holocaust continue to receive reparation payments from Berlin. The past is gone. But it is also right in front of us.

Did my father know that playground? Was he taunted there, as a Jewish child of the Third Reich? Did he understand things that we never will?

***

As I walk, every step leads me deeper into the past, and into the future. As an Israeli diplomat I have been blessed to inherit a century-long tradition of a unique kind of diplomacy—a tradition that helped to bring about the most astonishing reversal of national fortunes in human history. And I am personally charged with carrying this tradition forward.

Let me go over a few of the key lessons of this tradition.

Power flows from respect, and respect flows from dignity. If you act with self-respect, stick to principle, and act from a position of presumptive strength, you will gain the respect of nations—even if your actual power is limited. The unique quality of statesmen like Herzl, Weizmann, and Eban was their ability to represent compellingly not a weak people, begging for sympathy and struggling to find their place in history, but an ancient and proud nation whose return to the world stage was inevitable. I think of Eban's immortal words to the UN Security Council just two months after Israel declared independence: "The State of Israel," he said, "is an immutable part of the international landscape. To plan the future without it is to build delusions on sand." Every Israeli diplomat must carry this ancient dignity into every speech, every meeting, every negotiation.

Be forever creative, energetic, and determined. We are a small nation in the world, few in number but rich in achievement. Our greatest strength lies not in our tanks and missiles, but in our ability to act creatively, to break the rules, to take risks, to generate new ideas, and invest resources quickly—as the Silicon Valley saying goes, to "move fast and break things." But for this to happen, we have to make sure that we encourage entrepreneurship and risk-taking at every level, which often feels like the opposite of what diplomats are supposed to do. Our greatest achievements have always flowed from this combination of creativity, energy, and determination.

Take advantage of informal networks of support around the world. The Jewish state enjoys a vast array of sympathetic individuals in positions of influence—Jews and non-Jews alike—who are willing to act for Israel's benefit when called upon. The challenge of Israeli diplomacy is to maintain those relationships and, at the moment of truth, successfully recruit them in an almost military-style operation, bringing a coordinated campaign to bear on the world stage. Israel will never have the inherent voting power enjoyed by the Arab League, or once enjoyed by the Soviet empire. It is but one voice in a world of 200 nations, many of which are indifferent or hostile to our fate. But when rallying the support of nations really matters—as we saw in the run up to the UN Partition plan vote of November 1947—our fate can stand or fall on our ability to put our friends around the world to good use.

Ignore the allures of Diplomacy-land. Every diplomat, at every level, faces a daily tension between fidelity to the nation's interests and the desire to "go along to get along," especially at the UN and other international forums. Diplomacy-land is, however, a viper's nest hiding behind beautiful tapestries, perpetually trying to convince you to put less than your best efforts into advancing your nation's interests, to enjoy the ephemeral benefits of praise and collegial popularity at the expense of your mission. But while agreeability is an important personal skill for any diplomat, the ability to refuse is often far more decisive. To repeat: *A diplomat who is unwilling to say "no" will have difficulty getting others to say "yes."*

Never forget the difference between access and influence. Knowing people, networking, being able to get a meeting with those who have power—all of that is only a first step, even if it's a crucial one. No less important is what happens once you're in the room with them. The ability to persuade, to successfully read the power map and apply the right kinds of pressure at the right moment—that is the key to changing history. I think of how Chaim Weizmann changed Lord Balfour's mind about the Uganda Plan and brought him to support establishment of the Jewish national home in Palestine. I think of how Shimon Peres, facing a new French government determined to cancel its predecessor's nuclear agreements, threatened to make those agreements public if they were cancelled—and fundamentally altered the course of Israel's history in a single meeting.

"Mr. Balfour, you meet the wrong kind of Jews." In his very first meeting with the man who would provide the keys to the Jews' return to their homeland, Weizmann revealed the central tenet of Zionism: that Jews, accustomed to so many centuries of relative powerlessness, would have to evolve if they were to survive. The "right kind" of Jews would be those who stood tall in the face of incalculable animosity, fought for their historical rights, and won. The Zionist revolution was, before anything else, a critique of life in exile and an assertion of an ancient honor, organized into a political movement that would restore our sovereign place in the world. And in a world where so many today are, alas, still the "wrong kind" of Jews, Zionist diplomacy must always remind itself of the bedrock principles on which Zionism was founded if Jews are to thrive into the future.

***

Such is the past, and the future, of Zionist diplomacy. And yet, I am in Berlin, where the European present, always in motion, never stops imposing itself.

The 2022 Russian invasion of Ukraine has been an earthquake. Being in Berlin right now is, on top of everything else, oddly familiar. I cannot escape a sensation bizarrely similar to what I felt in Washington more than two decades ago, in the autumn of 2001.

In a profound sense, Ukraine has been Europe's 9/11. Russia's aggression has had a similar effect on European decision-makers and public thinking as the al-Qaeda attacks on New York and Washington had on America. A shattering of illusions, a sudden clarity, an end of a dream, a time to gird for battle.

And in both cases, a fundamental change in the place Israel holds in their minds.

Nations allow themselves to live under comfortable misperceptions for a long time—even for decades or generations—when doing so carries no immediate burden or threat. Since Israel was founded, it has often struggled to pierce the veil of these misperceptions, even among its closest allies, to help them to navigate the complicated realities of life. Such was the case with the United States before 9/11: Americans did not understand the threat that Middle Eastern violence—whether from brutal regimes like Iran or Saddam Hussein's Iraq, or terrorist groups like the PLO and Hamas—posed to America itself. It was, in their view, a Middle Eastern problem, one that affected allies abroad and expressed itself only in terms of instability, rising oil prices, and military deployments abroad.

When the Twin Towers came down, so did the illusions. Amid the horror was also an awakening. Many Americans suddenly understood what Israelis had been saying all along and began to seek our help—through intelligence sharing, airport security, weapons and tactics and technology and more. It is awful that immense tragedy must sometimes occur before misperceptions are corrected. But so it is.

When Russia invaded Ukraine, a similar process began to take place in Europe. Over the past seven decades, generations of Europeans had convinced themselves that strategic defense was no longer a necessary investment. They believed that the fall of the Soviet Union and unification of Europe heralded a new order, one in which wars and "militarism" were relegated to other parts of the world. In Europe at least, an age of reason had taken hold—and perhaps would take the rest of the world with it.

The reality, of course, was that throughout the Cold War and for some time after, America was taking care of Europe's strategic defense, with major U.S. bases, a nuclear umbrella, and a disproportionate contribution to NATO's budget. Americans, however, have grown tired of being the world's policeman and Europe's protector, and three consecutive presidents—Obama, Trump, and Biden—tried to tell the Europeans that in the absence of a Cold War, the nation's priorities had shifted and they needed to step up. Europeans heard the words but did not get the message.

Until Ukraine.

Europeans woke up to a reality in which an authoritarian regime with a centuries-long history of expansionism had ripped the post-World War II order to shreds right in their back yard. American withdrawal had stoked the darkest tendencies of Russian imperialism, and Russia had attempted to swallow a country whole—something the world had not seen since Iraq invaded Kuwait in 1990. Suddenly, European nations felt vulnerable in a way they hadn't since the fall of the Berlin Wall.

Just as with 9/11, Europeans began to wake up to a reality that resembled what Israel has had to deal with every day since its independence. The world, it seems, really was every bit as chaotic and violent as the Israelis had long claimed. Civilization, law and order, human rights, democracy—these were not a natural and inevitable progression of humanity, but an artifice, a bubble, which could survive only if protected through military might, deterrence, and the credible threat of force.

In practice, this has meant that Europe is now arming up—not just sending advanced weaponry to Ukraine but building its own capabilities as well. For the first time in three-quarters of a century, Europeans are realizing that the best way to prevent a third world war is not to lay down arms and call for dialogue, but the opposite. That the most important thing preventing the deluge of rapacious imperialism, invasions, and mass death would be their own might.

What is Israel's new role in this changing world? It remains a small country—similar in population to a mid-sized European state. We have many problems of our own, surrounded by authoritarian regimes of varying levels of instability, in the thick of an intense proxy war with Iran on both our southern and northern borders, stuck in an unresolved Palestinian conflict and torn by internal struggles that come to the surface every few years.

Yet despite it all, we survive. A single democratic state defying the odds, remaining the same country with the same constitutional system for longer than most European states. We arose from the ashes and have absorbed immigrants and built and prospered and grown. And we have done it without illusions about the world around us. We have fought hard for what we have.

Perhaps that is our role right now. To give Europeans some hope—that amid uncertainty, it is possible to thrive without self-delusion. To dream without sleeping. To make a better world, but to do so incrementally, iteratively, *l'at l'at*—slowly, slowly. To look past the painful setbacks that inevitably arise, to a better future.

***

I continue walking. Germany, like all of Europe, has layers upon layers. Past and future, good and evil, blood and hope—a kaleidoscope of shifting realities, and we Jews both see it and are seen by it.

As Germans have woken up to the reality of Russian tanks, however, they seem blind to another threat, no less real—and one which my Jewish "spider-senses" detect with utter clarity and alarm.

Antisemitism is back.

Germans, more than anyone, think they've taken care of antisemitism. Denying the Holocaust remains a serious crime. Neo-Nazis are reviled. Unlike some European countries, Germany views the evils of its past with astonishing clarity and remorse. Yet it is precisely this confidence that risks blinding them to the newer forms of antisemitism, those that do not brandish swastikas or march in parades, instead presenting themselves as the most rational, progressive of ideologies. Antisemitism from the Left is the new Germany's blind spot—or at least it was before October 7 thrust it into streets and campuses across Europe.

The new antisemitism does not deny the Holocaust, but instead accuses the Jews of carrying out a new one. It does not claim Jews should leave Europe, but rather Israel. It does not prey on our weakness, but curses our strength.

Take, for example, the international art exhibition known as Documenta, held in Kassel, Germany, every five years—most recently in the summer of 2022. It is one of the largest, most prestigious events in the art world. This time, scandal erupted when it was discovered that several major works of art—including an enormous mural in one of Kassel's main squares—contained blatantly antisemitic imagery. Indonesian artist collective Taring Padi's *People's Justice* ostensibly was about the 1965 Indonesian genocide but for some reason had soldiers with pigs' heads and "Mossad" on their helmets killing Indonesian children. Additional works had Jews with sidelocks and skullcaps committing atrocities. After a public outcry and a halfhearted response by the curators, the head of Documenta, Sabine Schormann, was forced to resign. A few months later, Documenta's "scientific advisory panel" issued a 133-page report, and the results were damning, calling the exhibition "an echo chamber for Israel-related anti-Semitism, and sometimes for pure anti-Semitism."

The stream of such moments is constant and growing. There is no effective deterrence against this kind of antisemitism. Often it seems that the entire academic-cultural sphere in Europe has become an "echo chamber" for antisemitism. Demonstrations are held calling for both "Death to the Jews" and the annihilation of Israel. But for some German politicians, "Death to the Jews" is the epitome of incitement and punishable by law, whereas calls to destroy the Jewish state fall under "freedom of speech and opinion," and are to be tolerated. A so-called academic panel is held on the anniversary of Kristallnacht, drawing comparisons between the Naqba and the Holocaust. And on it goes.

It is a constant drip, drip, drip, like Chinese water torture. Sometimes it triggers outrage, sometimes it doesn't, but it never ceases. If anything, it's only getting worse.

That's because unlike classic antisemitism from the Right—people who tell you outright that they don't like Jews—when it comes from the Left, it deliberately takes advantage of two ambiguities to which the cultural-academic world is especially vulnerable. First, it takes advantage of the prestige and mystique surrounding art, academia, and culture, and the insistence that criticism of anything expressed in that world is an affront to artistic or academic freedom and a form of censorship. And second, it hides behind a thin veneer of "legitimate criticism of Israeli policies," as though it were comparable to criticism of any other democratic government.

But if you look carefully, the symbols invoked by such "criticism" are identical to those of the old antisemitism (pigs' heads, conspicuous Jewish figures with hooked noses, scheming brutality against non-Jews, and so on) as are the effective results (justifying violence against Jews), but the context, it is claimed, is about Israel, not Jews per se—and therefore it's somehow acceptable.

It's not. Over and over again, these two arguments are used to shield the most vicious sort of antisemitism, and the result is that while its intentions, symbolism, and results are identical to those of the more traditional antisemitism, a great many Germans, Europeans, and Westerners in general have a much harder time putting a stop to it.

This strategy is not especially new—again, it was a central part of the Soviet Union's cultural assault on the West half a century ago—but it persists, and lately seems to be gaining strength in a country whose extreme sensitivity to the dangers of the Right sometimes blinds them to very similar dangers when coming from the Left.

This is something that cannot be fought only with the tools of civil society. Antisemitism threatens vulnerable Jewish communities throughout Europe and beyond. Fighting it requires a broad combination of efforts, and responsibility falls on many of us—not just Jewish communal leadership across the Diaspora, but also Western and especially European national leaders, and of course the State of Israel, which has a variety of tools at its disposal. An important part of the burden falls on the shoulders of Israeli diplomats, us all. Indeed, fighting this kind of antisemitism, especially among our democratic allies, is one of the greatest challenges facing Zionist diplomacy moving forward.

***

We live in a new world. Europe has stopped unifying and has begun arming up, whereas Russia—a pillar of the post-World War II order—has become a reviled rogue state. An enemy of global stability still holds a veto in the UN Security Council, the most important postwar body for the purpose of maintaining global stability. The structure that has held the world together for seven decades has begun to collapse.

But what this all means is that diplomacy matters more than ever before. The ability to rapidly, creatively, and aggressively pursue solutions to problems great and small, the ability to communicate between and among states, to share perspectives, brainstorm solutions, and resolve contradictions; the ability to mobilize collectively the allies of freedom and democracy worldwide—these skills are needed more desperately than at any time in recent memory.

And it is especially the case for Zionist diplomacy. With every day that passes, our nation's position in the world grows stronger—and our enemies try to adjust to the new reality, constantly crafting new weapons, new narratives, new alliances through which to attack us. But the evolution of our enemies' tactics is not a sign that they're winning. On the contrary, it's a symptom of their failure.

For Israeli diplomats, however, this means that the main battleground for our national survival has shifted—and thus the role of diplomacy has changed. The failure to destroy Israel by force of arms has meant that the new efforts are at the level of culture, ideas, values, media, and messaging. Diplomats—among others—are on now on the front lines, requiring a constant mastery of a constantly growing and shifting set of skills.

Zionist diplomacy, perhaps unlike that of any other nation, requires permanently filling two contrasting roles simultaneously: defending the nation against those who would destroy it, on the one hand, and at the same time deepening its relations with countries, corporations, and communities that understand the value Israel adds to the world.

These two roles are not, of course, disconnected. If anything, there is no greater response to the endless attempts to paint Israel as a blight on the world than to highlight the immense contributions our country in fact makes—whether in artificial intelligence (AI) and cyber-defense, rapid response to humanitarian crises, defense technology protecting democratic nations, innovations in energy, medicine, science, and every field of policy from education to reducing road fatalities. In our day, "a light unto nations" is neither spin nor messianism, but a simple fact.

Europe is awakening to the importance of its alliance with Israel. So are the Arab states. So is India, now the world's largest nation in population. The world was overtaken by a pandemic—and Israel led the way both in innovation and policy, being among the first to immunize its population and return to normal life. The world is stunned by advances in AI, driverless vehicles, pilotless drones—and finds Israeli companies at the forefront. The world is rocked by natural disasters and finds Israeli rescue teams on the ground before anyone else. The world is shaken by a massive invasion by Russia of Ukraine—and looks to Israel to mediate a solution.

Yes, it is true that no nation is as reviled and falsely accused on a daily basis as the Jewish state. But it's also true that a great many people see through the lies. The reality of Israel, properly explained, is more powerful than any of the conspiracy theories invented by our adversaries.

It is common to see Israel as an upstart in global affairs. And indeed, the idea of Israeli leaders being asked to mediate major global conflicts is relatively new. But in the diplomatic sphere, we have more than a century of astonishing success under our belts, from Herzl to Weizmann, from Eban to Peres to Netanyahu. We have learned how to build key relationships, to mobilize them in the hour of need, to take advantage of new media and new technology, and to safeguard our nation's interests.

Israel's success is first of all the product of its people—scrappy, creative, entrepreneurial, hustling, street smart, humanitarian, and visionary. But when you are under perpetual assault, from bombs to blogs, you have no choice but to fight back, and to do so effectively with all the means at your disposal. Israeli diplomats are the tip of the spear in our people's battle for effective, positive relations with the rest of the world.

***

The journey on foot from my grandparents' apartment at Eisenzahnstrasse 3 to the Israeli embassy on Auguste-Viktoria-Strasse 74 takes no more than half an hour, if you're walking directly and quickly. But my journey today has taken longer, spanning days and years and the better part of a century.

The embassy building, built at the turn of the new millennium, is stunning: utterly modern yet containing sharp hints of the past. It was designed by Orit Willenberg-Giladi, the Israeli daughter of Samuel Willenberg, who was the last survivor of the Treblinka revolt. He escaped in 1943, moved to Israel in 1950, and lived a full life, passing away in 2016 at the age of ninety-three. After designing this embassy, Orit was selected to design the Holocaust educational center at the site of the Treblinka camp. Knowing Orit's backstory injects the building's commanding presence with a historical and human complexity, as beguiling and poignant as the very fact that such an embassy exists at all.

But there is also reference to a far more ancient past. For alongside its monumental curves and angles and glass, alongside its large, vertical Israeli flags hanging astride the grand entrance, and alongside the architect's personal connection to the German story, this magnificent building is also faced with Jerusalem stone—the unique limestone that adorns most of the buildings in the ancient Jewish capital, a stone that turns to gold as the sun sets and which inspired the famous Naomi Shemer song "Jerusalem of Gold."

Like my own role and that of the other Israeli diplomats inside it, the building itself offers layers upon layers of complexity, of past meeting future, of survival and prosperity and hope.

And as I walk through the building's massive doors, reporting for work, I realize that such, indeed, is the meaning of our nation's presence in the world—and nowhere more so than in Berlin, the heart of the world's darkness in the middle of the past century. Israel's role is to be—at once and in the same breath—a glow amid the darkness, a glimmer of gold answering every sunset, a cutting edge of hope and betterment, and the reinvigoration of an ancient vision.

We, the emissaries of the Jewish state around the world, contain within us a microcosm of the spirit of our people. Our task, at once impossible and irreplaceable, is to encompass both futuristic visions and stubborn memories, suffering and thriving, vulnerable and expansive, filling the world with dreams as we fight to survive—and above all, never, ever giving up.

The Ambassador speaking at a solidarity rally for Israel at the Brandenburg Gate, following the October 7th massacre.

The Ambassador laying Stolpersteine (stumbling stones) in Berlin in memory of his family, who fled Germany in 1933. The stones were placed at the family's last freely chosen residence on Eisenzahnstrasse, commemorating Alfred and Berthold Proskauer, the Ambassador's grandfather, and their children, Lieselotte and Ulrich. For Berthold Proskauer, a proud Prussian patriot who served in the German army during World War I, leaving their home behind was a particularly difficult decision despite the dire circumstances.

The Ambassador speaking at a rally in Berlin calling for the release of the hostages.

The Ambassador presenting his credentials to German President Frank-Walter Steinmeier, accompanied by his wife Hadas, his mother Nechama, his sister Sigal, and his eldest son Lior. Credit: Presse- und Informationsamt der Bundesregierung

The Ambassador with President Frank-Walter Steinmeier.
Credit: Presse- und Informationsamt der Bundesregierung

The Ambassador, immediately after presenting his credentials, brought a group of young people to Bebelplatz, the site of the infamous book burnings. This was his first official act, emphasizing the importance of educating and empowering the next generation. Strengthening youth engagement and fostering exchange programs were central to his mission of deepening the connection between Israel and Germany.
Credit: Boaz Arad

The Ambassador with long-time friends from the IDF Battalion Commanders Course, Benny Gantz and Nitzan Nuriel, at the Herzliya Conference.
Credit: Gilad Kavalerchik

The Ambassador with President Frank-Walter Steinmeier.

ACKNOWLEDGMENTS

Writing a book is akin to bringing new life into the world.

This work reflects the story of my life and the beliefs I've cultivated over the years. While the content is ultimately my responsibility, its creation would not have been possible without the support of many remarkable individuals.

First and foremost, I wish to express my deepest gratitude to Yaniv Cohen, a close friend and the founder of the Tachlith Institute, Israel's most influential policy institution today. Yaniv's exceptional guidance, wisdom, and unwavering dedication were instrumental from the book's inception to its completion. I would also like to thank Danielle Leumi, my excellent chief of staff. Her commitment and professionalism were crucial in overcoming the challenges along the way.

I am immensely grateful to David Hazony, whose mastery of language and relentless dedication were key to bringing this book to life. He made sure that the essence of my thoughts and experiences was conveyed with clarity and precision. David's meticulous attention to detail and creative insights transformed the manuscript into the polished work you hold in your hands. His contribution is evident on every page, and he was instrumental in shaping the narrative, especially in the aftermath of the October 7 events.

Special thanks also to Adam Bellow, the book's publisher, whose support, friendship, thoughtful feedback, and commitment to excellence were essential in shaping the final manuscript.

I am also deeply grateful to those who worked tirelessly on the English version and provided invaluable feedback: Raphi Schutz, whose thoughtful comments and support as a trusted friend and advisor were deeply appreciated; Douglas Feith, whose extensive knowledge and wise insights greatly enhanced the manuscript; David Sable, a dear friend whose feedback was both insightful and constructive; Gerald Steinberg, whose observations and keen insights were instrumental; and Gadi Blatinsky, a loyal companion whose thoughtful suggestions were invaluable. Lastly, special thanks to Eylon Levy, who expertly translated the original book into English and played a crucial role in shaping the version you've just read.

As this is my "second child," I cannot proceed without thanking those who helped bring the Hebrew version of this book to life. During that journey, several individuals played crucial roles, including Ella Tkach-Dreazen, Savion Medaleion, David Krikler, Yaniv Khalili, Rafi Shamir, and Aviva Klompas. Their expertise was invaluable in refining ideas and sharpening the message. Many friends and family members offered invaluable feedback on this book, including David Noam, Yaki Dayan, Dr. Dan Schueftan, Gideon Frank, Dr. Eli Levite, Attorney Ben-Dror Yemini, Dr. Gadi Taub, David Sable, Nadav Tamir, Dr. Dore Gold, David Roth, Gil Bringer, Yacov Hadas, Oren Anolik, and Oded Joseph. Their insights significantly enriched this work.

I would also like to extend my heartfelt thanks to the Kirsh family for their steadfast support throughout this journey. Their encouragement and belief in my work were a constant source of motivation.

Finally, my deepest thanks to my family—my wife, Hadas, my children, Lior, Tomer, and Oren, my daughters-in-law, Maya and Noa, and my grandchildren, Amit, Daniel, and Dean. Your love and support have been my anchor, and I am endlessly grateful for the strength and joy you bring into my life.